Richard Clynton

The Life of a celebrated Buccaneer

A Page of past History for the Use of the Children of to-day

Richard Clynton

The Life of a celebrated Buccaneer

A Page of past History for the Use of the Children of to-day

ISBN/EAN: 9783337178390

Printed in Europe, USA, Canada, Australia, Japan

Cover: Foto ©ninafisch / pixelio.de

More available books at **www.hansebooks.com**

OF A

CELEBRATED BUCCANEER

A PAGE OF PAST HISTORY FOR THE USE OF THE CHILDREN OF TO-DAY

BY

RICHARD CLYNTON

LONDON
SWAN SONNENSCHEIN & CO.
PATERNOSTER SQUARE.

1889

LIFE OF A CELEBRATED BUCCANEER.

CHAPTER I.

ONCE upon a time there lived on an island, separated from the main land of Europe by a silver streak of the ocean, a celebrated Buccaneer.

There was a rugged grandeur about the rock-bound coast of this island, with its bluff, bold headlands and beetling cliffs, where the sea birds loved to make their nests high up above the spray; mingling their cries with the voice of the ocean as it rushed into its wide and deep throated caverns. The waves, too, worked ever, and for ever, a broad fretwork collar round these rocky shores. Unlucky was the ship that found this island on her lee in a gale of wind. Many a child had been made fatherless there, and many a wife a widow. But to those who knew how to thread their way through the many channels, numerous bays, creeks, and rivers, offered a safe retreat either from the storm or from an enemy.

This island was a fit home for one following the profession of a Buccaneer. Its natural advantages were extremely great; for not only was it difficult of access, but its innumerable big throated caverns opened their wide jaws ready to receive anything that floated in from the ocean. However, this bold pirate did such a good business, that in a short time these caves became too small, so he had to build wharves and warehouses to hold his plunder; for he lived in such an age, and was surrounded by such unprincipled people, that he could not leave his things lying about on the shore. Besides which, the climate was not good, being frequently visited by fogs, gales of wind, and very heavy rains.

Soon villages rose up; then towns, which in their turn grew into great cities, the principal of which were generally planted by the side of some one of his many rivers. Soon the bays and rivers became crowded with ships, and the shores were busy scenes of industry. Cargoes were being landed. Sails were being made and repaired; ropes overhauled and restranded, and the smell of the pitch caldrons rose up and mingled with the salt air blown in fresh from the sea. Shipwrights' hammers resounded along the shores, and were echoed back by the beetling cliffs. While the men worked, the women sang, and the chubby-faced, fair-haired children played about on the beach.

To those who ask how our bold Buccaneer acquired most of his property, it must be answered that it came to him in a manner usual in those times. Everybody laid their hands upon what they could, and then devoted all their spare time and energy to the keeping of it. Title deeds were for the most part written in blood, with a sharp-pointed one-nibbed steel pen. When we live in Rome we must do as the Romans do, and we must not set up to be better than our neighbours, that is, if we wish to prosper, and when all the world is going in for universal plunder it does not pay to stand on one side, with hands idle, arms folded, and eyes upturned to heaven, saying that people are wicked. Needs must when the devil drives.

It has been a time-honoured custom to rob and kill, so that riches may be laid up; then it becomes the duty of all to watch lest the thief breaks through and steals. This primitive method of doing business is now justly condemned, and all nations pay at least a tribute to virtue, by flinging a cloth over any shady action. But nations even now have to maintain their dignity. Insults have to be resented, and ambitious designs have to be frustrated. Battles are fought, and people are slaughtered, and some one, as the saying is, has to pay the piper.

It would almost seem, by a contemplation of things in general, that man by nature is a robber, the action changing its colour according to the atmosphere that people have to live in. In barbarous ages the act of plunder is done openly, and a fellow-creature is sent about his business, either with a broken head or with a spear through his body, and there is an end to him, and perhaps the world is not much the poorer. That honesty is the best policy is, by experience, forced upon us; but even now, in our most enlightened age, the individual will at times adulterate his liquor, sand his sugar, and sell short weight, though he may try to sanctify the deed by saying his prayers before and after; thus adding somewhat to the general stock of humbugs, hypocrites, and Pharisees. But to our story.

It was a noble sight to see this bold Buccaneer getting under weigh with his fleet of ships. Clack, clack went the windlasses, and his brave lads could be heard singing as they lifted their anchors a peak—

> Merrily round our capstans go
> As we heave in the slack of our chain,
> Into our sails the north winds blow
> As we bear away from the main.
> Yo ho, my lads, heave ho!

Home went the sheets. Up went the yards, and the sails bellied out to the wind. On the shores crowded the women and children. The little ones with shock heads of curly hair, the sport of the breeze, crying after their fathers, holding up their tearful little faces for the sea-breeze to kiss. The wives wishing their brave lads a prosperous voyage, and a safe return, with plenty of plunder. Silks and spices from the East, and gold and silver from the West, or wherever they could find it. Away went the ships, with their white canvas spread like the wings of a seagull. Soon the hulls were down, and the white specks, after lingering for a while upon the far-off horizon, sank beneath and vanished. Then sending a sigh after their mates on the wings of the north wind, the women returned to their homes and sang their young sea whelps to sleep, with lullabies tuned to the daring deeds of their fathers.

CHAPTER II.

THINGS in this world do not remain shady long. Time works wonders and throws the halo of romance over the darkest deeds. See what time and romance have done for William Tell. Look at your Alexander and your Frederick; are not they both called great? Ah! these two were conquerors not plunderers; and there lies the difference, though perhaps Maria Theresa and one or two others might have had something to say against one of these fine fellows. Then there is Robin Hood. Have not time and romance completely changed the aspect of that, at one time, bold and notorious outlaw? For over fifty years did this jolly robber enjoy himself upon other people's property. Look too at the numerous other gentlemen of the road; your crusaders and adventurers in early times. What were the hardy Norsemen, of whom we love to sing? There is something very attractive about your robber, no matter whether he carries on his profession by sea or land, the only thing needful being, to study him at a distance, and through the halo of this said romance. If it were not for the world's great robbers what would historians have to record; what would poets have to sing about? If they had to confine themselves to the virtuous actions, to the good that is done, their occupation would be gone. The chronicling of small beer is a waste of labour.

But there comes a time when the very worst of sinners are troubled by that mysterious part of the human economy known by the name of conscience. This conscience is at times a veritable tyrant, saying what we shall eat, what we shall drink, and what we shall do. To the many the matter is not one of difficulty. If they have to make their way in the world, conscience is either thrown overboard, or put under hatches until such times as it is wanted. Then it comes up all the fresher for its temporary retirement, and is, generally speaking, very exacting.

The disposition to repent of the evil we have done is not confined either to age, time, or sex happily. The call comes perhaps, more often, and earlier, to women than it does to men. Jezebel was not altogether as good as she ought to have been, but even she might have turned over a new leaf, and have become a most respectable saint, had not misfortune thrown her across the path of that impetuous fellow Jehu, with the result that she was, as every one knows, thrown out of a window. Had Jezebel lived in the Buccaneer island in his later days, and had she been young and beautiful, and the paint not too thick upon her face, she might have been tried for some small act of indiscretion, such for instance as that trifling incident about Naboth; but probably she would have been acquitted, when no doubt she would have left the court without a stain upon her character, and would have been an object of sympathy ever after. This lady has left a numerous family of daughters behind her, many of whom, however, turn over new leaves, and having been considerable sinners, become the most straight-laced, unpitying, and uncharitable of sour-faced saints. Poor Jezebel the first was never given a chance. She lived too soon.

But to the point. The time came when our bold Buccaneer received, as the saying is, his call, and it was brought about in the following manner. In early times when saints walked about the earth calling sinners to repentance, one found his way over to the Buccaneer's island, induced to go there, not by the hope of any worldly gain in the shape of church preferment or salary; and here lies much of the difference between a modern saint and an ancient one. But the one, of whom we wish now particularly to speak, was impelled by the hope of snatching this burning brand from the devil's fire. Some of the Buccaneer's neighbours had tried to convert him before this, by means of the sword, but without effect, for the pirate's nest was a hard one to take, and the eggs burnt the fingers of all those who attempted to touch them.

The precise spot where the saint landed is open to doubt; so is the exact time and the method of his transit. Some declared that he came over on a broomstick. Others again, said he used the ordinary means of conveyance, and this is the most worthy of credence. About saints there is generally something that is legendary. He preached his gospel to the Buccaneer, and told him in the plainest language that he was going to the devil, about whose dominion he drew such a glowing account that the Buccaneer was moved.

He repented, and determined to turn over that wonderful leaf, that the world is for ever hearing so much about, and seeing so little of. To show his earnestness, the Buccaneer built churches and endowed them, and not unfrequently out of the money that he took from other people. This was but right. Belfries rose up in every nook and corner, and their iron tongues could be constantly heard calling all pious buccaneers to prayer.

But that befell the saint which sooner or later must happen to us all. He died, but left behind him a book, which he told the Buccaneer was to be his rule in life, for between its covers there lay the seed of all that was good, and the gentle spirit of one, who though dead would live for ever. The precious gift was handed over to the safe custody of the Buccaneer's church, and the old saint with much sorrow and ceremony was laid in his narrow cell, to await there the sound of the last trump.

CHAPTER III.

THE days of mourning were barely over when difficulties arose. The faith left behind by the old saint was extremely good, and even beautiful, but it was not at all adapted to one who occasionally robbed a neighbour's hen-roost. Indeed, it was not at all fitted for one who followed the profession of a bold Buccaneer. It was a trifle hard to sell all that he had and give it to the poor, who might be a lazy lot of skulking rascals. Then who could expect to get on in this world, if, when one cheek was struck he turned the other? Beautiful, yes, but not practical. If our fighting Buccaneer did this sort of thing, every daw from the mainland would invade the nest of the eagle, and peck him to death, and suck his eggs.

Then the command not to lay up riches upon earth; and to live in peace and charity with all men. This was all very well, but then when you are surrounded by a lot of people, who will not live up to these fine sentiments, what is a poor fellow to do?

The Buccaneer had a coxswain, who was his right-hand man, and whose name was Jack Commonsense. He took him into his confidence. Old Jack scratched his head, which was a sure sign that he was in trouble, and he told his master that he did not see any way out of the difficulty, for, if they sailed by the instruction as laid down in the Book the saint had left behind, they had better give up the buccaneering business at once, and try something else. The end of the matter was, that it was handed over to the Buccaneer's Church to settle, for, as he said in his quaint sea-faring language, it's no use keeping a dog if you have to bark yourself. To his clergy he deputed the by no means easy task of shaping a course in accordance with his book, the Bible, and at the same time not altogether antagonistic to his worldly interests. In fact, some kind of a compromise had to be made.

Obedient to the command of their earthly master, the most learned of the Buccaneer's divines assembled together in solemn conclave, and having opened the proceedings with prayer, they fell to arguing upon the grave questions before them. The Scriptures were searched, and very much learning and piety were displayed, and very much heat, with a little temper, was introduced; but there seemed to be little probability of their coming to a satisfactory conclusion. Some said the word must be adhered to, others said that the word killed, and that it was the spirit that must be taken into consideration.

After very much argument, which at times cleft asunder the matter in dispute, thereby forming schism and even sects, a satisfactory conclusion was arrived at, and the foundation was laid of an edifice, which in time was to grow into most beautiful proportions. The foundation rested upon the Book, and the corner stones were those which Christ had laid in Galilee. The superstructure was built to a large extent by human hands, and of earthly material. Still it was a noble edifice, and thus the Buccaneer had manufactured for him a good every-day religion, somewhat worldly perhaps, but eminently suited to his mode of life.

There were slight incongruities, but it mattered little to the subject of our history, and we may presume that he did not see them; or if he did he did not notice them, which answers the same purpose. Such things are at all times more apparent to other people than to those especially interested. Besides, any little shortcomings on the part of the Buccaneer were amply made amends for by his solicitude for the religious welfare of others, whose eternal happiness seemed indeed to be more to him than his own. Wherever he went he took with him his Bible, and as he had not been able to swallow it wholesale himself, he soothed his conscience by thrusting it down the throats of other people. If they would not take it quietly, then he would help them over their difficulty with the point of his sword. It was a principle of his that if people would not go to Heaven, that they must be made to go there, and accordingly he sent a good many to the other world very much against their will, and very much before their time.

This bold Buccaneer was perhaps originally intended for a Mahommedan, but being spoilt in the making he became an indifferent Christian. Tell him this, and it would be wise to clear out at once, and make tracks for the remotest part of the world.

As a matter of course he must follow the example of all other Christian people, and enroll himself under the protection of some saint. Now, whether it was by chance, or whether he was possessed with a grim kind of humour, it would be impossible to say. Indeed, he may have had a genuine admiration for the man. The fact remains that he chose as his patron George of Capadocia, who seems to have done a very good business in the way of bacon. It is at all times a difficult matter to form a true estimate of a character far back in history; but it is probable that the whole saintly calendar does not contain a more disreputable blackguard than this self-same George; but he is now a saint " de mortuis &c.;" the bold Buccaneer having now had a good serviceable religion manufactured for him, and having also been fitted out with a good elastic and easily worked conscience, he was himself again. Away the merry rover went, cracking a head here and a crib there, and returning home with whatever happened to fall in his way.

CHAPTER IV.

ALL the Buccaneer's neighbours had adopted some characteristic emblem or device with an appropriate motto. No people, of any degree of self-respect, can get on without such things. The device generally takes the form of some beast or bird of prey—eagles and vultures being greatly favoured. The bold Buccaneer with a characteristic modesty adopted the lion as his emblem, and as his motto "God and my Right." It is wonderful how he made both ends of his motto meet to his own great advantage. These two principles seldom seemed to clash, and if they did, he generally overcame the difficulty in a most satisfactory manner. This perhaps was the effect of his having a good conscience.

Now the lion is a noble-looking animal. His appearance is ferocious, while his roar is terrifying in the extreme. Those who have watched, and studied his habits, say that in spite of all this, he is about as mean a beast as ever stole a meal or entered upon an unequal fight, being ever ready to rob and plunder the weaker inhabitants of the jungle. Of course, the animal had his good points; all animals have, and, no doubt, it was these that attracted the Buccaneer's attention. How delighted he was when his lion's roar frightened any one of his neighbours! What pleasure too it gave him when he put out his large paw and snatched a handful of feathers out of any of their birds! But then what a terrible screeching there was, and very often a fight.

Not to be behind his neighbour in anything, he created high sounding titles, and honourable distinctions, to reward those of his sons who did well in the buccaneering trade. Then to support the weight of their newly acquired dignity, he either allowed them to levy blackmail on whom they could, or he sent round the hat amongst his own people. This hat was with him a cherished institution, and was used on all kinds of occasions. It was hung up in all his churches, but taken down and sent round after every service. Of such importance was it that it must be deemed to be worthy at all times of a capital to begin with. For length of titles he could not approach many of his neighbours, who frequently found consolation for empty pockets, ruined castles, and extreme poverty in a long string of names.

The bold Buccaneer grew in strength, in riches, and in righteousness also. His family increased and multiplied as all good people's families should; but still he fought, and for the most part conquered. Thispr oved to his own satisfaction that God was generally on his side. When the enemy was handed over to him he despoiled him, thus following the example set him by most other peoples and nations, in olden times and in new. It is a good thing to pluck a beaten adversary well, lest he flies again too soon, and sticks either his beak, or his claws into you. Do not believe him if he says he will not do it. To his beaten foe the Buccaneer was kind, for he gave to him spiritual consolation; giving his Bible and selling him his strong and intoxicating drinks. He fully believed that those who did not live up to the teaching of his book would be eternally damned, though he did not at all times show a disposition to live up to it himself, it being very much too inconvenient to do so. There was occasionally such a difference between his preaching, and his practice, that his neighbours wondered whether he was a knave or a hypocrite, or a good honest gentleman who saw no incongruity in his line of action.

Sometimes in his encounters with his enemies he came off second best, as the saying is. Then there was nothing he was so sure of as that the devil was fighting against him. It was his custom then to look about for a scapegoat, and if he found one he sacrificed him to appease the Divine anger. Then having bound up his broken head and dressed his wounds, he took down his book, read a chapter or two, said his prayers, and then waited until the Lord handed his enemy over to him. Then he quickly wiped off old scores, adding or taking something, by way of interest. Thus he became very much respected by all who knew him. As he prospered, so did his church, for he was very generous as most sailors are. Whatever the edifice was within, it was beautiful without, and had a complete organisation. The High Priest, not Caiaphas, stood at the head of all things, and he was the keeper of the Buccaneer's conscience. It was the duty of the High Priest to keep all his subordinates in order. This was a task which at times he could not perform, for the members of the ecclesiastical body showed themselves to be true chips of the Buccaneer block, and though essentially men of peace, they proved themselves at times to be equally men of war. His priests being the keepers of his conscience, frequently took upon themselves to lecture him; not hesitating even to tell him of his transgressions. Having brought the ardent old sinner upon his knees, and prescribed for him prayers, mortifications, and fastings; having also bled him, they cleaned and repaired his conscience and sent him on his way again. Thus did the priesthood grow in power and in self-respect.

Comparisons, it is said, are odious; but they are necessary at times, and if we compare our friend with any one of his neighbours, we find him not a bit worse; he himself thinking, indeed, that he was infinitely better. To exterminate the heathen, or to bring them over from their evil ways, and to burn all heretics was at one time the pious object of his life. The weak, too, had to be protected, and those who cannot take care of themselves ought, at all times, to be extremely obliged to those who will do it for them, and of course they must expect to pay. Then the evil doer had to be punished and fined, and the pride of the arrogant and haughty had to be humbled, and surplus populations had to be worked off, and anybody undertaking these very disagreeable, though necessary duties, is deserving of the thanks of those who have neither the taste, nor the leisure for the occupation. There is nothing strange in all this. Did not Moses sit upon the hilltop with Aaron on one side and Hur on the other, and while these two held up his hands did he not look with satisfaction upon Joshua discomfiting the Amalekites? and very well Joshua seems to have done his work.

Who then will blame the Buccaneer? As in Joshua's day, so now such things are necessary. And if the Buccaneer did burn a heretic or two, what then? He was strictly impartial. To-day it was what was called a Holy Roman that he fried, to-morrow he varied the bill of fare by roasting a Protestant. That was in his early days.

Our Buccaneer was essentially a fighting man, and though the Book he swore by preached peace on earth and good will towards men, his habit was to mix himself up—in early times at least—in every pot-house brawl that he could, and a cracked head was to him an honourable distinction. He as often as not took the wrong side, and he was frequently found fighting in very queer company; but to his honour it must be said that the weakness of a neighbour, who was put upon, was more to him than any abstract principle of right or wrong, and though he was not above pitching into a fellow smaller than himself, he would not allow anyone else to indulge in the luxury if he could help it.

The ill-natured—those who are for ever ready to find out spots and blemishes in other people, to the utter neglect of their own, said all kinds of things. Called him a hard fighting, hard drinking, and hard swearing Christian. He did swear; it was a bad habit, no doubt; but then his climate was enough to make any man swear, and drink into the bargain. He had his failings, and he did not mind being told of them, and he would sit patiently in church, whilst his priests thundered at him from their many pulpits. He took it all in; said his prayers devoutly, and when the inevitable Hat came round, he gave liberally. Perhaps he experienced some slight regret on such occasions that some of his wicked neighbours were not present to partake of the spiritual food that was thus given freely. He felt sure it would have hit some of them very hard. It might perhaps have made them mend their ways, though, as it did not seem to have a permanent effect upon the Buccaneer himself, there may be a doubt upon the subject. It is said that eels get accustomed to skinning.

In passing it may be mentioned that his women—at least in early times—were honest, virtuous, brave and true, and in every way fitting mothers for a race of warriors. It may be presumed that they had their faults. Indeed, some of his laws and customs would lead us to believe that such was the case. For instance, it was laid down as a rule that no husband should beat his wife with a stick of greater diameter than one inch. There was very great humanity here. Scolds he sometimes ducked. If that did not stop the rancour of their tongues he tried the effect of an instrument called the "branks." This fitted over the head something like a dog-muzzle, and was fastened behind with a padlock, while an iron plate rested upon the tongue, and kept it quiet. This was found to be effective.

Judging from our present high state of civilization when women are allowed full liberty of speech, these early habits and customs of the Buccaneer will not bear looking into. Occasionally in later times some one of his sons, not conspicuous for chivalry, knocked down his wife, or his mother-in-law, and then jumped upon her; but as a general rule his manners were very much softened, and his women were treated with very great indulgence. Perhaps those who suffered were deserving people. If, in his ruder age, the women did not love their lords and masters, they at least respected them, and this feeling in the long-run brings the most happiness. In his latter days a deep suit of mourning, with much crape, and a becoming widow's cap, often covered a joyous heart, and a fresh campaign was commenced. But what is love? You have it; you have it not. It is sometimes near, then again it is obscured by distance. It wanders about like a sweet and gentle spirit above the earth; soaring sometimes with outstretched wings to heaven. It seems brightest when afar. Touch it, and it will shrink and fade like the delicate petals of a flower. It often haunts a grave-yard and makes a home amongst the tombs. You fly from it, and it follows; you turn and chase it and it flies. What is love? It is a veritable Will o' the Wisp.

CHAPTER V.

HONOUR to whom honour is due. In speaking of the Buccaneer and in briefly sketching his early life, it would not be right to pass by, without some slight comment, a people who occupied an island situated not many miles from his shores. They were called the Ojabberaways. They came of a spirited and highly sensitive race. They were imaginative in the extreme, quick of temper, and very prone to insult. The smallest slight they would look upon as a grave injury. They were also a quick-witted, clever, and merry people, and fighting was the joy of their life. They were not total abstainers.

Somehow the Ojabberaways and the Buccaneer, though near neighbours, did not get on very well together. This often happens, more especially amongst relations, but the Ojabberaways would not admit that they were of the same blood as the Buccaneer. They maintained that they came from a far nobler stock. In fact, it would appear from what the people themselves said, though history is silent upon the subject, that the island was at one time inhabited by one or two kings, who left a progeny sufficient to people the whole place, and that consequently, every Ojabberaway had royal blood in his veins. No wonder then that they were high-spirited and proud. Now they looked upon the bold Buccaneer as a tyrant, whose chief aim in life was to tread under foot, and otherwise insult them. Nothing would induce them to believe the contrary. They sucked it in at their mother's breasts. The origin of their name is wrapped in mystery, but it is probable that it had, in some way, a connection with the chief produce of their country.

The Ojabberaways were not a united people. Though for the most part they were inimical to the rule of the Buccaneer, and groaned under what they considered the chain cast upon them by an alien and an oppressor, there were many who were comfortable and even happy and contented under his rule. Between these two sections of the Ojabberaways there was no love lost. The wild Ojabberaways as they were sometimes called—of course behind their backs—looked with peculiar hatred upon what were called the loyal Ojabberaways. Speaking of the people generally it may be said, that when you came across one who was a thorough gentleman, no finer specimen of the class could be found in the world; but nature is not at all times prodigal. There are some flowers that only bloom once in a hundred years.

For the ordinary occupation of life the people had little or no taste, and in his own country, if you found one Ojabberaway working, you would always find two at least indulging in the luxury of looking on. And at all times an Ojabberaway would give over any labour in which he might be occupied, to follow a fellow-countryman to his grave, to whom in life he would not have lent a single sixpence. This respect for the dead is touching; but the Ojabberaways were a sentimental nation.

They were also a peculiarly constituted people, generous to a fault as long as they had anything to give; but they, for the most part, lived beyond their means, for a man with a thousand a year would generally spend two, and this in time brought them into the usurer's hands and into difficulties. Then some one had to suffer, and it was generally the tenant of the land and the peasant. The usurer at all times drives a hard bargain, and what bowels he has are not those of compassion. What is in his bond he takes care to have. This gave an opening to the agitator, and he took advantage of the state of things to stir up strife.

Then the Ojabberaways had peculiarly formed eyes. To the outward appearance just like other peoples; but inwardly quite differently constructed. An object that would appear to an ordinary individual in one light would impinge upon the retina of an Ojabberaway's eye in such a manner as to distort some things and magnify others; but most of all a grievance. On the other hand an obligation would appear as small as if it were looked at

B

through the wrong end of a telescope. They were extremely romantic and were given occasionally to romancing. In fact, it has been said by those who like to summarise and put a whole history almost into a nutshell, that the lower orders of the Ojabberaways were liars by nature and beggars by trade. Allowing for that exaggeration which is common to all such sayings there is still a residuum of truth left. Though brave at all times when out of their own country, in it their courage generally took refuge behind a bank or a stone wall. Their food was simple and their favourite drink was strong; so much so, that when taken in too great quantities, it made them perfectly irresponsible beings and extremely dangerous and disagreeable neighbours. Their women were the most virtuous in the world and amongst the most lively, and the men, though in their revenge they would have recourse to the assassin's dagger, would never assail the chastity of a woman, who might walk from one end of their island to the other without the slightest fear of molestation.

The lower orders of this devil-me-care people were joyful in their rags. They preferred dirt to cleanliness, and as has been already said, truth with them was not a highly prized virtue, though if they did lie, they did it more to please than deceive. The Ojabberaways had taken up patriotism, and made it into a regular trade, and they had cultivated it until it had become a most lucrative employment. But with all their faults, and Heaven only knows they had many, one could not help liking them. They had worked for the Buccaneer; they had fought for him, and had helped him in many of his predatory excursions, and they were inclined, at the time of which we are speaking, like many another people, to do a little robbing on their own account; but it must be owned that they were a regular thorn in the Buccaneer's side, and the thorn was working deeper, and deeper, into his flesh every day he lived. It must also be owned that in time past he had not treated them over-well, and retribution was galloping after him in hot haste.

CHAPTER VI.

WHAT am I? I am a whitened sepulchre; a cloak which covers a multitude of sins. Who am I? I am a masquerader a thorough hypocrite and a Pharisee, for I am a worshipper of forms and ceremonies. I move in the very best society. I am a stickler for social laws and etiquette, and I love a lord. I am the guardian of public morals, and in all my dealings I exercise a strict propriety, and I punish severely, not so much the crime, as its detection. At church I am regularly to be seen; but I worship more in public than in private, my devotion being more to attract the attention of my fellow beings than for the sake of God. If I pray, it is openly. If I give, it is before the eyes of all men. It is not so much to me what I am as what I appear to be. On my way home from church I put on a demure, and downcast look, and enjoy in secret my worldly thoughts. I contemplate with inward pleasure, though I outwardly condemn, the shortcomings and failings of my neighbours. I put a check on honest, robust mirth, for its loud, and consequently vulgar laugh offends me. I keep aloof from all questionable society. A poor relation I never see, should he present himself at my door, I promptly have him kicked into the gutter. I dread the touch of an impure hand; but when in the society of the great I sometimes condescend to visit the slums of the poor, though the atmosphere is not congenial to me. An erring sister I pass by as the priest and Levite did the man who fell amongst thieves. I am a social tyrant, more feared perhaps than loved, though few are so independent as not to pay me homage. To the indiscretions of the great I am a little blind, for the vices of the vulgar crowd I show no pity. The nakedness of the fashionable world does not distress me; but immodesty amongst the common herd I visit with my severest displeasure. I keep my eye on all my neighbours; should any of them trip, unless they are saved by their position I let slip my dogs and hound the miscreants outside my social pale. I ride rough shod over society, and no one dares to turn upon me. Who am I? I am society's uncrowned queen, Respectability.

It would be difficult to say at what precise period this uncrowned queen took up her abode under the roof of the bold Buccaneer; but she did, and winked at his goings on; because she looked upon him not as a robber, but as a brave sea-king, who went in quest of venture, and was far removed from the common and vulgar thief. There are other reasons which perhaps induced her to take him under her protection. The Buccaneering business was beginning to fall off, probably because other people had taken to it more thoroughly, and it is well known that competition interferes considerably with the very best of trades and professions. It is possible also that our friend having made a large fortune, was beginning to see the truth of the maxim, that honesty is the best policy. Property does undoubtedly alter ideas; take the most rabid socialist, who is for ever preaching a community of interests and endow him with a fortune, and the burden of his song is speedily changed and in a most wonderful manner. Before it was, "*I take*," but now it is, "*I hold*."

The Buccaneer's wealth had steadily increased, and so had his towns and cities. The hum from a busy multitude rose up like the murmur of the distant ocean as it dashed against the rock-bound coast. On his rivers and bays he had built dockyards, and his shipwrights' hammers could be heard sounding over the waters far and wide. His ships became celebrated for their build and rig, and his sailors were considered not only the bravest, but the most skilled in all the world.

He was a man of great resource and enterprise, was our Buccaneer, and when he found the one business falling off he at once turned his hand to another. If no one wanted either beating or robbing, they wanted their merchandise carried, so he became a carrier to the universe at large, and combined with it the business of trader. One thing begets another, and he soon found out other industries. Tall, tapering chimnies pointed like great black fingers far into the sky and vomited out thick volumes of black smoke. Then he built mills, and put up machinery, and the rattle of thousands of wheels could be heard all over the land, and the uncrowned queen moved about amongst his people and leavened them. But even in his peaceful pursuits the natural bent of his genius discovered itself, for he would frequently, for the want of a more worthy object, steal an idea from a neighbour and then set himself to work to improve upon it, and he generally turned it to good account. The Buccaneer's mind was not inventive, but it was eminently adaptive, and this is very much better, because it generally manages to suck the marrow out of the bones of genius.

Having been the greatest Buccaneer that ever ploughed the briny ocean, he now became a mighty trader—a fighting one perhaps;—fetched and carried for the whole world, and became in fact a universal provider. He often built and fitted out a ship for some neighbour who turned her guns against him; but he did not mind so long as he got his price, and he not unfrequently got the ship back into the bargain in fair and open fight. So things went merrily on.

As is well known success breeds envy and jealousy, and the Buccaneer's neighbours soon began to eye his superior good fortune with hatred and much uncharitableness. They said all kinds of hard things, as people will. Said his gains were ill gotten. But who will ever believe that vast wealth has been honestly acquired? Somebody must have been robbed say they. But if it is only a fool what matter? He and his money must sooner or later part company. At least, so it is said by those people who know everything.

The Buccaneer, of course, put his prosperity down to a different cause. He was a God-fearing and good man. Went to his church regularly; gave of what he had to the poor; and sheltered himself under the cloaks of Respectability and Religion. It is true he could not altogether divest himself of his buccaneering tendencies, and on one occasion he even robbed a church, which is considered about the last thing a man ought to do; but then if he did rob Peter he made ample amends by paying Paul very handsomely. That the Buccaneer was innately a most pious man there can be little if any doubt; he had none himself. He loved to carry his religion with him into his everyday life, and even into his business, and in this perhaps we see the reason why he selected George of Cappadocia as his patron saint. He loved to adulterate, as it were, all his merchandise with it, and he succeeded in a marvellous manner. He was very fond of texts taken from his Book, and these he would hang up in all suitable and unsuitable places. He regulated his trading transactions with his neighbours upon the principle laid down in the parable of the talents, and he took for his especial guide the man who turned his five pieces into ten; for he considered he must have been an excellent man of business; a clever fellow in fact, and one well worthy to be followed. No doubt the parable above alluded to has carried comfort to the soul of many a Jew, Turk, and even infidel. Trade is at all times, and in all places, and by all people, considered for some reason or the other dirty work, and yet it is the founder of great families, who, however, try as soon as possible, to blot out all recollection of the source of their greatness. Trade, too, is the founder and supporter of great nations. Why then is there such a prejudice against it? Is it not honest? Is its first principle, namely, to try and get the better of your neighbour in a bargain, condemned by a virtuous world? Scarcely, for to do your neighbour, to prevent the possibility of being done by him, seems to be implanted firmly in the human breast. It is a principle, in fact, which is well adhered to, and it helps considerably that law of nature which demands the survival of the fittest. Perhaps it was as a precautionary measure that the Buccaneer besprinkled himself, as it were, with holy water, before entering upon his everyday life.

CHAPTER VII.

It is said by the wiseacres of the world that you should always set a thief to catch a thief. Whether it was from a belief in this principle of nature, or whether it was from an innate liking for the business it would be difficult to say; but it is a fact that the Buccaneer made himself for some considerable time a policeman, to keep order amongst his neighbours, and prevent the strong from robbing and setting upon the weak. Oh! the trouble the man had! Big fellows pitching into little ones, to get either their marbles or apples! Then he not only had to keep his neighbours from robbing each other, but he had to keep them off his own property; for had they dared they would have stripped him as naked as the desert is of vegetation. The rascals!

During the time that the Buccaneer was thus doing policeman's duty he was generally pretty well employed, for there was always a row on somewhere; either some hen-roost being robbed, or some pot-house brawl to be quelled, so that all things considered he was not doing a good business. Indeed, he was getting for his trouble little more than hard blows, more kicks than halfpence, in fact.

After a while he determined to give the policeman's duty up; finding no doubt that it did not pay; and he was very much too sensible to conduct business upon such terms for any length of time. So he allowed people to mind their own business as far as they could, while he paid more attention to his own. Of course this state of things was not brought about all at once, for the force of custom is great, and for the life of him, the Buccaneer could not refrain from having an occasional finger in the pie.

The Buccaneer now doffed his pirate's dress, which, though picturesque, was not altogether respectable. People will have prejudices, and if they see a man constantly going about with a brace of pistols in his belt, and a cutlass by his side, they will think that that man is up to no good; so he hung these weapons up, quite handy, for there was no knowing when he might want them to keep off robbers either by sea or land.

But, gentle reader, do not for a moment imagine that the old man was dead—not a bit of it. Beneath the peaceful dress he now assumed there still beat the old heart. You may cover the lion with the skin of an ass but you cannot change the nature of the beast. Our friend was as ready as ever to tread upon his neighbours' toes, and to fight with anybody who trod upon his. Then the peaceful stillness of his shores would be broken by the clack, clack of his many windlasses, and the "yo heave-ho" of his merry men. Up would go his sails, out would go his guns, pokirg their black, angry-looking snouts through the port-holes, as if they sniffed the enemy in the offing. Away went the Buccaneer for the main. His priests prayed; his merry seamen swore, and his women and children cried, as it was their duty to do, upon all such important and interesting occasions.

CHAPTER VIII.

It was the boast of our Buccaneer that he never turned his back upon either friend or enemy, but in this perhaps he romanced a little, as the very best and bravest of men will. The accusation was certainly brought against him in after years. In dwelling upon our own actions a little latitude is always allowed, and the disposition to boast a little must be considered to be a pardonable weakness. Indeed, why should we detract from ourselves when there are so many kind friends and bitter enemies ever ready to render us the service and all for nothing?

He did love to dwell upon his past actions, many of which were glorious, and over his pipe and his glass he would spin many a yarn, and he would declare that there was no nobler sight than a good sea-fight, no finer music than the clash of arms, no finer scent than that which came from the muzzle of a freshly discharged gun. All this is, of course, merely a matter of opinion.

If his sons were successful, he rewarded them well, if otherwise they frequently had to play the part of the scapegoat, and were driven out into the wilderness of neglect. He worshipped success and there is nothing like it. It changes the aspect of the blackest deed, and under its mellowing influence rank rebellion, it is well known, comes out oftentimes, if not always, in the pure and beautiful light of patriotism.

It has been mentioned that our bold Buccaneer had engendered a certain amount of jealousy amongst his neighbours, who were for ever calling him hard names, and always retained the privilege of adding to the number. Such things do not break bones or otherwise injure people, more especially if nature has endowed them with good, thick, serviceable skins, and in this respect she had been considerate to the subject of our history. A good thick skin is, in this world, a tower of strength, from the top of which the fortunate ones can defy ill-nature. At times, however, a shaft did pierce through some soft and indifferently guarded spot in the Buccaneer's armour. He had fought many a good fight both by sea and land, and against long odds, and he could not bear to think, that there should be a suspicion even, that he was a bully ever ready to pitch into one smaller than himself.

There is something very offensive about the above term. Schoolboys are for ever requesting their fellows to pitch into boys their own size and calling them bullies if they will not. But has not the bully been somewhat put upon, misunderstood, and subjected to unjust obloquy? To attack one your own size is a mistake and worthy only of the immortal Don. As a rule for everyday life it would never do, and might be fraught with injustice. All virtue does not lie on the side of the small boy, who frequently by his self-sufficiency and conceit deserves a thrashing. Oftentimes he presumes upon his smallness and makes himself as disagreeable as a drowsy fly in cold weather. If a small boy be put upon by one bigger than himself, he can in turn set upon his inferior, and thus the chain of responsibility can be carried on " ad infinitum," and in the end justice will be done to all.

We are all children of nature and she has established bullying as a principle which is, by the aid of the microscope, to be detected from the mite to the man. The small of each species which she wishes to preserve, she guards and surrounds with especial attributes. The skunk is not a large animal, and yet enemies and friends alike approach him with extreme respect. Was there ever a nation yet, that was kept from thrashing and robbing another on account of its size?

Does the bully never walk about in public offices, or in private dwelling-houses? Is he never to be found on the domestic hearth? Ask the humble swain of yonder fair-haired, blue-eyed, and angel-faced damsel, if he knows what it is to be bullied? Ask the husband of many years standing if he has ever experienced the feeling? All things have their allotted functions to perform in this most complex world of ours, and no doubt the bully is as necessary as many of those minute insects whose presence is only known by the energy of their actions. So much for the bully.

His neighbours also said he was a money-grubber; a mere tradesman, but withal a proud and even prosperous man. That he could fight well had been proved on many a battle-field. What then, if now, he made a goodly income by means of trade? All love this money, yet so many pretend to despise the means by which it is obtained. To march your thousand into your neighbour's country; to lay waste his lands, to filch from him his money, and to ravish, perhaps, his daughters, has ever been considered more noble and honourable, than to sit quietly at home and allow the gold to trickle into your coffers through the peaceful channels of trade.

We have touched upon this subject with the tip only of our pen before, for we fear pollution. The trader is looked upon askance. The uncrowned queen of society turns up her dainty nose at him. The poor man knows it, and as soon as he can hides all trace of his calling. Frequently enrols himself in some civic guard and calls himself a colonel, and tries to hide under his military plumes all signs of the desk and high stool. Then as to our Buccaneer's pride. Such a thing is, no doubt, to be condemned, but its next-of-kin, namely, self-respect, is very much to be esteemed. The Buccaneer maintained that his pride amounted to this and nothing more, and he gloried in it; took it with him everywhere, more especially to his church. When he prayed he might humble himself before his God, but as regards his fellow-man he must hold his head up and claim that consideration which he considered his due. If you wished to see pride fully displayed, there could be no better place than the debatable ground of a church pew in the Buccaneer's island.

When his sons visited his neighbours or any parts called foreign, they were perhaps a little haughty and had a good-natured contempt for the people they found themselves amongst. But that they did not hail from their own fair land was, however, more their misfortune than their fault. Perhaps it is the vulgar ostentation that sometimes accompanies the acquirement of great wealth that renders it so offensive to the less fortunate.

Pride, no doubt, is not a Christian virtue, yet have I found no Christian entirely without it. The Buccaneer's High Priest and other great church dignitaries, were they humble? Yes, humble enough if you paid them the respect they thought their due; if you approached the ecclesiastical breeches and gaiters with modest diffidence. Did not contradict them—not the breeches and gaiters, but the divine beings inside them—or doubt the superiority of their learning, wisdom, and virtue, or presume to make use of that intellect which God has given you. Humble enough then; but your ordinary, and sometimes your extraordinary priests cannot brook opposition. Admit also that our Buccaneer was great, good, rich, generous, brave, and a few other things barely worth the mentioning, and he was humble enough, heaven knows. What he was almost entirely without, was that offensive pride which apes humility.

CHAPTER IX.

IN our preliminary remarks it is necessary to mention two individuals who played a conspicuous part in the Buccaneer's realms.

We have already mentioned one honest sailor, the old coxs'n, Jack Commonsense by name; but there were two women, not to say a third, who also had a permanent abode in his island. The one was called Patriotism, the other Liberty. The first of these was allowed to live for the most part in neglect, and though at times she was made much of, her position was little better than that of a beggar woman, to-day she would sit at the table of the great, and be taken into their councils, to-morrow she would be thrust aside, and occasionally thrown into prison. She was made a shuttle-cock for the battledoor of Madam Party, who was the other celebrity above alluded to, and who pretty well ruled the roast in the Buccaneer's island. Everything had to give way to her, whilst except on extraordinary occasions the beggar woman, Patriotism, was thought but little of. Everybody swore they loved her; but men were deceivers ever, if not liars.

With Liberty it was quite a different tale, she could do pretty well what she liked, and had over our Buccaneer for good and for evil a wonderful influence. At her instigation he allowed the island to be made an asylum for rascals of every kind, who having been kicked out of their own homes, came over and plotted, and sowed broadcast among his people the most pernicious seeds, which bore their fruit in due time. Indeed, Madam Liberty played the part of a veritable wanton, and flirted with blackguards of the deepest dye. The consequence of this was, that one fine day, she gave birth to a boy, named Demos, the father being King Mob. This boy grew to be a most unruly fellow, and caused much trouble wherever he went.

It is said that neither man nor beast can stand prosperity for any length of time, the horse becomes restive, and occasionally kicks his stall to pieces, or otherwise misbehaves himself. Even the ass; the gentle and long-suffering ass, if too well fed, disturbs the whole country round, braying out in his husky tones of repletion his discontent at the very best of corn, when at one time he would have been glad enough to fill his stomach with thistles. So it was with Madam Liberty. It was through her that the Buccaneer first opened his doors to a host of cheap-Jacks, and to merchants and ped'ars from all parts of the world, until in the streets of his principal sea-port towns and chief city, could be seen a strange mixture of costumes and features. Swarthy Orientals with their finely cut profiles, and proud bearing. Broad-faced, oval-eyed Mongols, who always look half asleep, but are generally found to be very wide awake. Flat-nosed, thick-lipped, woolly-headed negroes, and as a matter of course, the ubiquitous Jew was well represented. The Jew is found everywhere, but stay, exception must be made to the northern-most part of the Buccaneer's island. A Jew could not live there, not on account of the severity of the climate, though that was bad enough; but on account of the habits of the people. It is said by some that the object of the Jew is to skin the Christian and the Gentile, with the view of buying back Jerusalem, or, perhaps, the whole of the Holy Land. Many wish that this laudable desire may be accomplished, and that quickly. With all these different nationalities it was a wonder that the Buccaneer retained his individuality, or even kept his language from corruption, but he did, though a broken patter often saluted the ears, while the signs of many different races were stamped upon the faces of the people. There is a belief in the world that mongrels and cross-breeds will not fight. This is a mistake. Our Buccaneer was made up of ever so many nationalities, and yet he had fought in his day well enough. Showing, indeed, an absolute love for the fray. May not the very best blood, of the bluest kind, which flows through the veins of some haughty descendant, have taken its rise in some sturdy cur of low degree, who snapped and snarled himself to the front?

It would be as well to mention that our bold Buccaneer had had a quarrel in early times with one of his sons, who had emigrated and established himself, after the fashion peculiar to his father, on a large and fertile tract of land in the far west. This son, who was called Jonathan, was a tall, lanky, raw boned fellow, with a good head upon his shoulders and a strong will of his own. Modest diffidence had never been a stumbling block in his way. As to whose fault the quarrel was, well, some said it was entirely the old man's, but it is probable there was much to be said on both sides, and that Jonathan was not altogether blameless. At any rate blows were struck, and Jonathan handled his father somewhat roughly, and so there was an estrangement, and a separation, and Jonathan set up business for himself upon the old man's lines; except perhaps he was not quite so religious, and a great deal sharper.

Jonathan did wonderfully well. He had a keen eye for the main chance, and at driving a bargain, or getting the better of a friend, he could not be beaten. In this, to make use of an expression of his own, he pretty well licked creation. In his early days, he was not altogether scrupulous; but what he called sharp practice, other people might put down as something approaching more closely to dishonesty. The proof of the pudding is in the eating. Jonathan prospered, and cheating, it is well known, never does, so he must have been an honest fellow. He loved to do his old father; to get the better of him in a bargain, to get his money out of him either by fair means or foul. Talk to him of honour and he would laugh in your face at your squeamishness. He had many of the eminent qualities of his parent, had Jonathan. He generally managed to keep what he laid his hands upon, and as the saying is, he was not altogether the man to drink with in the dark. By trade he was a packman, or a cheap Jack.

Between Jonathan and the Ojabberaways there was a great friendship. The former used to send over money to the latter to help them in their campaign against the old gentleman. Then the Ojabberaways used to plot, and make infernal machines in Jonathan's country, and come over to the Buccaneer's island, where they frequently carried out their designs, and occasionally used the knife into the bargain.

CHAPTER X.

The family of the Buccaneer in time increased to such an extent that it began to overflow the narrow limits of his island home. His sons therefore carried their zeal and energy and their manners and customs to unknown countries. Under their hands forests disappeared, lands became cultivated, and the aborigines changed their habits or cleared out. It was no business of the young chips of this ancient block, that the soil had already its owners, if not its tillers. If these people did not like the new order of things, they had an alternative. Of course the young chips would commit no act of flagrant injustice, for such would have been against the teachings of their parent's Book, but it was generally noticed that where they went they staid; and that they succeeded in the long run in clearing the land of all rubbish, using for this purpose the toes of their boots as well as their hands. Should the aborigines elect to stay, they could; but then they were made clearly to understand that they must live respectable lives. If they had anything to sell the Buccaneers bought, putting upon the articles their own price, for it could not be expected that the simple children of the soil could know the value of things. They generally gave about half of what was asked, and when the natives, to correct this, put on, to begin with, double the price they intended to take, the Buccaneers were horrified at such innate depravity, which could, as they thought, only come direct from the devil himself. The antidote was their Book. This they immediately presented to these vicious, ignorant, and immoral people, with many of the pages turned down for reference.

Wherever the Buccaneer's sons went they always took a cargo of their intoxicating drinks. These they sold to the gentle savage who showed his readiness to be civilized by getting as drunk as he could, as often as he could, thereby manifesting again his shocking depravity. The Buccaneer at home, when he heard of all this, turned up his eyes to heaven in pious horror, and immediately sent out a cargo of missionaries to counteract the evil effects of his cargoes of drink. These good people wrestled with the devil; prayed for the savages and preached to them, gave them more Bibles and explained it to them; told them to fear God; to shun the devil and all his works; begged them to give up their wicked ways and to lead new lives; to be honest and just in all their dealings; not to be extortionists; not to seek after riches, for that heaven was for the poor. Begged them to do unto others as they would be done by. In the meantime the Buccaneer's sons gave a practical illustration of this beautiful doctrine by selling strong drink and other merchandise at double and treble their value.

These missionaries were godly, self-sacrificing men, but their teachings to the untutored mind must have sounded strange, supplemented as it was by the actions of the Buccaneer's traders. Then again, they found that rival sects, although they pro'essed to follow the same great Master, preached rival doctrines, and hated each other with a peculiar fervour. At one time they painted God as the God of love, at another time they implanted fear and horror in the heart by depicting Him as a revengeful and malicious demon, full of the worst of human failings. They taught these simple savages that life was a kind of tight rope, along which they had to walk; holding in their hands the balancing pole of religion. If they slipped, which likely as not they would, then there was God's rival underneath ready with his net to catch them, and to throw them into a fire that is never quenched.

It could not be expected that the ignorant savage would understand, all at once, the many nice distinctions of modern civilization. No doubt it must have seemed strange to him that the Buccaneer, in the face of what he preached, seldom went away empty-handed—taking indeed at times a goodly patch of land, just by way of recompense; for it was generally found, that, wherever his sons placed their feet, some of the soil always stuck to the soles of them.

Thus were the first seeds of civilization sown; but other and better things were to follow. The nakedness of the savage had to be clothed, and the long black coat and tall hat of respectability had to be introduced. The result of all this was not far to find. It was a natural consequence; for where the Buccaneer found simple human beings, worshipping God after their own way, dark if you like, but at least honest, he frequently left an accomplished lot of hypocrites, drunkards, liars, thieves and rascals generally, who having cast off the few rags of virtue which their own benighted religion had clothed them in, had put on a garment made up of most of the vices of civilization, and only stitched together with the thinnest threads of Christian virtues, which threads were liable to snap at any time. Of course this was not the fault of the Buccaneer's sons. It was entirely due to the wretched soil they had to work upon; you cannot grow figs on thistles, nor can you make a silk purse out of a sow's ear.

What is civilization, do you ask? It is a veneer, sometimes thick and sometimes thin, which is thrown over human nature by culture and what not. From under this cloak the old Adam will from time to time peep out and take a good look round. Did he not peep out to some purpose amongst one of the Buccaneer's neighbours, and playing the part of Cain did he not draw his knife, called the guillotine, across many a brother's throat, kicking them unshriven into eternity? It is right to give every one their due, and it must be owned that the Buccaneer's footsteps were not always written in dust. He often found a people at war amongst themselves, and tearing each other to pieces. These he brought under subjection and gave them law and order, and if he could have kept his sons from selling strong liquors to them, and teaching them some of the pernicious principles of trade, he would have done very much good, but with his Book he took his bottle, and the latter was more readily received than the former.

It sometimes so happened that the ignorance of the heathen was so great, and their minds so clouded by prejudice, that they misunderstood altogether the nature of the missionary. Experience had taught them that the Buccaneer's Bible was generally the harbinger of the Buccaneer's sword, which cleared the way for the Buccaneer's man of business, who, it was found, generally got the advantage in any bargain that was made. What wonder then, if the simple children of nature, the gentle savage, mistook food that was meant for the mind, as food meant for the body, and consumed the missionary instead of his teachings? This is an expensive way of converting a people, but it might be expected that a devoured missionary would not be without its effect upon the consumer. The disposition is naturally affected by the state of the body, the latter by the food that is taken in to nourish it. A violent fit of indigestion might bring on a deep remorse, and then the body would be in a proper state to receive the good seed, which taking root in the heart of one man even, might spring up and spread amongst a whole people. There is consolation here for those who have lost a friend or relation in the above manner.

By the simple methods thus related the Buccaneer managed to get an outlet for his surplus population, and he then increased his dominions, until it was his boast that the sun never set upon them. There was not a clime too inhospitable for him. He conquered not only the people but every natural disadvantage. His sons too travelled into every land as the bearers of the veneer called civilization. Their footprints could be traced upon the desert sands of Arabia. The ring of their rifles was to be heard in the remotest parts of India; on the wild prairies of America, and on the untrodden plains of Africa. They loved to beard the lion and the tiger in their native lairs; to shoot the alligator on the banks of the Nile, and the wild goats high up on the slopes of the vast snow-capped Himalayas. This to them was a pleasurable recreation, while for pastime they loved to climb the highest ice-bound peaks, and the mangled corpse of some adventurous comrade lying at the foot of some precipice in no way damped their ardour. They recovered the body, sang a pean in praise of his temerity, gently placed him in the tomb of oblivion, where so many good people lie, and then commenced their dangerous climb. They were a brave and adventurous lot were the sons of this bold Buccaneer.

CHAPTER XI.

OUR Buccaneer from his earliest times had always kept his Sabbaths in a manner peculiar to himself. He put on his best clothes and a long hat, shut up all his shops but kept open his pot and public houses, and allowed no other recreations than going to church and drinking. Six days had his people to enjoy themselves and his tradesmen to adulterate their different articles of merchandise, the seventh day he decreed should be given up to worship and to pious meditations. All his museums were shut up and all his picture galleries were closed, and his chief city would have been like a city of the dead, if it had not been for the howling mobs that occupied his parks, and other public places, and either shouted sedition or spouted religion. Entire freedom of speech he considered absolutely necessary to the entire freedom of the subject. Many of his people who were not thus engaged passed their time in an inoffensive manner in their favourite pot-house and boosed their holiday away. This from a pecuniary point of view was very much more profitable to the Buccaneer than the opening of any of his museums or libraries; for from drink he derived a goodly income. It is sad, but it must be owned that this rich man had his poor, and where there is poverty there is discontent. The skirts of his garments did trail in the mud. The most distressing thing about this Poverty is that she will bring forth and increase, in an altogether unnecessary manner, thereby providing food for the jail, the hangman, and in the end, the devil.

Some sinned in this respect who ought by example to have taught a better lesson. It was no uncommon thing in the Buccaneer's island for one of his priests to ascend the pulpit, and preach from there the efficacy, and even necessity, of practising self denial. He would then descend from his throne and point a moral to adorn his tale, by marrying and bringing into the world a number of children that he had no visible means of supporting; your priest's quiver is generally full, and he seems at times to have a beautiful faith in God's mercy. Thinking, perhaps, that as He fed the Israelites in the days of old, so would He feed him and his numerous progeny now, with manna fresh from heaven.

It was said that our Buccaneer frequently forgot to look at home, and raising his eyes over the heads of his own poor, fixed his sympathetic gaze upon other people's. Perhaps he did experience a certain amount of gratification at seeing his name at the head of subscription lists, when any of his neighbours suffered from either fire, famine, or pestilence; and to clothe the naked savage of the sunny south, where clothing, except the smallest amount for decency's sake, is absolutely unnecessary, seemed to be to him a more meritorous action than the mending of the rags of his own poverty stricken people.

Then as if he had not enough poor of his own, all his neigbours paid a flattering tribute to his good nature and generosity, by emptying their human sweepings into his dust bin; until in time his island became—and he prided himself upon the fact—an asylum for all the cut-throats, thieves, blackguards, assassins and idiots of the whole world. Madam Liberty had a good deal to say to this. But our Buccaneer, or fighting trader as he had become, was generous even to his own poor in a spasmodic kind of way, and when in his church he heard the oft told story of Dives and Lazarus, it made him sympathetic and opened the bowels of his compassion, and could he have laid hands upon that rascal Dives he would have been made to suffer. This Dives does not appear, however, to have been a monster of iniquity. The only sin he apparently committed, was to fare sumptuously every day, and clothe himself in fine linen. Who amongst us will not do the same if he has but the chance? Do modern Christians live the life of anchorites? Does Dives never sit at the priest's table? Did the Buccaneer's priesthood, from the head down, eschew fine linen, and even at times gorgeous raiments? Do they turn their faces against the luxury of the table on which delicacies temptingly repose. Suppose the Buccaneer on his way home from his devotions had found Lazarus on his door-step, would he have taken him in? not a bit of it. He would have sent him quickly about his business, and if he did not hurry himself the officer of the law would have been called in and Lazarus would have been marched away as a rogue and vagabond. Would the Buccaneer's high priest or any other of his ecclesiastics have taken Lazarus in and washed his sores; tended to him, and fed him? Yes, yes, but times have changed and the story of Lazarus does very well as an example to hold up before the people for pious admiration, but Lazarus' case does not apply to our present high state of civilization, with all its complex social machinery for the benefit of the poor. The proper place for Lazarus now would be the sick ward of a poor house.

Having thus briefly sketched the early history of our Buccaneer or fighting trader; his conversion, the manufacturing of his religion, and the method he had of persuading the heathen to become Christians, it is necessary to relate how he conducted his business. His old sea-faring instincts stuck to him, and he moored on the river that flowed past his principal city, a ship which he called the Ship of State, and by her side he moored another, which he called his Church Ship, and these two rode side by side and stemmed the current of time.

It could not be said that either of these ships were rapid sailers. Indeed, both of them were somewhat bluff in the bows, but they were excellent sea boats, and the old Ship of State had weathered many a storm, and had experienced in her day much foul weather. Her figure-head was a crown. Her crew all told numbered some six hundred and seventy hands, and was divided into two watches, Starboard and Port, each having its captain, lieutenants, petty officers, able and very ordinary seamen, cooks, bottle-washers, swabbers, and adventurers. Of the latter there were a goodly few in each watch, and they had but one star to steer by; but that one was of the very first magnitude. These adventurers were a very busy body of men, and by keeping up a great noise, and pushing themselves to the front, they tried very hard to feather their nests, or drop into some well-paid but sinecure office. They were frequently successful.

In the after part of the Ship of State the Buccaneer had placed his second or Upper Chamber, into which he sent all those of his sons who had done well. Here they enjoyed in peace and extreme quiet their well-earned repose. When thus shelved they were given titles, and were frequently endowed out of the public purse. In early times some of the members of the Upper Chamber had endowed themselves, but there were very few of the old stock left. The principle that our Buccaneer had of promoting his sons to the Upper Chamber was peculiar. It was not based upon personal merit, nor at all times upon services rendered to the State. Success in trade, or fidelity to a party, was generally considered to be, by him, of the very first consideration.

The power that this Upper Chamber once had was extremely great, but now all this had changed, and the old ship was worked entirely, or nearly so, by whichever watch happened to be on duty. Besides, as will be shown, the Upper Chamber had the misfortune to fall under the displeasure of one of the ship's crew.

The Buccaneer dearly loved a lord, no matter whether he was spiritual or temporal, and the women, with few exceptions, adored them without distinction. There is perhaps too much obloquy bestowed upon the toady and tuft hunter. Why should they be so despised? To love and revere the great is surely a commendable action. Are they not the salt of the earth? Sometimes, indeed, the salt has a little lost its flavour, but what then? Much that is good must still remain, to which homage is due. It is the birthright of those who, by their superior intelligence, wisdom, and virtue, have placed themselves high up on pedestals, for common humanity to bow down and worship them.

Who does not love a lord? This esteem for the great is universal. Even the democratic cheap-Jack Jonathan dearly loved a lord; but as he had none of his own he had to make the most he could out of other people's, and he did. It was thought by many, that such a clever fellow as this Jonathan would not be long without lords of his own; but that he would manufacture a few out of the cheap shoddy that he always had on hand.

The Upper Chamber ought to have been extremely wise, and their councils even inspired, for their deliberations were sanctified and leavened by the presence amongst them of a certain number of Lords Spiritual. This gave a sort of Divine authority to the great affairs of State. The priest's kingdom is not of this world; it is therefore all the more wonderful how in every age, and in every clime, he becomes clothed, hemmed in, and perhaps hampered by temporal power, which no doubt he wears as a garment of sackcloth and ashes.

The Church Hulk, which was moored on that side of the Ship of State away from the shore, was commanded by the Buccaneer's High Priest, one celebrated for his piety and learning. His crew was numerous and very able, though at times a mutinous spirit showed itself on board when the authority of the High Priest was openly defied; but then it must be remembered that the church was a church militant, and the priests true chips of the fighting old Buccaneer block. The power of the Buccaneer's priesthood grew, and waxed in strength, and gained such an influence over him that he was not allowed to do anything scarcely without their sanction, and before he set out on any of his predatory expeditions he always asked the blessing and the prayers of the church, and was very seldom if ever refused. This practice is followed even now amongst brigands, in certain parts. These picturesque cut-throats say their prayers before their favourite shrine, and then sally out, slit a gullet and steal a purse with a clear conscience, and take some of the spoil back—if they be pious brigands—to their favourite shrine.

In time the Buccaneer's State Church became so extremely rich that envious eyes were cast in her direction. Those on board of the old Church Hulk denied her wealth, and they should have known. Some of her crew were poor enough, heaven knows, and the Great Hat was constantly sent round. The priest, he is by nature a beggar. It is perhaps one of the few relics we have of that time, when a pure religion was planted by a small band of mendicants, who had neither shoes upon their feet, nor money in their scrips.

How beautiful is poverty at a distance. Songs have been sung in its praise, but no one likes it. It pinches so, and in the Buccaneer's island it was as the mark of Cain. There is something to be said on its side though, for is it not written? "Happy are the poor, for theirs is the kingdom of heaven." Twice happy are they, for not only is theirs the kingdom of heaven, but they are free from the social parasite who never leaves the rich man alone. One attacks him and begs, because he has a large family born to genteel poverty. Another has a church to be roofed or renovated, or some distressing object of charity which he would willingly hang round the neck of the rich man instead of his own, until the rich man being tormented by a thousand and one importunate beggars of high and low degree, feels inclined to exclaim, "Oh! unhappy indeed am I, for not only is it harder for me to enter the kingdom of heaven, than it is for a camel to go through the eye of a needle, but also on earth I am not unfrequently set upon, and despitefully used by the common and vulgar thief, while the hand of the whole world is against me."

CHAPTER XII.

On the mainmast of the Ship of State, high up above the domes and minarets of the Buccaneer's chief city, he had placed his crow's nest or look-out tub, where the look-out man was stationed. This man had, as a matter of course, the usual number of eyes; but one was an official eye, the vision of which was peculiar; for it could see into far distant lands if so inclined; but if not, there could be no eye more blind, not being able to discover what was going on under the nose placed by nature to its immediate front.

Then the Buccaneer had wonderful inventions, by which he could communicate with all his foreign relations and receive in turn what information it was their pleasure to give.

The way the Buccaneer filled up appointments on board of his Ship of State was peculiar to himself. Adaptability, or knowledge of the particular department, was of little or no consideration in his eyes. If the hole to be filled was a round one, he took a square man and jammed him into it, and left him to fit in as best he could. This might appear difficult, and even detrimental to outsiders, but to those accustomed to the peculiar system, things soon settled down and worked pretty well.

He had a distinct objection to anything new. Change had to be brought about slowly and by degrees. If there was any haste in the matter, he started up at once, took fright and cried out "revolution!" and then any necessary reform was thrust back and considerably delayed. He loved patchwork. His Ship of State was patched. His Church Hulk was patched, though of course this was not admitted by the generality of her crew, who declared that the order they sailed by had come down without interruption from the fountain-head; but there were differences of opinion as to this even on board the Church Ship, and sometimes even heated discussions took place on other matters when charity, and brotherly love, were either sent below, or kicked over the ship's side for the time being.

The Buccaneer loved to mend and mend, not from any love of economy, for his public expenditure far exceeded that of any of his neighbours, and he gloried in the fact. If some article of his own manufacture wanted repairing he would not take any of his own material, but he would borrow or buy from his neighbours, and clap on over his own product something peculiar to other people. It was nothing to him whether the thing suited or not, he still held on the even tenor of his way with a doggedness that was in him almost a virtue, because it overcame so many difficulties. In course of time he became famed as the very best tinker that the world had ever produced; and this trade he guarded with a jealous care and kept it entirely to himself.

Then the way he had of relieving his watches was peculiar. He had no regular shifts, but when one of the watches displeased him he just kicked them over the ship's side and sent the whole crew about their business, and a fresh lot had to be selected by the people on shore. It was also another peculiarity of his that whenever the most learned, and wisest of his sons, could not solve some difficult question of State, he appealed at once to the most ignorant, and generally abided by their decision. On such occasions his old coxswain took the helm and generally brought him successfully out of his difficulties.

During the time the crew were on shore soliciting the suffrages of the people they were ready to promise almost anything, if they were only sent on board in charge, but memories were often proved to be very short. The crew often abused each other soundly, making use at times even of very bad language. This was in a measure to be attributed to those who managed to creep on board amongst the crew, who had not all the characteristics of gentlemen; and also to the establishment amongst the Buccaneer's people of a new university called Billingsgate, the language and manners taught at his two ancient seats of learning not being strong enough for the necessities of the age. There were always Ojabberaways on board, and some of these had neither the refinement of manner, nor the delicacy of feelings peculiar to the thorough bred gentleman.

At one time the old Ship of State was the scene of polished debate and pointed epigram, while the satire was delicate and keen; but now things had materially changed and the language too often descended to gross personal abuse.

CHAPTER XIII.

THE means the Buccaneer had of gaining his information, namely, through the medium of his daily press, was confusing in the extreme; for all his papers took sides and showed the fighting instincts of the head of the family. Columns were written upon the same subject which was so decked out in party colours as to baffle all efforts at recognition. Each paper acted the part of an advocate, and by fixing upon the weak parts of an adversary tried to conceal its own shortcomings. Under these circumstances it was very difficult, if indeed it were possible, to find out the true merits of a case.

Every day a battle raged, and frequently an opponent was allowed neither learning nor knowledge, while occasionally he was denied common honesty and even decency. The gentlemen of the Buccaneer's press were a mighty power. Fall under their displeasure, and it would be wise to make peace with your enemy quickly, or you would have a whole phalanx of quills charged to the very tips with ink, levelled at you. Kings even were censured and nations chided in the most patronising manner; being occasionally set at each other's throats, causes for quarrel being found when none really existed. And often where a sore existed between two people, it was not allowed quietly to heal and sink into the regions of forgetfulness, but was kept open until perchance it ended in an open rupture. Then having done this, the press frequently sat in judgment upon the belligerents and censured them for their bloodguiltiness; and by persisting in being present at the row, and chronicling the actions of each combatant, the gentlemen of the press frequently did considerable damage to both.

As information could not possibly be legitimately acquired to keep so many papers going it had to be manufactured. Then when a false rumour was started, there was soon a hue and cry after it, and it was either run to earth, or caught and worried to death in the open. Although the dailies gave themselves great airs and many graces, posing often enough even as prophets, they were a mighty power for good. They often redressed wrongs; brought abuses to light, and kept a rod in pickle for the back of the evil doer. The press was not, however, without its inconveniences, and even evils. Taking a page out of Jonathan's book, the Buccaneer had allowed the system of interviewing celebrities to creep in. Distinguished persons were considered to be fair game, and they were badgered, and bored to disclose their inmost secrets. What they had had for breakfast, how they conducted themselves in private life, whether they ate, drank, slept and dressed as other people, or whether they had any peculiar way of their own, was considered to be of the utmost interest to the people. The method by which we conduct our everyday life is somewhat confined. We can only sit in one way, which we may perhaps slightly vary; but the centre of gravity must be kept within certain small limits. As a rule, there is but one mode of getting into bed, namely, on either one side or the other, though we have known cases in which the individual preferred to crawl in at the foot.

Amongst other inconveniences must be named the newsvendor, who every day, and at all hours up to late at night, rushed through the street and cried up his wares in tones perfectly unintelligible, and which ranged from the shrill pipe of the tender-aged gutter-grub, to the deep gin-and-water voice of the full-grown and matured drunkard.

High above the heads of the rest of the dailies stood the Great Thunderer, as it was called. Every day it belched out dense heavy columns from its paper throat, and it ploughed in amongst the smaller fry and did occasionally great damage, this big gun worked upon a pivot, and by the direction of its smoke you could tell which way the wind of public opinion was likely to blow.

Once a week the weeklies sat in judgment upon the dailies.

The monthlies pitched into both of these, and four times a year the giant quarterlies strode in amongst the combatants, and dealt destruction all round; overcoming all obstacles by the sheer weight of their columns. It was said that one of these big bullies killed a man once, but this is one of those assertions that requires confirmation. What one paper affirmed, another denied, and that which to begin with was tolerably clear, soon became overclouded with prejudice and party feeling.

CHAPTER XIV.

As is frequently the case in histories strides have to be taken, and bridges have to be made over the river of time, so that we may walk over in ease and comfort from one age to another.

At the time of which we now wish to speak, the Starboard watch was in charge of the old Ship of State. The captain of this watch was one William Dogvane, a celebrated sailor, and as shifty a salt—so it was said—as ever trod a plank. His first lieutenant was one Harty, as fine a sailor as ever chewed a quid, or drank a tot of grog. A good hand all round and a thorough gentleman. Then there were the other officers and petty officers, of whom it is not necessary to make particular mention. Strange as it may appear, some of the foremost hands will play a conspicuous part in this history. To begin with, there was Pepper, the cook of the Starboard watch, a great admirer, and supporter, of Captain Dogvane's. Then there was Billy Cheeks, the burly butcher, Joseph Chips the carpenter, and Charlie Chisel his mate, all of the same watch. Pepper was a merry clever little fellow, full of quips, jeers, and jokes, but like most cooks he was a bit uncertain in his temper. Put him out, and stand clear, or you would have a bucket of water over you, either hot or cold, dirty or clean, just whichever happened to be nearest, before you knew where you were, and from his language, a stranger might infer that he had taken high honours at the university of Billingsgate. He was a great admirer of the Ojabberaways.

The cook had a keen eye for the failings of others, but he was a merry fellow with all, and excellent company, and though no one really believed in him, all were ready enough to laugh, either with him, or at him. It is true that such people do not, as a rule, figure in history, but such things have been known. A dancer was once made prefect of Rome. Besides your cook is no ordinary individual, for indirectly he rules the universe. He is the foundation of peace and happiness, and the cause often of strife, sorrow, and great suffering. A bloody war even may be indirectly the consequence of the indiscretion, carelessness, or want of skill on the part of some cook who has to prepare the food for some kingly stomach. A little too much of one thing, or a little skimpiness in another, brings on a fit of indigestion, accompanied by mental irritation, and general loss of temper. Ministers are abused, and have to bow their heads before the fury of the royal anger. The bearing of some rival potentate assumes an altogether offensive aspect. Heads are cut off; the prison opens its gates, and many poor subjects are thrust in to contemplate in silence the fickleness of fortune, or their own sins. Wars are declared. Battalions are ranged against battalions, and human blood flows like water, and all this commotion springs, may be, from the kitchen, where the cook sits calmly; bakes, stews, and fries as if nothing had happened.

Most assuredly the cook holds a most responsible position in the world, and it is not too much to say that the safety, honour, welfare, and integrity, yes, and even the happiness and intelligence of a people, depend in a great measure upon the head of the kitchen. The cook should, therefore, take his place amongst the high ministers of every state, for it is in his power to do far more good, and to give far greater pleasure to the many, than your prating philanthropist, who with meddling and muddling manners, large heart, but, generally speaking, small head, tries his best to make paupers of a people, and do harm generally. Your cook is the prime minister to the greatest potentate in the whole world, namely, king stomach, and therefore your cook, if he be a wise, skilful, and virtuous cook, should hold a high place in every community. My lord bishop do you cavil at my statement about his majesty, king stomach? Does he not dwell in the monastery? Does he not sit even at the priest's table, and say to the company, eat, drink, and be merry? Does the priest more than the layman turn his back upon the succulent oyster, the truffled turkey, the barded quail, the plover's egg, which may have cost a shilling, though the honest tradesman only perhaps gave a penny for the rook's egg, which he substitutes for it? Is the voice of our mighty potentate never heard in the bishop's palace? The priest is but a man. True, but too often he looks upon himself as the Lord's anointed who is to be approached with respect, and listened to with reverence, when from his throne, the pulpit, he preaches a self denial to others, that he does not find it convenient to practice himself.

As the Port watch were not on deck at the time of which we are speaking, it is not necessary to say much about the men that composed it, further than to mention that Bob Mainstay was the captain, and a most experienced seaman, quite equal, many thought, to old Bill Dogvane, and very much more certain, though he had not Bill's command of language. Indeed, few had, for Bill could spin a yarn many fathoms long. The first lieutenant of the Port watch was Ben Backstay, a safe steady going seaman, universally respected, and both he and his captain had had no finishing touches put on by the university of Billingsgate, and in consequence they were courteous gentlemen. The captain was perhaps a little imperious and keen of speech. Then, of course, there were all the other officers and able seamen, and there was a merry, clever little fellow, who though only a middy, must not be lost sight of: for he was destined to rise step by step, and even jumps to a high position in the old Ship of State. And he will play no mean part in our present history. Random Jack as he was called, delighted annoying old Dogvane, in fact, he buzzed about the whole of the Starboard watch like a mosquito, and was the merriest, and most cheery little devil that ever put on a sailor's jacket. People at first laughed and jeered at the middy, but he cared not. Only those laugh in the end who win, and he was contented to bide his time, and through fair weather and foul, in ups and downs, he never lost confidence in himself, and herein lies the mainspring of greatness and very much of the world's success.

It has been shown that the old fighting instinct of the Buccaneer was present amongst all his children, and that it was not absent even on board of the Church Hulk. No wonder then that it showed itself to a marked degree amongst his ship's crew, which, however, had not as yet advanced so far as to run an opponent through with three feet of cold steel or plug him with an ounce of lead, like some of his neighbours ; nor was his ship's deck strewn about with spittoons, like, it was said, Jonathan's at one time was. In a matter of expectoration Jonathan was great. A spittoon, if properly aimed at the head of an antagonist, political or otherwise, might bring a debate to a speedy, and perhaps a satisfactory conclusion.

Though Captain William Dogvane swore he was essentially a man of peace, his life proved him to be a man of war, and he displayed a marvellous aptitude for getting into rows and then swearing that they were none of his making. Then if he found that he was getting the worst of a fight he would at once give in ; own himself in the wrong, and apologize all round, and sometimes tread on peoples' toes in doing so, and consequently getting more abuse than thanks for his disinterestedness. Dogvane said it was a noble and magnanimous thing to own oneself in the wrong, and so save bloodshed ; but his enemies said it was generally due solely to cowardice, and they had some reason for saying this, as far as Dogvane was concerned, for he never owned himself wrong until he had been two or three times beaten in the open, and then the enormity of the action—not the beating—became apparent to him. This shifty old salt would at once ware ship, and put all the blame for everything upon the other watch, the members of which, if they only did a half of what old Dogvane accredited them with, deserved to be hanged, drawn, and quartered. This skilled old sailor could sail on any tack and before any wind. In his lifetime he had been many things and had served in both watches ; but there was nothing out of the way in this, as it was no unusual thing for a man to commence in the Starboard watch and finish up in the Port, and the reverse. Then old Dogvane could do almost anything. There was nothing too great for him to tackle. He could talk for hours upon the Mosaic

Cosmogony. Science would try to knock him over with facts; but Dogvane would, to his own entire satisfaction, prove that science was altogether wrong. He would discuss religion, philosophy, ethics, in fact, anything, with any past master in the craft, and he had the quality, said to be peculiar to the race from which he sprang, of never knowing when he was beaten.

The Ojabberaways who served on board the old Ship of State were for the most part in the Starboard watch, and if by any chance they changed over to the other side to serve their purpose, the alliance was never of long duration nor was it altogether of an honourable kind.

CHAPTER XV.

A TIME came when things were said to be as they ought not to be; discontent became very prevalent. It is always thus; but the people, it was said—and with some show of reason—had quarrelled with their prosperity. Labour had combined against capital, and the workers refused to work except upon their own terms. They demanded shorter hours and more pay. Nor would they, if they could help it, allow others to labour. The Buccaneer's system of education had perhaps something to do with this state of things, for it taught his children almost everything, except how to gain a living, gave many of them exalted opinions, crammed their heads, but left their stomachs empty, until in time the serving class bid fair to be educated out of his island. All wanted to be masters and mistresses, and the kitchen was looked down upon. Things came to such a pass that it was far easier to obtain a governess who could teach almost anything, for thirty pounds a year, than a cook for the same amount, whose knowledge of her trade barely soared as high as boiling a potato, or grilling properly a mutton chop, and who even with this small amount of professional skill was insolent if found fault with.

Then the Buccaneer's tradesmen, being true chips of the ancient block, were frequently extortionists, if not actual robbers. They were certainly well imbued with his first principle of trade, namely, the turning of their five talents into ten, and some at least were not above selling short weight and adulterating their merchandise; but these of course were the dishonest ones, the black sheep that are said to exist in every flock. Then before things reached the consumer they had to be dealt with by the middle men, a species of vampire who sucked a good deal of the profit out of the article; so the consumer was driven into the hands of the foreign cheap-

Jack, who soon began to sell more than ever. The Buccaneer's old coxswain, who, it must be owned, was a bit of a preacher, and like all such a little prosy, spoke up as was his wont: "Mates," he said, addressing a lot of grumblers, who had assembled together to air their grievances, "don't you see you've got your ship's head lying in the wrong direction? You are cutting your throats, my hearties, like a swimming pig, for while some of you are quarrelling with your masters, and others of you are going in for keeping up the prices, these furrin cheap-Jacks are doing a thriving trade. Shipload after shipload of their merchandise is coming in. They are ousting you, my lads, out of your own markets, while you stand by, pipe in mouth and hands in pockets, demanding your shorter hours and higher wages." "What would you have us do, mate?" cried a burly fellow from the crowd, as he held his pipe in one hand and a quart pot in the other. "Are we to work our souls and bodies out, day after day, and year after year, while our masters are building up a pile, and palaces to put it in? We ain't agoing to work like some of our neighbours for a mere nothing; neither are we agoing to live on black bread and sour crout; so unless our masters are going to cave in and come down with the needful, we are going to hold out. As for the cheap-Jack fellows, let our master make 'em pay toll. Let's have everything fair and above board. Put that in your pipe, old man, and smoke it." "Lads!" cried old Jack, "you are killing your goose that lays the golden eggs; or, you are frightening her over the water, which amounts to the same thing." "Let her go, mate. If she stays here and stops laying eggs, we'll wring her neck, and divide her carcass amongst us. We shall have a good feed then anyhow, and be equal all round." So there were strikes, and a great cry out against capital, and trade began to work down towards the seashore, and unfolding her wings, prepared to take flight to other and more congenial climes.

Whenever the old coxswain got his master's ear upon the subject, his favourite, Liberty, was sure to be on the other side, telling him to let things alone. This aggravated old Jack, who one day exclaimed: "Pray, madam! how far are you going to take our master along this road of freedom?" "Good, honest Jack, that is for you to say," cried madam, with a smile and a curtsey. "Aye, aye, that is all well enough, my fine lady. But there is not a place you don't go to with those doctrines of yours. You commenced upstairs in the parlour, and now you have gone down into the kitchen, and heaven only knows where you intend to stop. What is the use of my saying anything? Where you lead my master follows; no matter whether the road you are on goes to the devil or not. It is no use my holding on to his coat tails, when you are coaxing him, cajoling him, and pulling him forward by both his hands." So saying the old coxswain went his way, muttering something about women in general, that was not altogether complimentary to the fair sex. But the honest coxswain, when ruffled, said, like many other people, very much more than what he meant.

In the general running down of things the Buccaneer's women did not escape. At one time they had been famed both for their virtues, and their beauty. Of the latter it was said there was a falling off. Indeed they were so pulled to pieces all round, by the sharp talons of ill-nature, that they were not left too many virtues to plume themselves with.

Beauty it is well known is only skin deep, and in very many cases it does not penetrate even so far. It can be laid on in the morning and dusted off at night without much trouble, though no doubt many beauties prefer to go to bed with the bloom on. This kind of beauty has its merits. It withstands to a certain extent the ravages of time; art following close in the footsteps of nature with the paint brush filling up the crevices, and washing out the marks of the years that have hurried by. But it was said that a good deal of the bloom on the young cheeks was not a constant quantity, and that the cherry lips were not a fast colour. That eyebrows and eyelashes were pencilled and hair dyed. If this was not a foul libel how much was it to be regretted? Youth requires neither putty nor paint to deck it off. For the old it matters little; the only people deceived are the artists themselves. You may disguise the age somewhat, put back the hand of time a year or so, but you can never make an old face look young; paint it up and putty it as much as you like. In the Buccaneer's island there was indeed to be seen strange contrasts, such as dark eyebrows and fair hair, but then nature does at times play sad tricks, giving to animals more heads than one, and occasionally more than the usual quantity of tails, and even legs.

Suppose the Buccaneer's daughter did call in the aid of art. They all do it, and in doing it, a woman only follows the instincts of her nature, though some are so strong minded as to pay little or no attention to personal adornments. The instinct above alluded to is to be found in the daughter of nature, as well as in her civilized sister, and is the one great link that binds female humanity together. Is there a part of the civilized world yet discovered where the female mind does not turn towards the embellishment of the outward form? No doubt the first act of Eve after the sad catastrophe in the garden of Eden, when she recovered from the temporary fit of despondency, was to seek some smooth sheet of water, on which her fair face and form might be mirrored, and with as little doubt her second act was to procure the most becoming fig leaf, that the whole garden of Eden could produce to deck herself in. In the general effect perhaps she found some slight consolation, though she might regret there were not more Adams than one. While in the West the female head is decorated with hair taken, perhaps, from some one, who having paid the debt due to nature has no further need for it, her sister of ruder climes utilizes the bushy end of a cow's tail. While the one uses cosmetics, pomades, and dainty perfumes, the other uses earth, or clay, or things that by no means, or under any circumstances, can be called dainty. In passing, we may perhaps call the attention to the strange perversion of the order of things that seems to run through the civilized male mind of the West. Hairs pulled from a horse's tail decorate the wise heads of judges, while feathers plucked from the nether end of a cock, float over the heads of Western warriors. Is there any subtle influence of nature at work here? But to return to the ladies.

The female child of nature, instead of hanging round her neck precious stones, wears thin strings of beads, or berries, or even shells, and this in many climates is no inconsiderable part of her attire. Then where she places a bunch of reeds, or dried grass, her civilized sister places tastefully a bunch of ribbons. The same parts, present the same difficulties, as to picturesque decoration. The progress of civilization is also shown in the use of nose, lip, and ear-rings. The two former have vanished from the fair faces of the West, but ear-rings still remain as a link to bind us to the past, and though ankle rings have disappeared except on the legs of French poodles, bangles are still worn.

As to the modesty of the Buccaneer's women. This is a delicate matter and we pass over it with the remark that in this respect they would bear favourable comparison with any of their neighbours, though their language perhaps at times, and even their manners, left somewhat to be desired. The modesty of a woman must not be treated lightly, for it is to her, or should be, as a diadem studded with precious stones, and a garment as lovely to behold as the mantle of our Creator when dipped in Autumn's rich and ever varying colours.

What for the most part attracted the eye of censure was the manner in which the fashionable daughters of the Buccaneer dressed of an evening. Then, in many cases, there was very little clothing on above the waist; but ample amends were made by the length of the skirts, which trailed many yards in the dirt behind.

This display of what are usually called the charms of a woman, could not have been from any base motive; for had such been the case the middle aged and old, would not have indulged in the practice. There may be something very attractive about the well-shaped neck and snow white bosom of a young and pretty girl, when modesty is not altogether outraged, but there can be nothing pleasing about too fleshy middle age, or the skinny old. Besides had the desire been the base one of exciting the worst of man's passions, the skirts of the fashionable dresses would have been considerably shortened. A pretty foot and shapely ankle is every bit as pleasing to the eye of man, as a naked bosom, though here again the beefy heels of maturity, and the fleshless pegs of age must be excepted.

We rather see in the above fashion an innate modesty born in the female breast, and we detect in it a disposition ever present to go back to the far off past. To that time, when the clothing of our first mother was conspicuous by its almost entire absence. It was all the more commendable on the part of the Buccaneer's daughters to endeavour to re-establish this early state of innocence, because his climate was dead against the movement, and it says no little for the hardiness of his women, who could thus lay bare so much of their bodies in a temperature notoriously inclement, without suffering any ill effects.

CHAPTER XVI.

THERE was a lively discussion going on now on board the old Ship of State about the state of things in general. As to whether trade really was depressed at home, and as to whether the Buccaneer's relations were all as they should be abroad.

The Port watch, who wanted to get charge of the old ship, swore that things were at sixes and sevens. Their part of the press gang took of course the same view, while the Starboard watch, headed by Dogvane, declared with great zeal and certainty that things were never better.

There was discontent even amongst the Starboard, or Dogvane's watch, some of the hands, namely, the carpenter, the butcher, and the cook, and, of course, the carpenter's mate, thinking that the old ship was out of date, and much too slow for the times. The carpenter was for altering her, and for cutting adrift the old hulk alongside. The cook was for breaking the old ship up, and for building an entirely new one on lines of his own. The new craft, he declared, would be a rapid sailer, very easily managed and cheaply worked. These ideas grew and took root, and were productive of certain fruit, as will be hereafter shown.

When the captain of the Port watch drew the Buccaneer's attention to the general, as he said, unsatisfactory state of things, old Dogvane shut one eye—not his weather one—that was always open. "It does you credit," he said, "it does you credit; but bless you, my master isn't going to be taken in, in that way. It is a trick, sir; just a party trick," he said, turning to the Buccaneer, who with his cox'sn was standing on the quarter-deck, wondering, as was his custom, whom he was to believe.

The Port watch now began to abuse old Dogvane, and many of the long shore hands freely damned him; but quite as many blessed him, and were ready to crown him with laurels; but he was called by the Port watch a double-dealing, sly, foxy, old fellow, who would commit any crime from pitch-and-toss to manslaughter, though not a soul had ever seen him indulging in either of these games.

The carpenter declared that the Buccaneer's people were doing a rattling trade in boots, shoes, and watches, while woollen stuffs were all up. What a carpenter could know about such things it would be difficult to say. Had it been nails, or screws, it would have been quite a different thing; but on board the old ship a want of knowledge never kept a tongue quiet. Indeed, under the system of a square man for a round hole, how could it be otherwise?

There was a lengthy and animated discussion on the matter, which Random Jack, of whom mention has been made, took advantage of to scud up aloft to the look-out tub. The shaking of the rigging woke up the man on duty, who, from a matter of habit, sung out "All's well."

Random Jack declared it was nothing of the sort, and he accused the look-out man of being asleep. Then the middy hailed the deck. "Below there!" he cried, "I see clouds in the East." This was a safe thing to say, for there were always clouds there of some sort. He added, "Dust and smoke show there is a heavy storm there. I see, too, a city in flames, and people are being massacred."

The Buccaneer turned upon old Dogvane, the captain of the watch on duty, and asked him what all this meant. Dogvane was not in the least taken aback, no good sailor ever is, so he said, "I cannot believe, sir, that anything is going on in the East that should not be, because we have no official information on the subject." It was a well known fact, that in the Buccaneer's island, his official information was about the last that was ever received. People often wondered what kind of an animal carried his mail bags. Some said it must be a mule, or perhaps an ass.

Dogvane, to reassure his master, hailed the mast-head, and asked the look-out man how the old ship was heading. This was the usual way of asking for information. The man on duty in the tub immediately placed his official eye to the telescope, while he firmly closed the other, and answered that the distant horizon was quite clear. Then he added, "Some people are so precious sharp that they stand a chance of cutting themselves." This sarcasm was levelled at Random Jack, but he treated it with a contempt that was peculiar to him.

When the little middy reached the deck he had a pretty tale to tell; but the cook said it was a parcel of lies, that the other watch could scarcely be believed on their oath, and this depravity very much distressed him; for Pepper was an upright, and an honest man. Billy Cheeks said that the young Tory Bantam, as he called him, was a deal too fond of crowing, and that if he came within striking distance of his fly flapper, he would take his meals standing for some considerable time. The Ojabberaways on board were highly delighted at the prospect of a row, for nothing they liked better than a free fight, and they were always ready to join in any devilment that would cause the old gentleman annoyance.

Dogvane, seeing how things were going, delivered himself of one of those speeches, for which he was celebrated. Having hitched up his trousers fore and aft, like the good sailor that he was, he said:

"All this stir, sir, is about nothing. As I said before it is just a trick of the other side to shift watches. Clouds in the East? Of course there are. It is the very place we generally look for them. I am creditably informed that all our relations are for the most part friendly, and taking into consideration how interfering and meddlesome relations usually are, this must be considered highly satisfactory. At home the bright sun of prosperity shines over all the land, while the songs of a contented people rise up in a grand chorus to heaven." The cook hearing this winked at the butcher, upon whose placid features there was a smile of approval and self-satisfaction; but the good impression left by the above beautiful language upon the mind of the Buccaneer, was slightly clouded by a parting shot on the part of the captain of the Port watch, who knew as well as Dogvane how to arouse his master's suspicion. It could always be done by drawing attention to what were said to be the ambitious designs of some old rival. Then our Buccaneer from a state of indolent indifference, would often fly to the opposite extreme and suffer something in the nature of a panic, under the influence of which he would for the time being storm and rave. If he could, he would make a scapegoat of some one. Perhaps he would kick his watch on duty over the ship's side, and think to put all things straight by lavishing his money upon every conceivable object. The fury of the storm being over, he would again sink into his usual happy-go-lucky state, and rest quietly until some one stirred him up again. As some rusty old weathercock will not condescend to move for anything less than a gale of wind, so it took a panic to rouse up this wealthy and easy-going old gentleman.

CHAPTER XVII.

In the East there dwelt at this time a mighty Bandit, Bruin by name. He was an old rival of the Buccaneer. It is said that birds of a feather, either do, or should flock together; but as a matter of fact it is frequently found that they do not; the feather being too often a bone of contention. People would have thought that these two celebrities, following as they did the same profession, with the exception that one pushed his trade more by sea, and the other more by land, would have lived peacefully one with another; more especially as they were separated by a wide tract of land and sea. Many old saws and sayings would justify this belief; but the Bandit and the Buccaneer could not hit it off together. The latter being quite a reformed, God-fearing and respectable man, no doubt looked with horror upon the life that the former was leading. It was strange too; because the Bandit was an eminently pious, and Christian gentleman also; but he had not as yet made his pile, which of course made all the difference; and his people, though many of them were slaves, were beginning to be unruly.

As to whether the Bandit was as cruel and as bad as he was said to be, is open to doubt. It is well known that the devil is not as black as what he is painted. Evil things were said even of the Ojabberaways, and we know that once give a dog a bad name, and you may as well hang him, or tie a string round his neck, and fling him into the nearest pond. Some people no doubt would have gloried in seeing this Eastern Bandit run up on the nearest tree; but then he required catching.

Of the living why not be truthful? There seems to be a prevalent opinion that this should be the case when we discuss the characters of our enemies, and more especially of our friends to whom we can make amends by saying nothing but what is good of them when they are dead. This old sea king whose history we take a delight in relating, had as has been shown a very quick eye for the shortcomings of his friends. Looking over the heads of his own little peccadillos, he fixed his keen gaze upon those of his neighbours, and no one could find out an act of robbery sooner than could this Buccaneering trader; then his virtuous indignation knew no bounds.

It was indeed a belief of his, that most of his neighbours were ambitious and designing, ever ready to feather their own nests at the expense of other peoples. Yet they were all eminently religious, prayed often, and professedly were all followers of the same great Master; but they all slept in armour, and were ready on the slightest provocation to fly at each other's throats. Our pious Buccaneer had learnt to look upon the East as a sort of devil's playground, and the Bandit as the arch fiend himself who he frequently thought was up to no good when the poor gentleman was perhaps actually engaged in his devotions.

The slightest allusion to the Eastern Bandit always alarmed him, so the command was given on board the old Ship of State to pipe all hands, and presently the bo'sn's whistle, followed by those of all his mates, sounded merrily along the decks. Those below hurried up, while those on shore hastened on board, and the scene was soon one of the liveliest. Just as the last man tumbled over the ship's side, there was a great commotion at the Port gangway, and on looking over, a very queer powerfully made fellow was to be seen trying to get on board; but the rest of the ship's company would not have him at any price. Pepper, the cook, said the man was a friend of his, in fact, his mate; but Pepper spoke to deaf ears; for the fellow would not swear, and it is a well known fact that a seaman who will not swear cannot be a good sailor. Several of the hands seized upon the intruder, and suiting an old rhyme to the occasion, they commenced to sing—

"Here comes a queer man
Who will not say his prayers,
So we take him by his two legs
And chuck him down the stairs."

And they did, much to honest Pepper's disgust, who rated and accused them well for their trouble. The man himself as he swam ashore affirmed that he would return and serve yet on board of the old ship. He kept his word; was posted to Captain Dogvane's watch, and became very much respected.

As was their custom, the Ojabberaways tried very hard to monopolize the whole of the conversation, with their numerous complaints, and they swore most stoutly that not a stitch of business should the Buccaneer do until they were given their independence and freed from the yoke of the tyrant. When they were told that all was being done for them that could in justice to all interests be done, one of them said, "Indeed a mighty deal too much has been done; but in the wrong direction. We ask for our freedom, and you give us a rope and bid us go hang."

Here some one amongst the crew who apparently had caught a cold, sneezed, this the Ojabberaways took as an additional insult upon their unhappy country, and because the insult could not be withdrawn, they created a great disturbance, to quell which, two or three of them had to be thrown overboard. The ship thus lightened rode all the better, but the cook said it was a sinful waste thus to sacrifice the Ojabberaways, when there was the whole of the Buccaneer's Upper Chamber weighing the old ship down by the stern. The discussion on board now took a lively turn, upon an assertion which the carpenter had previously made about boots and shoes being brisk. Some interested person declared that if the trade was brisk the boots themselves were bad, as could be seen by the Buccaneer's soldiers who were fighting in the East.

All the fat was now put into the fire, and there was a heated argument as to whether the Buccaneer was or was not engaged in warlike operations. There ought to have been no doubt about such a thing, but there was. It was also asserted that the rascally contractor was at his old game of starving both men and animals, or giving them bad food, and so amassing a large fortune and qualifying himself for promotion to the Buccaneer's Upper Chamber.

The Buccaneer turned for information to his trusty Captain

Dogvane. "How is this, Master Dogvane?" he asked, "I thought you said my relations abroad were all good."

"Sir," replied the captain, "ever since the old Ship of State was built have there been these differences of opinion, and God forbid that it should be otherwise; it will be an evil day for my master when his watches take so little interest in his affairs as to cease to have wordy battles over them."

"But, Master Dogvane, whom am I to believe?"

"A straightforward question, sir, demands a straightforward reply. Believe in me."

At this there were loud jeers from the other watch, and many voices were heard to say: "Believe in him and he will run you pretty soon into shoal water."

"Aye! aye!" cried Dogvane, "the same old cry. I have been man and boy on board this old craft for many a long year, and these hands have held the helm and so the old ship rides safe and sound. Her bluff old bows riding superior to every storm. Have not gales and hurricanes swept over these decks, and yet she has risen superior to all? Some say the old craft alongside is in shallow water, and yet she seems peaceful and safe enough."

Here Random Jack said the captain was, as usual, drifting from the point.

"Of course, my little man, you must have your say. It was you that first set this ball a-rolling; but hurry no man's cattle is a safe cry. I was merely clearing my decks, as it were, for action."

Upon being pressed, Dogvane was obliged to admit that he was engaged in operations of a warlike nature; but he went into so many subtle distinctions as to the different kinds of warfare that nobody could follow him. He swore that in the footsteps of the other watch followed gratuitous and unprovoked war. "We are not now at war," he cried in great warmth, "though I will not say that we are not engaged in some kind of military operations which, however, though offensive in form are purely defensive in essence." Dogvane being apparently afraid lest he should be called upon for an explanation turned the conversation by appealing to a weak part in his master's nature, namely, his religion.

"Can we ever forget," he said, "the Divine Master we follow? Can we forget the principles of peace he taught us? The operations I am now engaged in are only a part of that terrible inheritance that the other watch left me." This of course brought down a storm upon him from the other watch. "My aim," he continued, "ever has been to maintain a friendly footing with all your neighbours, and by keeping them in union together to neutralize, fetter, and bind up the selfish aims of each."

"And the result of your labours," cried the captain of the Port Watch, "has been to estrange our master from all his friends and to land him in incessant troubles. Have you not bombarded a friend's town?" he added, "have you not massacred his people?"

Dogvane could not altogether deny this, so he said: "It is true that a few forts have been knocked down, but they were better down than up; and a few people have no doubt been killed, but what of what? Accidents will happen in the very best regulated undertakings."

Thus did the argument continue to the utter confusion of the bold Buccaneer who cast his eyes towards the Church Hulk alongside, and he inwardly wished that all was as peaceful and secure as it seemed to be there; but scarcely had the thought crossed his mind than a great hubbub rose up and the sound of controversy became loud. All eyes were turned towards the Church Hulk, and many feared they were about to witness one of those religious disputes which occasionally are so bitter and even disastrous. Some thought it must at least be a mutiny. Considerable relief was felt when it was found upon inquiry that it was nothing more serious than a discussion as to the shape and colour of the vestments in which our Creator was to be worshipped in, and a rival sect nearly came to blows over the form of an ecclesiastical hat. All this seemed strange, because the Church Hulk professed to sail by orders which said: "Take no thought for your life, what ye shall eat, or what ye shall drink, nor yet for your body what ye shall put on."

If people squabble amongst themselves it soon becomes known, and it soon began to be noised abroad that the Buccaneer's

Church Hulk was in danger, both from jealousy without and the want of Christian charity and brotherly love within. It is certain that some of the crew of the Ship of State had their eyes upon her, and it got rumoured abroad that some fine morning people would wake up to find she had either slipped her moorings or been cut adrift. But has not this rumour ever been a lying rascal and a fit lieutenant for the devil himself?

CHAPTER XVIII.

THE Buccaneer paced the deck of his old ship in a thoughtful manner. Suddenly he stopped and addressed his captain. "Dogvane," he said, "I have trusted you; beware lest you deceive me."

"Sir," said the captain, "the man who would deceive so good and great a master would be base indeed."

"Is all this true that the other watch have said about my ships? Am I in the wretched state they say? Where has gone all my money?"

"Master, allow not the idle shafts of the Port Watch to trouble you. They are greedy of office, and to gain their ends, they magnify some things and totally misrepresent others. Believe not what they said about your ships and about your trade. Bloated armaments, sir, are a source of danger; exciting the fear, jealousy, and suspicions of your neighbours; draining your exchequer, and feeding like a foul canker upon the fair flower of your industries. You are no longer a bold Buccaneer, sailing the seas in search of plunder. You are no land stealer. The object of your life is not now to carry fire and sword into your neighbour's country. You are a respectable trader, peaceful and industrious, a Christian, with religious principles to act up to."

"Yes, Master Dogvane; but there are those about, who, if I am not ready to protect my own, will save me the trouble."

"Sir, it is not right to have so base an opinion of the world; but your armaments are fully equal to all your needs."

"In this, Master Dogvane, I must perforce believe you. But how about that rascal Bruin? He has committed depredations in the past. He is a grasping fellow too, and I have my suspicions that there may be some truth in what I hear. He may be casting sheep's eyes at my fair Indian Princess."

"So long as they are only sheep's eyes, sir, where is the harm? The lamb which is the forerunner of the sheep is the emblem of peace. Suspicion, my master, is the attribute of either a base or weak mind, and is unworthy of you, The Eastern Bandit I have always found a pious and truthful man; only requiring to be known to be appreciated. Honest too, as times go; but awkward when vexed."

We must leave the Buccaneer in the hands of his skilful captain and take a turn ashore. The Port Watch having collected crowds of idlers addressed them on the general depressed state of affairs, and they found ready listeners. No one considers himself so well off but that he wants something more. There was a general and continued cry out against the foreign cheap-Jacks. The blackguards who take advantage of every breath of discontent to preach their doctrine of universal plunder had merry times, and their tongues wagged at the street corners, in the parks, and other public places. These fellows had a following, for they held up before the eyes of the poor a picture of plenty, while the criminals saw in them instruments to help them on in their trade. The sound of their many voices surged up like the angry roar of wild beasts in some distant jungle.

But now all eyes were turned towards the old Ship of State, for a sight was to be seen that had not been seen in the memory of living man before. It was nothing more nor less than the portly form of the old Buccaneer struggling with difficulty up the rigging, and behind him came the lithesome form of old Dogvane; both of them were evidently bound for the crow's nest, below which the legs of the look-out man could be seen hanging like the legs of some huge stork.

There was a look of anxiety on the captain's face, as though he feared the consequences of that climb up aloft. It might upset the gravity of so portly an old gentleman as his master had grown to be, and he might look at things with a temper somewhat clouded by anger. Then the look-out man might be found asleep at his post. That some such thoughts occupied old Dogvane's mind was evident, for, making some excuse, he passed his master in the rigging and hurried to the top. The man in the tub was so lost in his own meditations that he did not see the captain enter; but a kick startled him, and he cried, "Look out!" "I am going to," was Dogvane's reply. He then added: "Now, look alive, my hearty, and show me the official slides."

The Buccaneer arrived in the top, puffing and blowing and quite exhausted, for it was a stiff climb for one so stout. He was breathless, and his face was as ruddy as the setting sun. As he sat swabbing himself, as the sailors would say, he heard the murmurs of the crowd down below on shore rising up. "What noise is that?" he asked of the captain.

"That, sir, is the lowing of your many herds," was the reply. Dogvane was a ready man.

Now, when the people on shore had recovered from their first surprise, their tongues began to wag freely.

"At last!" cried one, "the old man is roused; now we shall see what happens."

"Not much, my mate," cried a second, "don't you see old Dogvane is up aloft too." Of course this was either a Port watchman, or one with Port watch sympathies.

"It is a pity," cried a third, "that the old gentleman did not mount aloft before and take a look round for himself; then he would have seen how things were going on. For, drat my buttons if you can believe any of these land lubbers below."

"Ah! it's all very well to talk," said another, "but the old gentleman is not so active as he used to be. Prosperity has made him lazy too, and good living has made him thick in the wind."

"There is life in the old man yet," cried another. And so it went on through the crowd. Several levelled their telescopes at the mast head of the old ship, and there were general regrets at the apparent absence of the Buccaneer's old coxswain, for the people believed in him. There was now what bid fair, at one time, to end in a general free fight between partisans of the two watches, and of course the Ojabberaways were quite ready to join in, for wherever heads were to be broken there they were sure to be; but a peaceful turn was given to the affair by Random Jack jumping upon an empty beer barrel and declaring, as he took off his jacket, that he was ready to meet in single combat, any man double his size of the Starboard Watch, and bid any one who liked to carry his challenge on board, either to the cook or to Billy Cheeks, the burly butcher.

"Listen to the lad!" the people cried and laughed; but no one took up the challenge.

"Well, my mates," cried an old salt, "let us wait and see what comes of it all. For my part I doubt much good, with old Dogvane up there too."

"What can he do, pray, if the old man takes a look for himself?" said another.

"What can he do?" cried Random Jack. "Look here, my hearties; that is a difficult question to answer when old Bill is concerned. For there is little he can't do, and there is not a trick or a dodge that that old fox is not up to. Why, he would get the weather side of the devil himself. Now, listen to me, my lads. Ah! it's all very well for you slavish followers of old Dogvane to put your tongues in your cheeks and flout and jeer, but those laugh in the end who win, and my merriment is yet to come. Now I will tell you what old Dogvane will do. He will make our master look through the wrong end of the telescope, or he will put in coloured lenses, or glasses with pictures painted on them, or he will do something to deceive; and whatever he does his crew will swear it is right, more especially the cook, the carpenter, and the burly butcher; but I have my eyes upon them; and I will smoke them out yet."

People laughed out right at these bold words of the little middy's. Many of the old salts said the boy would grow into no ordinary man, and that if he lived he would achieve great things. This Random Jack fully believed himself; and perseverance as is well known conquers all things. It is only necessary to be constantly dinning into the ears of people our own particular merits, and in time the most obstinate will give in and take you at your own valuation. In no other way can very much of the success we see in the world be accounted for.

If you are an impostor, the course of events may perhaps find you out, but it is hard to overthrow even a humbug when once fully established, and if he is knocked over he is sure to retain some of his followers and believers, who will worship him as a martyr, and he may even finish up by being canonized as a saint.

CHAPTER XIX.

THE look-out place at the mast head of the old Ship of State had many names, and amongst the rest it was called the owl's nest. This bird is sagacious looking; but by some people it is considered stupid, though perhaps rats, and mice, and other like vermin, think he is sharp enough for them. From this point of vantage Dogvane was bidding his master to behold the bright things that lay beneath him. " Look around you," he said, "and your eyes will rest upon a beautiful picture ; upon fields of golden corn bending their heads ready for the sickle of the reaper ; upon pastures well stocked with flocks and herds and upon a contented and a happy people." Just as the Buccaneer was stooping down to adjust his eye to the telescope, Dogvane very deftly slipped in, as the clever little middy had said he would, a slide beautifully painted with rural scenes, for what he had said existed only in his imagination, for a good deal of the land was lying fallow. The Buccaneer seemed lost in wonder and admiration, and was silent ; but Dogvane kept talking all the time. Conjurors always do this to distract the attention of their audience, otherwise their imposition might be found out. " Your eyes rest, sir," the captain said, " upon a peaceful scene ; no one would think that all those quiet looking villages, with their churches, stand over the bones of dead pirates." The Buccaneer did not like this allusion to his past life so he said :

" Master Dogvane ! there are but few men that have not had their early indiscretions. Even the very best of us in looking back wish some things undone. Many a saint has commenced life as a sinner; then let the dead past be buried, and often the greater the sinner the greater the saint. The first public act of Moses was a murder."

Dogvane took advantage of this diversion to slip in another slide. "Behold!" he cried, "your happy villages, with their churches, nestling in amongst the trees. Behold your towns and cities, the monuments of your industry and intelligence! See the tall tapering chimneys rising far into the murky sky. Look down, my master; look down at your rivers thickly studded with innumerable ships." Dogvane said not a word about the nationality of those ships. He did not tell his master that they belonged, a good many of them, to the innumerable cheap-Jacks that infested the shores.

"Dogvane!" cried the Buccaneer, as he wiped the small glass of his telescope, "I see chimneys enough; but I see no smoke coming from them. They seem to me to be mute monuments raised to a dead industry." The artist had quite forgotten to put the smoke in. Perhaps he painted from nature—some artists do. Dogvane was quite equal to the occasion, "We compel all your subjects, sir, to consume their own smoke."

This of course was not the case, if it had been, the Buccaneer's people would not have had to live at times in a gloom that made mid-day scarcely distinguishable from midnight.

Do I accuse a high official; a man whose character was as that of the wife of Cæsar, of not adhering to the truth?

Heaven forbid, that we should be so profane. But even truth at times must be suppressed, and though this may be considered by the straight-laced and sickly minded to be lying by implication, it is not so. It is done in the very best and most pious society; and in a high state of civilization it is absolutely necessary; because truth hurts the feelings of the refined.

The tinkling of many bells rose up on the air, and hovered for a while over the crow's nest. "What sound is that?" asked the Buccaneer. "The bell wethers, sir, ringing out their glad tidings of large and multiplying flocks." It was nothing of the sort. It was the muffin man going his constant and monotonous rounds.

"Listen, sir!" exclaimed Dogvane in high glee, "to the merry, but perfectly unintelligible cry of your happy costermongers. From dewy morn till dewy eve they vend their wares."

"If their cry, Master Dogvane, is unintelligible, why allow them to disturb the quiet of my people?"

"For all that I do, sir, there is a goodly reason. One of the favourite cries of our enemies is that we are revolutionists, upsetters, and destroyers of cherished customs. We refute this base slander by pointing to your costermongers. Here is a time-honoured institution that we have left untouched, and if the merry voice of the costermonger is to be silenced the guilt shall be on the head of the Port Watch, for old Bill Dogvane will have nothing to do with it." After this burst of impassioned eloquence the captain of the Starboard Watch wiped a glistening tear from his eye, took a little time to get his breath and then continued: "Look at your sanitary arrangements! In a matter of drains you have not an equal."

"All this is very well, Master Dogvane, and at home things may be sound enough; but how about my neighbours?"

"Your neighbours, sir? oh! I am credibly informed that in a matter of drains they are not good. I believe they have none; or if they have, I have no official information on the subject."

"Confound their drains, man! How do I stand with them?" Saying this, the Buccaneer turned his glass to distant parts. Dogvane tried very hard to distract the attention of his master, so that he could turn the telescope round until the small end might be where the big end ought to be; but he had no opportunity; neither had he any foreign slides. This was an oversight, and Dogvane was disconcerted. He tried to persuade his master by all manner of devices, not to trouble himself about other people's affairs. Told him that he was looked upon with jealousy, as all great and good men are; but that he ought to be too wise to mind what people said.

This rather flattered the Buccaneer's vanity. So long as he was feared and respected that was all he cared for. This was not right from a Christian point of view; but we must not expect too much; for the flesh is at all times weak, and man has been endowed with certain qualities that will occasionally assert themselves. Was not the Hulk alongside the old Ship of State, the custodian of all Christian principles? Would you find charity and humility reigning supreme there? Good people all, beneath the priestly frock there sometimes beats a hard and unforgiving heart. Saint Chrysostom was a godly but outspoken man; one of strong convictions. He expressed an opinion that in his day the number of bishops who might be saved bore a very small proportion to those who would be damned. We live in better times, and the balance now would be no doubt against the devil. At least let us be charitable, and hope so.

The Buccaneer kept his gaze fixed upon the East, and Dogvane was not experiencing an ecstasy of delight. Presently his master cried, " Eh! what is that I see?" Dogvane seized the glass and placed his eye to the hole, " It is nothing, sir, but a dust storm. Such things are of frequent occurrence in the East, and very trying and disagreeable they are to those who have to live there. This is no doubt what that youngster, Random Jack, made such a fuss about."

" But who is kicking up the dust?" the Buccaneer demanded. Dogvane ran through a number of common and ordinary causes for such things, which however did not seem to satisfy his master, who said to the captain's surprise, " Dust storm, or no dust storm, Master Dogvane, I am going to take a look there myself. There is no knowing but what the Bandit of the East may be behind that cloud."

" Ah! the old scare!" muttered Dogvane. " Down on deck and pipe my yacht's crew away!" cried the Buccaneer as he prepared to descend. Dogvane was for making a thousand excuses, the manufacturing of which was to him a matter of the greatest ease. But it was of no use, and so down he went to comply with his master's bidding. He was still more horrified when he learnt that it was his master's intention to make a few calls on his neighbours on his way to the East.

" What do you want to leave home for now, sir, when all your people are so happy and comfortable?" Dogvane asked as he went down through the lubbers' hole.

" And what better time, pray, could I choose?"

"But your neighbours may not like to be taken thus unceremoniously?" Dogvane said as he began to descend.

"A friend, Master Dogvane, is always welcome, and by our reception we shall see in what estimation we are held."

"But, sir," cried Dogvane, looking up from the rigging.

"But me, no buts, Master Dogvane, but do as you are told; so down you go."

Dogvane seemed to have lost somewhat of his alacrity, for he took a terrible long time in reaching the deck, and kept up a running accompaniment to his thoughts, which, however, was not loud enough to be heard, and therefore cannot be recorded; though it is safe enough to assume that so good a man made use of no bad language. Something evidently troubled the old captain's mind, for when the two of them reached the deck, he said, "Master, you must not listen to everything you hear against the great Bandit of the East. People are not all honey behind your back. In the past you have ever been too ready to draw the sword, following the example of those who fight first, and argue afterwards."

"Because, Master Dogvane, experience has taught me that if you thrash your enemy first he is the more amenable to reason."

"That, honoured sir, was all very well in an uncivilized and barbarous age. When the mind was not open to reason, and when the manners had not been softened by Christianity, then the sword was, no doubt, a good major premise; but now, sir, it should never be drawn except through dire necessity. In a just and good cause I am ready to shed my last drop of blood for you."

"Nobly said, Dogvane! nobly said!" exclaimed the Buccaneer, as he slapped old Dogvane in an approving manner on the back, thereby nearly knocking all the wind out of his body.

"But, mind you, master," Dogvane said, "I must be assured that the cause is just. An appeal to arms should only take place when the noble art of diplomacy has failed. Then, sir, by all manner of means draw the sword."

"Master Dogvane; tell me what is Diplomacy?" asked the Buccaneer.

"Diplomacy, sir, is the polished and courteous method that one nation has of conducting business with another."

"To my mind, Master Dogvane, it is the polished method by which one nation tries very often to overreach another. Strip it of its courtly paraphernalia and you often find this Diplomacy to be a lying, intriguing, cheating, and unprincipled rascal, that every honest man ought to shun. Look you! it has been said that by this self-same Diplomacy I have lost a good deal of what I have won in fair and open fight."

Dogvane sighed over his master's want of enlightenment. But he knew too well that in his present mood he was not to be reasoned with, so what could a poor sailor do? What cannot be cured must be endured. Dogvane felt assured that everything was to be put down to the fallacious teachings of the Port Watch, and had he not been the pious man that he was he would undoubtedly have damned all their knavish tricks, if nothing else.

The cook, the butcher, and the carpenter, could see that something was amiss by the troubled look upon their captain's face, so they were not at all surprised to hear the bo'sn's whistle pipe the crew of the bold Buccaneer's royal yacht away; to be one of the crew of which was esteemed a great distinction, as it was a sure road to preferment. The cook only hoped the old man, meaning the Buccaneer, was not going to make a fool of himself; but he had his doubts, of course. Had the sagacious and learned Pepper been one of the party to give his master the benefit of his advice it would have been a different matter altogether.

But where is the old cox'sn all this time. Is the Buccaneer going to make his round of calls without his right-hand man?

Good people all, the cox'sn was on shore moving about amongst the people, doing good after his humble fashion, wherever he could. He did not always accompany his master, more is the pity; but the truth must be told. He could not at all times get on with Captain Dogvane, and old Jack Commonsense was not much of a traveller.

CHAPTER XX.

JUST as the Buccaneer was about to start upon his round of calls, the snowy white sails of a large ship were to be seen gliding, as it seemed, over the fields that hemmed in his principal river; the hull of the stranger being hidden by a bend. From her masthead flew a star-spangled banner, and the well-known strains of Yankee Doodle came floating up on the southerly breeze. "Ah!" exclaimed the Buccaneer, "Here comes Jonathan, our cheap-Jack cousin: been home to refit and reload I suppose." Presently a long black hull with a good sheer forward came, as it were, out of the low lying land below the city.

In days long gone by, such a suspicious looking craft would have made the bold Buccaneer beat to quarters, when out would have gone his guns, but times had greatly changed, and pirates of the open and declared type were not to be seen on Western waters. The black flag with death's head and cross-bones is never boldly run up now to the masthead as in the good brave days of old. It frightens people. So all robberies both on sea and land are done under more respectable looking flags; and very much more genteelly. No walking the plank, no running up to the yard arm. Now a whole crew are sent to the bottom of the sea at a single shot, and there is an end of them.

The stranger finding a comfortable berth, rounded to, as sailors say. Splash went her anchor, rattle, rattle went her chain. Down came the yards, clewlines and buntlines were well manned, and up went the snowy sails. The nimble seaman scudded up aloft, and rolled up the canvas, and everything was trimmed down, and hauled taught, and his yards squared in proper ship-shape fashion. "Bravo, Jonathan!" cried the Buccaneer. "Nearly as well done as I could have done it myself. True chip of the old block; eh! Dogvane?"

"Yes, sir: and at driving a bargain, or getting the better of a friend, our Jonathan has not an equal."

Presently a boat impelled by lusty arms and hands shot round the stern of the old ship, and brought up alongside, and a tall lanky fellow with a big pack on his back stepped on deck. In an easy tone of familiarity he saluted the old Buccaneer. "Wa'al, old hoss, how are things with you?"

"Pretty well, Jonathan; pretty well," replied the Buccaneer.

"Glad to hear it; heard things wasn't quite O.K. Ever taste O.K. bitters? No! Wa'al, they would just revive a corpse, O.K. bitters would, you bet. Let us deal," he said as he took his pack off, and began laying his merchandise out on the deck. "I say, Boss, could you make it convenient to have this aire stream of yours widened? It puts me more in mind of one of our drains than anything else."

The old Buccaneer was highly indignant at his principal river being spoken of in such a disrespectful manner, and he replied with much dignity: "My river, Master Jonathan, is good enough for me, and if it is too narrow for other people, they can stay away."

"No offence, Boss, no offence. It does look small after our Mississippi, that would be an eye-opener for you, old hoss. But this ain't business. Now, here we have a lozenge that will cure anything, from a cough to a broken leg. Here's a pill fit to physic creation. Honest sailor," he said, addressing Dogvane, "try this pill. It will make your hair stand on end. Take a box for the sake of your family. Each pill is worth a pound, let you have a whole box for one shilling and a penny ha'penny. You have a son, a hopeful boy, give him a pill, if not a pill, try him with this pickle, it will sharpen his understanding and make him a credit to his family. Just you ask who cured Stonewall Jackson?" Dogvane declared he did not want anything; but Jonathan still cried up his wares. "Try this cocktail before going to bed, it will make your teeth curl. Talking about teeth; in teeth I guess we're tall. Now here is a set that one of your ecclesiastical big guns has asked God's blessing on, and they're up a quarter dollar accordingly."

"Jonathan!" the Buccaneer said, "I have long wished to have a little private conversation with you."

"All right, Boss, I thought something was up, chuck it off your chest, whatever it is, it will relieve you."

"I don't think it either neighbourly, or friendly, Jonathan, on your part to harbour people who plot against my life and property."

"What! Have you found out, old hoss, that snakes bite! You've harboured a good deal of vermin in your day, and you can't blame me for doing what you have done yourself. No, Sirree, that cock won't fight. Why, you've given an asylum to the cut-throat rascals of every nation under the sun, and when you could not find room for them, you have sent them over to me."

"I have only given an asylum, Jonathan, to the oppressed."

"That is only one way of looking at it, Boss. Too fine a name for a fellow with a bowie knife up his sleeve, and a six-shooter in his pocket; if he cries 'hands up,' old man, where are you? But this ain't business, honest sailor," here he again addressed Dogvane. "Buy this baby jumper for the missis. It will rock your child to sleep, wake it in the morning, wash it, dress it, slap it and feed it, and all for a few dollars. You have a son? No father of a family should be without this article." Then turning to the Buccaneer he said, "I reckon my gals are leaving your gals standing. They are just taking away all the cream of your men. Now, here's a notion, that may be will mend matters, try a cargo of these patent palpitating bosoms. They are warranted to go; they are as natural as life, and ever so much more convenient, for they can be taken off at night and put on in the morning. They never increase, and not like some cheap kind of article, you never see them under the shoulder, at the back, instead of in their proper places in front; buy a pair on trial."

"Stay, Master Jonathan, let us settle one thing at a time. Is it right for you to let the Ojabberaways hatch their infernal plots against me in your country?"

"Look here, old hoss, the Ojabberaways are blowers; then let them blow. It satisfies the darned skunks, and it don't hurt you. It aint safe in these high pressure times to sit upon your safety-valve. Let 'em blow off."

"I don't mind their blowing off, Jonathan; but I object to the skunks, as you call them, blowing up. As for blowing off; why, my parks and public places, are regular blow-holes, where democrats, demagogues, socialists, and blasphemers may, and do, howl themselves hoarse."

"It don't seem to me, old hoss, that you are altogether boss of your show. You are trying to run your ryal car on a democratic gauge, and you'll either run off the track or you'll bust your biler. But this ain't business, won't you buy? Honest sailor, here's a knife that will lick creation; and here's a watch—I reckon we are pretty big in watches. This child of nature is just leaving the rest of the world standing." Jonathan seeing that he could do no business, said, as he packed up his things: "Trade does seem dull; but I'll just look round shore. This island of yours is so darned small, and your cliffs are so high, that it is dangerous to walk after nightfall. You should just come over to our side of the water; you'd see something like a patch of land, you bet." Jonathan went forward to see if he could do any business amongst the crew. The carpenter wanted to deal with him in nails; then the cook wanted to clear out the Buccaneer's lumber-room; and the packman said that for a duke or two, or a couple of lords he would spring some dollars; for that he had none in his country, and accordingly they were very highly esteemed. He did love a lord. Then he wanted to exchange a dozen brow-beating barristers for one incorruptible judge; but the cook, the carpenter, and Billy Cheeks, the butcher, all said, that of brow-beating barristers, their old man had enough and to spare, and they could not part with any of their judges. As the cheap-Jack went over the ship's side, he said he had, he feared, mistaken the latitude and longitude, for he thought by the way things were going, he must be in the neighbourhood of Jerusalem. When he got ashore he had still greater reason for thinking this, for the

Hebrew element was so strong that he declared there was little chance of an honest man getting a living. Many of the Jews tried to modernize their names, but do what they would, they could not change their natures.

Just as Jonathan, the packman, was stepping into his boat, the cook looked through one of the port-holes and asked him if he had any need for the Buccaneer's lion. Jonathan said he thought the animal was not sound, but the cook declared that he was; only a little out of wind, having done a good deal of roaring in his day. Jonathan offered in exchange a skunk, which he declared was a most useful and valuable animal, respected alike by friends and enemies; but they could not deal.

Soon the voice of the cheap-Jack was heard mingling with the others on shore. The Ojabberaways, though they bought little, and sold still less, received a good many of Jonathan's almighty dollars, and as long as they lasted they were likely enough to love him and be friends.

CHAPTER XXI.

THE clack, clack of a windlass was heard one fine morning sounding over the waters of the river that hurried by the Buccaneer's chief city. Alas! the merry songs of his seamen, as they hove in the slack of their chains was no longer to be heard. Their cheering "Yo, heave ho!" was but a faint memory of the past. No cloud of sails was spread to catch the breath of the north wind; but the vessel moved stealthily down the river, leaving behind her a muddy wake and above a long winding black serpent of smoke.

Great changes had come over this old Buccaneer. Neither he, nor his ships were anything like what they were in the good old past. The past that we are always looking back to with such loving and longing eyes. Those huge wooden castles that had borne his flag to so many victories had been towed long ago to their last moorings. But ah! things change, and mountains even, if not moved by faith, are constantly being altered by that persistent worker, time. People looked back with regret to those grand old wooden walls, with their tier upon tier of guns; but it was all in vain. Science had condemned them. Amidst all the change that was constantly going on, there was one thing on board of the old Ship of State that bound the Buccaneer to the past. She was still impelled by wind, and consequently was not a rapid sailer. The Church Hulk alongside her, was also propelled in a similar manner, but considering the gales of wind that sometimes swept her decks she was a slow mover.

Away went the Buccaneer in his steam yacht, old Dogvane, of course, being at the helm. The cox'sn, however, for reasons already mentioned, was left behind. The captain's face did not wear an expression of happiness, but then he was one of those who take their pleasures seriously, and sometimes even in a melancholy manner; and often when he looked his saddest he was enjoying himself most. To judge from appearances, people might be pardoned if they thought that he and his master were bent upon some mournful errand, such as the burying of some dear departed friend.

But to return to the wonder-stricken people who lined the shore. Many were the questions asked and many were the answers given. Though our brave old Buccaneer hated anything secret, more especially in other people, yet he himself conducted all his public affairs by a secret council; being driven to do so, perhaps, by necessity. Then the reason for this sudden and somewhat mysterious departure was left open to all kinds of conjecture, some saying one thing, some another.

"What is in the wind now?" asked one. "Is the old man steering for peace or for war?"

"Ah!" cried another, "perhaps his spirit is at last aroused. Heaven only knows he has slept long enough!"

"The barking of curs, my lads," said a third, "does not disturb the slumber or the dignity of a bull-dog. Fighting, mates, it may be; for those who won't fight will fall."

The young hands looked hopeful and the hot blood mounted to their cheeks, for they had heard and read of fights by sea and land, and of the doughty deeds done by their forefathers, and they longed, too, for the fray. There was life in these young sea whelps yet. It was said that the wanton, Luxury, had touched them gently with the velvet tips of her fingers, but so far she had not taken away their manhood and put them to lie on downy beds scented with the perfume of flowers. No, no, she had not gone as far as that, and though the Buccaneer's women, some of them, had become masculine, his men had not surrendered up their position to them just yet.

The young expressed their hopes, the old men shook their heads. The Ojabberaways were wild with delight, and hoped that their tyrant master, as they called him, would get so embroiled that they might have a chance of shaking themselves free. Then, as many thought, there would be merry times indeed for those who lived in the green and fertile isle of the West.

The Ojabberaways now behaved themselves in a manner so peculiarly their own, that there was every prospect of a free fight. The leaders, or paid patriots as they were called, took up a strong position, behind whatever natural objects presented themselves, and from these points of vantage they commenced pelting their opponents with strong personal abuse. Of this they always kept a large supply ready on hand. Wise counsels prevailed, and the blood of the young Buccaneers was cooled down, and so a row was avoided and all attention was again directed to the head of the family and his doings. "Mates!" cried one sturdy fellow, "it's not for fighting he has gone with Captain William Dogvane on board. More likely he has gone to beg some person's pardon for some idle words spoken, or may be he's gone to hand over some patch of land that we got in fair and open fight. But let that pass, conscience becomes tender as a man grows old."

Here a square built old sailor with a patch over his left eye, and who was minus an arm and a leg cried out, "Who would spill his blood and stand the chance of being knocked on the head, if he thought that all he got in fair and open fight was to be given back, because a tender conscience pules and whines. Look at me, mates! The glim of one of my skylights is dousted, and is battened down for ever. My timber too I've lost, and have I been lopped of my branches for nothing? All, forsooth, because an old man's conscience pricks. Damme, lads! there's no justice in the like o' that. Do our neighbours give up what they have grabbed? not they; more likely to put the pistol to your head, as in days of old, and cry out, 'Stand and deliver?' That's the way of the world, mates, and we must not set up to be better than other folk. Haven't I a vested interest in the old man's conquests to the extent of one arm, a leg and an eye? Then damme, make all fast, say I!"

Another said, "The old Buccaneer is more fitted now to carry the staff of a pilgrim than the pistol and cutlass of a pirate."

"Vast heaving, my mates," cried a voice from the crowd, "no

hard names if you please. Our master's buccaneering days are over, and there is something so unsavoury about the name of a pirate, lads, that the word is now never used in good society. As to whether any little bit of business in that way is done on the sly, it is not for us to say. The wise man's eye is not always open; but his mouth, my hearties, is generally shut, so let us wait and see what comes of our master's peregrination." This was all that the old coxswain contributed at this particular part of the proceedings.

The Port Watch said there was no remedy for anything, but a shift of watches. Some even advocated a sudden raid on the old Ship, and by taking her by surprise to effect their purpose. Random Jack was for doing this, and he declared his readiness to lead the assault, and his courage was very much applauded, and not at all doubted. He was becoming a great favourite amongst the people, who had still so much of the old stuff left in them that they could appreciate pluck in any one. Just as they were going to put their plan to the trial, a soft sound of music came over the water. Music, it is known, has charms to soothe. Some uncovered their heads reverently for they thought it was the evening song coming from the old Church Hulk; but they were all very much disappointed when they found out that it was only the cook accompanying himself on his barrel organ to a hymn strung to his own praise.

This showed that the watch were not asleep. At the same time a spark, as bright as a diamond, rested, as it were, on the bulwark of the old Ship of State. This was caused by the rays of the setting sun impinging upon the glass eye of the carpenter. The burly butcher, fly flapper in hand, all ready for action, could also be seen. This made Random Jack thoughtful. Random Jack remembered the butcher's instrument of torture and he rubbed a part that had been more than once affected, and as he did so, he said that in his opinion things were not quite ripe for action, so the assault fell through, and the old Ship was allowed to ride peacefully at anchor. Hereupon the old coxswain took the opportunity of delivering an oration. "Mates!" he said, "let us do nothing rashly. Hasty actions often require much time for repentance. If so be that you can shift watches by fair means, do so; but give old Bill Dogvane a fair chance. He is an old hand, and an able steersman, and he has weathered many a storm." There was now a great outcry against the coxswain; he was called a traitor; a follower of Bill's; a carpet bag full of old wives' sayings; a bladder full of wind and such like things; one who, if he was struck on one cheek, would turn the other. All this abuse got old Jack Commonsense's back up, as the saying is, and whipping out an oath or two, he exclaimed: "Damme mates! I hope as how I am as good a Christian as the best of you, and as ready as any of you to do my duty to my God and my neighbour; but the man who strikes me, damme! I strike him back, or my name is not Jack Commonsense. Look you now! do you think if any of you blustering, railing lubbers, were to board the old Church Hulk there and strike, say, the High Priest on one cheek, that he would straightway turn the other? If you think so, go and try the experiment; I, for one, ain't agoing to. Mates! have we ever fought our enemies, that our clergy, God bless them! did not bless us, and pray for us? And while we fought with sword and pistol did they not fight for us with their spiritual weapons? Example, my mates, is the best precept, and our Church has never yet taught us in that way that fighting is wrong; or that too much meekness, except from outsiders, is to be very highly commended." When the old coxswain got upon his legs it was hard to get him down and every stump was to him a pulpit. He continued, "God forbid! that I should be a bully, going about the world seeking quarrels with the weak; but God grant, my lads, that I may be ever ready to lead you all on against the attacks of the strong, who threaten us, and a young woman as I keep company with will be well to the fore, and if you are not found ready to follow old Jack and the beggar woman, then, my lads, make ready your necks for the yoke of the foreign invader. And it is old Jack Commonsense that says so."

CHAPTER XXII.

WE are in these degenerate days singularly unfortunate in many ways. Our means of excitement are nothing like what they used to be. The Buccaneer's island was no exception to the general rule. Indeed time seems to have handled him very roughly. Not that he was altogether free from surprises. Occasionally an idiot obtained possession of a pistol, and either tried to commit or did commit a murder. Then at times a man was knocked down, kicked and robbed, whilst the mighty house-breaker prowled about with pistol and crowbar in search of plunder. It is also true that the Ojabberaways did all they could in the way of providing excitement of a lively nature for the benefit of the old Buccaneer and all his people; but gone were his highwaymen. The vulgar thief alone remained. A mutiny at sea, with the murder of a crew, was a thing of the past. Yet we have to relate a dark conspiracy, which will be for ever known as the Cabal of the Cook's Caboose, and which might have been productive of the gravest results. Mention has already been made of a slight defection amongst a certain section of the crew.

It was past eight bells, and the midnight watch had been set sufficiently long to allow all the look-out men to take up their positions of repose. Not a sound was to be heard upon the old Ship of State except the heavy breathing of the watchman aloft and the monotonous tread of the look-out man aft, who had not as yet secured a comfortable place to pass his watch in. The Church Hulk was wrapped in a deep sleep and the Buccaneer's Chief Priest, with all his ecclesiastical big guns, minor canons, able priests, and ordinary deacons, were fondly locked in slumber's arms. They kept no visible look-out, but angels with their silver wings, it was firmly believed by all devout Buccaneers, hovered over that old ship at night and kept the devil and all his minions away. It was only when the dusky mantle of midnight rested upon the island that silence ever reigned supreme upon that old Church Hulk.

The look-out man on deck hailed the look-out man aloft. "What, ho there!" he cried. "Watchman! what of the night?" The man up aloft had evidently been deeply meditating, for something very like a yawn broke the stillness of the air, but presently a voice came down laden with the words: "All's well! The twinkling eyes of Heaven look down upon a world wrapped in peaceful slumber. All's well!"

"All's well," went up from below in reply, and again there was a great stillness. The eyes of all the houses on shore except one here and there which sat watching for the setting out of some poor weary soul to the regions that lie beyond the grave, were out The dog that generally breaks the stillness of the night on such occasions was also silent; probably asleep. The wind even had folded her wings and had ceased to sing her lullaby to the accompaniment of her many stringed lute.

Presently a crouching form was to be seen creeping stealthily under the starboard side of the old Ship of State. The suspicious looking object who was enveloped in the dark cloak and slouched hat usually worn by conspirators and hired no doubt for the occasion, made for the cook's galley, and in a voice scarcely above a whisper, exclaimed: "Pepper!"

"Is that you, Chips?" came from the caboose.

"The same," was the reply.

"Where are the rest?" asked the cook.

"They will be here directly," the carpenter said, as he darted into the galley. Scarcely had he got well inside than his mate joined him, and shortly afterwards the burly form of Billy Cheeks, the butcher, was seen trying to conceal himself under the bulwarks. "Keep down, can't you?" cried the cook. "You'll have the look-out man see you."

"Can't help it if he does; can't make myself any smaller than nature made me," replied the butcher. "If I was as small as you, or a ringbolt chaser like Chips, I might be able to do it." This was sarcasm. The butcher loved sarcasm; but the cheery cook turned it off by saying that Chips, and Chisel, his mate, must spokeshave Billy Cheeks down to the ordinary and usual size of a conspirator. As the butcher did not see anything funny in this he did not laugh; and so the joke fell like a dead shell, quite harmless. But the cook, the carpenter, and his mate said that Billy Cheeks was far too big for a conspirator.

All was pitch dark inside the cook's caboose. The fire had long since been out, and it would not have been safe to strike a light. No doubt they had their dark lanterns, for conspirators would not be fully equipped without them, but for some reason best known to themselves, they did not for the present produce them.

"Your programme!" cried the butcher, who generally came at once to the point.

"Listen, my lads, and you shall hear," exclaimed the carpenter. "The old man being away and the captain with him, we must make this the high tide of our prosperity, and carry out as pretty a little scheme as ever entered the head of man, although I say it, as should not. The old coxswain is ashore amongst the landlubbers, so we have nothing to fear from him. For the rest of the crew on board belonging to our watch, well, if they will not join us, why, Billy, my man, you must do your duty. First and foremost we must lighten ship."

"That is easily done," said the cook, "by flinging overboard bodily the old man's Upper Chamber." It is wonderful what a hatred the cook had for this room in the after part of the old ship. He himself said it was on account of their ignorance, want of intelligence, class prejudice, and the airs and graces they gave themselves.

"As you all know, my mates," continued the carpenter, "things ain't as they ought to be on board this old craft; she is much too slow for the times. When a coat becomes too old to wear, what do we do? why, chuck it away."

The jolly little cook now had his say. "Without a doubt the

old ship is too bluff bowed for the rapid times we live in, and is more fit to drive piles than to make way against the swift current of events. So, my lads, I am for seizing the ship, and my little game—"

"What is that?" cried the butcher, as he laid his trembling hand upon the carpenter's arm.

"What is what?" exclaimed the carpenter, slightly startled. "Can't you give Pepper time to explain himself. Hurry no man's cattle, is an old and good proverb."

"I heard a noise outside, as if someone was moving," said the butcher.

"Then take a look round, Billy," said the carpenter.

"I am too big," said the butcher, with a sneer, which was felt, though on account of the darkness it was not seen. "Let Pepper go; he is the smallest; no one will see him, and if they do they will take no notice." This was veiled sarcasm, but the cook thought it better not to notice it, because he knew the butcher could not help it.

"Let every man stick to his trade," said the cook, "my place is inside the galley and not out."

Then up spoke the doughty carpenter. "What, my lads! is quaking fear going to be present at our councils? Look at me. I am not afraid." As it was pitch dark, of course nobody could see. "Chisel, my lad," he said, addressing his mate, "show these fellows the stuff you are made of."

"And why should I do what others won't?" replied Chisel. "It is no more my business than it is the cook's, and every man to his trade, say I, too."

"Why don't you take a look round yourself?" cried the butcher.

"Of course I will. Thus!" exclaimed the carpenter, "does conscience make cowards of ye all." Having delivered himself of the quotation, he took a hasty glance through the little square hole that acted as a window in the back part of the galley, and said there was nothing. "I knew that," said the cook. "That is why I did not take the trouble to look; but this is a grievous waste of precious time." "Well, my lads," the carpenter continued, ignoring the fact that the cook was, as the saying is, in possession of the house, or rather, galley. "First and foremost we must seize this old craft, run her ashore, break her up, and build a spic and span new one, upon entirely new lines. We will take a hint here and a hint there. In such a thing our friend Jonathan would not be a bad man to go by. Then we will board the old ship alongside, and make her disgorge, for the general good, some of her accumulated plunder. She is worth a pretty plum I can tell you. Been hoarding up for ages, and yet she is always crying out poverty. Bah! there must be something wrong somewhere, or where does all the money go? She does not apparently give too much of it amongst the poorer part of her crew; but as she renders no accounts we are all in the dark, my lads. It is a busy buzzing hive of drones, though."

"As you say, Master Chips," said the cook. "She does not seem to give much of her stored up wealth to her poor brethren, and Heaven knows that the priestly gabardine too often covers an empty stomach, while others amongst them lead the lives of a Dives. Does poverty and penury find clothing or food out of her riches? Not a bit of it. Too many of her crew, are they not proud? Have they not made an exclusive and an aristocratic high-cast priesthood of themselves?"

"So wags the world, my mates; so wags the world," cried the carpenter. "While one suffers from repletion, another starves. But that old Hulk is now out of date, and she will cut up well you may be sure. Having plundered her, and given every ecclesiastical dog a bone—no offence to the sacred calling—we will bore a hole in her and let her sink. Then, when we are well across the bridge that connects her with this old craft, Chisel, my mate, shall saw the bridge through, and thus lay a trap for the rats; let them either sink or swim."

"Rats, they say," remarked the cook, as he handled his three-pronged toasting-fork, "always leave a sinking ship, and the ecclesiastical rat will prove, I expect, no exception to the rule."

"Honest Pepper!" cried the carpenter, "you speak, as you always do, like a book."

"I've some doubt on my mind, which I should like cleared up before we go any further," said the butcher.

"Out with it, Billy, my man, out with it," exclaimed the carpenter. "Your chest is big, but no doubt it will be the better for being lightened, and an empty house is better than a bad tenant, any day of the week."

"Well, you talked about running this craft ashore, and then turning your attention to the Church Hulk; but if you do that, what is the use of sawing the bridge in two. The bridge would be the plank we should have to walk; with nothing but a drop of some fathoms deep into the pit we had dug for ourselves."

"Or rather the water, Billy," said the cook, who loved his joke.

"That little error can easily be rectified by our settling with the Church Hulk first; but these are mere details. The workers, my lads, shall have their reward; and the clerical Lazarus shall sit down at the same table as the clerical Dives."

"But robbing a church," said the butcher, "is about the last thing a fellow ought to do, is it not?"

"The end, Billy, will justify the means," the carpenter remarked.

"Our master, the Buccaneer," said the cook, "was not above robbing a church once, and who will say he did wrong? Of course his conscience-healers will find justification for the act if he pays them well, and as they read history by the light of faith, and not altogether by facts, they can prove all things entirely to their own satisfaction, and what would have been an act of robbery in others, would be, when they were concerned, a most laudable action. Faith, as is well known, my mates, can work wonders, and it can overcome a mountain of the most obstinate facts with the greatest ease."

"But suppose they turn to and curse us," asked the butcher, who evidently had some qualms of conscience.

"And suppose they do," cried the cook. "Are we a lot of old women to be frightened by such things. Know you not the saying, Billy, that curses come home to roost? Let them curse then."

"Where is Chisel?" the carpenter asked.

"I am here;" a voice said out of the darkness.

"Not hearing you, mate, I thought you must have slipped away."

"It appears to me," replied the carpenter's mate, "that there is little need for me to say much, considering that I am expected to do all the dirty work."

"Who will say that anything is dirty work?" replied the cook. "The worker purifies and elevates the work." Pepper was a philosopher. The carpenter continued, "Mates, rest assured of this; if it suits the Buccaneer to sacrifice his Church Ship, he will do it, for he has an elastic conscience, which he will satisfy by saying prayers before and after the act. And as for Dogvane, well, he will wait to see which way the cat jumps. If he sees the time has come, why, then, the State Church will be cast adrift. It is not the first time that old William has robbed a church. I am not the man to say he did a wrong. Why should the Church Hulk be kept moored alongsides of the old craft? All well enough when she ruled the roast; but now more than two hundred sects are outside her jurisdiction, and the Chief Priest and other officers under him cannot at all times keep the unruly crew in order. They have their mutinies, and their interior economy does not seem to be just as it should be; so, my lads, she will either have to mend her ways or end them, as has been said of another of our master's ancient establishments."

"Which, my mates," said the cook, "you may leave to me. I will have my knife into the Upper Chamber yet."

"After duty comes pleasure," continued the carpenter. "Having settled the Church Hulk we must turn our attention to old Squire Broadacre. His house is in a terrible state, and must be put in order. We must pare down his property a bit, for there is a family called Hodge, a good, decent, honest, and industrious, though perhaps ignorant lot, who are but poorly off. It is the squire's duty to look after this family; but, mates, it is well known that selfishness fills hell."

"But do you suppose that the Buccaneer is going to allow all this to be done?" exclaimed the butcher.

"It appears to me, mates," replied the carpenter, "that our friend Billy is going to throw cold water on all our plans."

"What is the use of our assembling here," asked the butcher, "if we are not allowed to speak?"

"Who wants to stop your speaking?" exclaimed the carpenter. "I certainly am not going to undertake the task, I can tell you. Our master must be talked and wheedled over, and as for old Dogvane, well, we all know that he has a damned tender conscience. (The oath must be pardoned. The best of carpenters, and all sailors, swear at times.) Look here, mates, I fancy I know as much about Captain Dogvane as most men. If he wants a thing done, and if so be that he has set his heart upon it, bang goes his conscience in that direction. Never was there a conscience under better control. It says to the captain's inclination, 'which way does my master want me to go, so that his servant may obey him?' Never yet did Dogvane's conscience prove him wrong, and he is at all times on the best of terms with it. Look you, our captain will say neither yea nor nay, and he will use so many words in saying so, that everyone will be at loggerheads, quarrelling over what he means, when in all probability he means nothing; but is only waiting to see which way the wind is going to blow."

Here the cook spoke: "I have great faith in the old man; but if he does not go with us, what then? All the talent is not in one head, and as for his first lieutenant, and one or two others, we can afford to lose them. They are too slow for the times."

"Lads, in cases like this," cried the carpenter, "we must not mince matters; and if the worst comes to the worst Billy Cheeks must do his duty."

The paleness of the butcher at these ominous words was concealed. There was a terrible hidden meaning in what the carpenter said, and it made the butcher's flesh creep and his blood run cold.

"I am at all times prepared to do my duty," the butcher said, "at fly-flapping the tail end of a Tory cockerel, or at stopping the cackle of the older birds, I will give way to no man; but I love the old captain, and I would not injure a hair of his venerable head on any account. As we all know, he is but lightly covered."

"Who wants you to injure his hair?" cried the carpenter. "Do you think we want you to be ship's barber as well as ship's butcher?" The carpenter, who began to fear that he had gone too far, thought it best to trim a bit, and therefore he advised the butcher not to be so sharp in coming to conclusions. "Of course," he said, "it's natural that you should put a professional aspect on things."

"There!" cried the butcher in alarm, "I heard the noise again."

"Then go and see what it is," the carpenter said in disgust.

"Ah! It makes no difference to me," the butcher replied. "If you other fellows did not hear it, I must have been mistaken." The cook, the carpenter, and Chisel his mate were extremely gratified at this generous admission on the part of the butcher, and they one and all said they never could remember the time when Billy Cheeks had owned himself in the wrong before. The carpenter was quite softened. Even Pepper was touched, and they all hoped that it augured no ill to the butcher, for sudden changes in disposition and character are often the unwelcome harbingers of speedy dissolution. They strongly advised Billy Cheeks to consult his medical man. This painful episode for the time quite damped the spirits of the conspirators. "If anything happens to you, Billy, where would you like to be buried?" the cook asked. They left the butcher to think the matter over, and after a while the carpenter continued: "Having got possession of everything, we will all live happily together ever afterwards." The butcher, who had recovered himself asked, "How about the old lion which keeps watch over the Buccaneer's affairs?"

"Your hand, Billy," cried the carpenter groping about in the dark, "I see you are better, and have taken up your character again of Chief Obstructionist. If you don't like to join our party, go over to the other watch. They are in want of men of substance."

"Why do you catch one up so precious sharp?" cried the butcher, irritated. "I suppose there is no harm in asking a simple question? Who wants to go over to the other watch? Haven't I always stood by you and Pepper, and defended you when you were both blackguarded and abused? One would think you two were the Buccaneer's darlings, but you are neither of you liked, though people may laugh at you, Pepper. What is the use of my being here, if I am to keep my mouth shut? Chisel may act the part of a dummy if he likes, but I will not."

"Messmate, your hand," cried the carpenter again. "No offence, old man. We are in the same boat, therefore we must pull together. There is an old adage that applies to us."

"It is no use our quarrelling over trifles," said the cook. "The old lion is asleep: or out of wind, and he is just about as harmless as if he were stuffed with hair or straw, and no one fears him now let him roar ever so loud."

"But to ease your mind, Billy," said the carpenter, " my mate shall draw his teeth and cut his claws."

"And pray why should I have all the dirty and dangerous work to do?" said Chisel again.

"What!" exclaimed the carpenter, in evident surprise. "Are you going to take a leaf out of the butcher's book, mate! It seems we commented upon your silence too soon; but if you are afraid to do the work; well let his teeth and claws remain. Thus the difficulty is got over with ease. After all, it is only a detail, and we will not come to loggerheads over a detail."

"There it is again," cried the butcher, "I swear I saw something like a hand spread out fan-shape towards me. The thumb was from me, and seemed attached to a human nose."

This was very terrible, and the conspirators felt a creepy sensation all over them. But the cook reassured them all, by saying, that very often people, whose stomachs were out of order, suffered from optical delusions. He said he felt sure Billy Cheeks must have eaten something that had disagreed with him; so they took no further notice, and proceeded with the business of the evening.

"Of course we shall want assistance; but we can count upon the Ojabberaways, they are always ready for anything in the shape of a row. They have their price, then we shall have the Hodges, and the Sikes with us. They are all ripe for action. Now another thing presents itself. We must have a head, no body can get along without a head."

"Some seem to get along very well without such a thing," said the cook. This also was sarcasm. The cook loved it, and his tongue it was said was as sharp as needles. "Well, my mates," he continued, "of course we must have a head; but mind you, let us have no hereditary fool to fill the office; and no baubles in the shape of crowns and court paraphernalia, no court flunkies, my lads, to eat the bread of idleness, no court pimps. I am dead against crowns. They are expensive articles, no matter upon whose head they rest. Kings too often are little better than blood suckers, and blood spillers, and all by the grace of God forsooth."

The subject of a head for the new commonwealth, or whatever it was to be called, was of so grave a nature that for some few minutes not one of the conspirators spoke. Evidently each one was revolving in his own mind as to upon whom the selection ought to fall, and no doubt each could have solved the momentous question to his own entire satisfaction; but modesty kept their thoughts locked up. Presently the carpenter spoke.

"It's a detail," he said. They all agreed, and so the matter dropped, not, however, before there had been a slight passage of arms between the carpenter and the cook. "Of course," said Chips, "you are out of the question, Pepper?"

"And why so, pray?" was the indignant reply. "I didn't say I would take the post if it were offered me; for I am not like some people I could mention, of an ambitious turn of mind. No matter who falls, so long as they mount." This must have hit the carpenter very hard.

"Whoever heard of a cook being made a ruler?" the carpenter asked.

"For the matter of that, whoever heard of a carpenter?" said the cook.

"Why Pepper, my lad, where's your schooling? Does not a carpenter's son, and one who was a carpenter himself rule the whole Christian World? But that is neither here nor there. You are too small; you would not command respect."

"Now I am surprised to hear a man of your ability, Chips, talk such utter nonsense. You seem to judge men as a butcher does his meat, by the pound. That is the sort of thing perhaps a woman might do. If that is to be your little game, you had better hoist Billy Cheeks up at once; he is not exactly a skeleton, and, no doubt, he would fill the place as well as any one else."

"No offence, Pepper, no offence, mate; it is a detail," said the carpenter.

"Then let it be a detail; and I care not who you hoist over us, so long as our head is neither expensive nor too highly gilded. But mind you, the lumber room must go."

They all agreed that this was a sensible way of looking at things, and to appease the cook, no doubt, they would there and then have lightened the ship by flinging over the whole of the Buccaneer's House of Lords, but the heavy tread of the watchman aft made them abandon the idea for the present; but as that ancient hereditary institution had fallen under the cook's displeasure, it was not likely that it could survive such a thing for long.

"What are we to do with our foreign relations?" asked the carpenter's mate.

"Ah! Chisel, my lad, you are coming to the front," said the carpenter.

"What have we to do with foreign relations?" the cook asked. "Let them mind their own business, and we will mind ours."

"The unfortunate thing is," said the butcher, "that they won't mind their own business; no people will." The butcher gave another start and declared he heard the mysterious sound at the back of the galley.

"Well, Billy!" the carpenter exclaimed, "for a big man, you have about the smallest heart of any man I ever met."

Thus did the conspirators settle the affairs of the Buccaneer's nation. But now another and most unmistakable sound saluted their ears. A cock crowed loud and long. It is a well-known fact that neither spirits nor conspirators can stand this sort of thing. "Ah!" cried the carpenter, "there goes the shrill herald of the morn." Conspirators generally speak in this florid manner. "The day has returned too soon. You have much to answer for, Billy; for by your incessant interruptions you have squandered our precious time. But no matter. My lads, one little thing before we part. We shall want money. We cannot get on without the needful. It is money that makes the old mare go."

"I have a scheme here," cried the cook, "of raising the necessary wind."

"Quick, Pepper, my man, where is that lamp of yours you are so fond of flaunting before the eyes of people in the broad light of day. The torch of Truth you call it."

"Ah! Master Chips, the light of that lamp is only shed on other people's business. It would never do here."

It could never for a moment be supposed that these conspirators had not their dark lanterns; and presently one was produced from the ample folds of somebody's cloak, and they all stooped down as the cook unrolled his plan and the light from the dark lantern fell upon the eager faces of Billy Cheeks, the carpenter, his mate, and the cook.

"Time, mates, is short, so I come to the point. This is a bill of sale."

"So, so, a bill of sale," they all said in a low tone as they eyed the piece of paper.

"We will have an auction," said the cook; "our foreign relations we have decided to let go; for we get more kicks than half-pence from them; but our colonies we will sell."

"Ha, ha!" laughed the butcher, hoarsely; "mind they don't sell you."

"At it again, Billy," said the cook; "but it shows you're recovering from your nervous attack. Lot No. 1. The Buccaneer's well-known property of India. A rich possession comprizing over 200,000,000 of faithful subjects, together with forts and garrisons fully armed and equipped, and a most lucrative trade."

"The Eastern Bandit no doubt will bid for that lot or perhaps he'll take it," said the carpenter's mate.

"Proceed, Pepper," cried the carpenter.

"That cock won't fight," remarked the butcher. "You don't suppose our master will allow his dusky princess to be bought or taken by his old enemy, the Bandit."

"Go on, Pepper," cried the carpenter; "Billy's state of health is rapidly improving. Haste, my lad, for the silver foot of day is advancing. In a short time his eye will be over yonder house-tops, and if he looks upon us plotting in the cook's caboose, then farewell to our plan and perhaps to our liberty as well."

"Lot 2. Egypt. We may expect bidders for that country and 'caveat emptor' say I. That is a country replete with articles of virtu, the only thing is to find them. It is the proud possessor of an ancient history. With this lot will go a discontented, harassed and poverty-stricken people, and one or more high military reputations, and may the devil fly away with the whole lot, say I. There are a few others—things scarcely worth mentioning—such as the royal robes, crown jewels, and other court paraphernalia."

Here the discussion was suddenly put a stop to by the butcher, who gave such a start that he knocked the carpenter's mate up against the cook, who in turn nearly overturned Chips. The lantern was upset and the light was put out.

"What the devil is up now!" cried the cook, recovering himself.

"I saw it again," said the butcher, in a terrified whisper. They all pitied the butcher and declared that he was, without exception, about as uncomfortable a member of a conspiracy as could possibly be found. There was something almost uncanny about his behaviour, and no doubt less doughty men would have been scared. It was now too late to continue with their plans. They one and all said that the scheme was good and wanted scarcely for anything except the carrying of it out, which they agreed was a mere matter of detail. They complimented the cook upon his suggested method of raising the necessary wind. They were all very well pleased one with another, and as the carpenter dismissed them, he said: "Bless ye, my lads! Away to your bunks, my honest fellows. The silver king treads close upon the heels of the sable queen, so away and snatch a few hours of repose. Then arise and buckle to your work. Mix well amongst the people ashore. Sow broadcast the seeds of discontent, and so prepare the way for action. The womb of time is big with great events. Be civil, my mates, to the wild Ojabberaways, for at times it is necessary to hold the candle to the devil himself. If we do not square them, the other watch will."

"The greedy office grabbers," cried the cook, "will leave no stone unturned to get the helm; but we must dish them. For my part I have always found the Ojabberaways a merry and clever lot of gentlemanly devils."

"To their many wants then," exclaimed the carpenter, "lend a kindly ear; but keep your own counsel. Be thrifty of your words unless you use them as our noble captain does, to conceal your thoughts. Away then, my lads! What, does no one move? It is too late for ghosts to prowl about, and of other things what have you to fear?"

"Who is afraid, Master Chips?" the cook asked indignantly, "I was only thinking."

"Vast heaving, my hearties, while the cook thinks," cried the carpenter. "In the meantime I will take a look round, the watchman may be about." Chips drew his cloak round him and pulled his slouched hat well down over his eyes; then with the stealthy walk peculiar to conspirators he took a look round. Just as he reached the back of the cook's galley, he heard what sounded like a splash in the water. It made him start; and his heart beat hard against his side, his hair stood on end, and he had to lean against the water-butt for support. "Pshaw!" he cried as he shivered in the chill morning air, "I am getting as bad as Billy Cheeks." The look-out man from aloft cried out, "All's well." Thus reassured, the carpenter told his companions that the coast was clear, so with cloaks well wrapped round them and hats well slouched they sneaked away to their beds.

CHAPTER XXIII.

It was but a narrow strip of water that separated the old Sea King, or Buccaneer, from his neighbours on the mainland. But narrow as the strip was it had been and it was of the greatest service to him; for it kept from his shores the numerous bands of robbers that infested the mainland. Of course things had very much improved of recent years, but still occasional robberies took place even now, and when an opportunity offered it was not allowed to pass by. Since the world began it has been said that honest men are few and rogues are many.

There can be very little doubt that the veneer called civilisation has done much for the world. It would appear, however, that when people are collected together into a nation, they cannot even now look upon the richness of a neighbour, without having some feelings of envy, and experiencing a slight itching sensation at the ends of the fingers.

Indeed, the study of history, and human nature generally, would lead us to believe that man is not only a very lazy fellow by nature, never working unless necessity compels him to; but that he is also a thief, and is only honest by compulsion, or by learning that it is to his personal advantage to be so. This much we may have hinted before. For mankind in general we have the highest admiration and consideration; but we cannot hide from ourselves the fact that it has with many virtues, also very many faults, and love of other people's property seems to be one.

Man we will not run down or decry. Look you at the savage! There is a great nobility about him, and in some things he compares most favourably with his highly cultivated and civilised brother. The latter is perhaps the proud possessor of a great intellect, of rank, of high position, having a long line of ancestors to decorate the walls of his ancestral hall. He may be the proud possessor of vast wealth, in fact, of everything that leads to human greatness, and yet see how he sneaks into a room as if he were some mean thing and thoroughly well ashamed of himself. Contrast with this man the noble bearing of the savage, every movement is as full of dignity, as, in all probability, his only blanket is of insects. This man feels himself a lord of creation. His mantle above alluded to he throws over his shoulders with an easy grace. His only possession perhaps is his spear or tomahawk which he is ever ready to bury in the stomach of an enemy or in the friendly earth. Then the savage is silent, and when he does speak, he does not prove himself a wind bag, but he speaks in measured tones, and with dignity and very much to the point. There is none of that senseless gabbling which is such a mark of Western civilisation, and which at times is so extremely confusing and even distressing. He does not wash, you say? Good people all, here the peculiar and special prejudice of civilisation presents itself. Yes, the tub crowns your Western edifice; but did your Saint James ever use the bath? The platter is well washed without, but within? The savage is a noble being, though perhaps the rain that falls from a generous heaven is the only washing he ever gets.

The imagination loves to dwell upon the ideal. It peoples the garden of Eden with beautiful and naked innocence. It loves to sing of the gentle shepherd, who, decked in ribbons and becoming fancy pastoral garments, pipes and dances to his flocks all day long, and in other ways wastes his employer's time. Strip the gentle shepherd of the clothing generously given him by the imagination and you find him a very rough fellow indeed, not given to singing so much as to cursing, and instead of dancing, is more ready to knock anyone on the head who interferes with his sheep-stealing propensities. We speak, good people all, of early pastoral times, of what we may call the ancient shepherd period.

Heaven forbid! that we should say one word against civilisation. Do we wish to live in a state of society which was so easily excited that if a man but sneezed some fiery fellow would fancy himself insulted and out with his bodkin and put it through one? Heaven forbid! we say again. But, good people all, the struggle for existence is great. The weakest at all times go to the wall. The noble savage allows his weakly and sickly offspring to die; perhaps even at times he assists nature, occasionally knocking an aged parent on the head, saving thereby much pain and suffering on the one side, and trouble and anxiety on the other. But see what your civilisation does. See how far superior it is; how supremely human. It calls in that eminent physician Dr. Science, and with his help your sickly human weeds are nourished and reared until they are old enough and strong enough to marry and multiply. Weeds produce weeds and quickly. A sickly body can only sustain a sickly mind, and so the world wags and whole peoples become undermined. What would we do? Nothing. We sit and watch things taking their course, and note the many advantages that civilisation has over barbarism.

It is an old, old tale, yet in the telling of it nature alone is not prosy. She has such a way of telling the same story over and over again and ever varying it some little in the telling. What wonderful powers of variation has our mother! Take a million faces and by some subtle combination of the same features she gives an individuality to each. But to return to our noble savage. In a rough and ready fashion he surmounts the difficulty of his useless members of society. By an extensive and well-organised system, civilisation finds out the exact amount of sustenance it takes to keep the body and soul together in an aged broken-down pauper. Then separating an aged couple, who perhaps have borne the brunt of many a misfortune together, it allows them to drain to the last drop the dregs of life, holding up to them as a consolation the plenty that lies in paradise. Civilisation justly condemns the inhuman custom of the otherwise noble savage; but does not deny itself the inward satisfaction of a sigh of relief when some person who, having lingered perhaps a trifle too long over his or her exit, eventually goes. "Poor soul," they say, "it is a happy release. Gone to a better and a happier world, no doubt." A pauper's funeral brightens a district and carries, if not joy, at least no sorrow to the hearts of the guardians of the poor.

We never said that civilisation was a gigantic workshop where hypocrites and humbugs are turned out by the thousands every day, whilst its religion occupies itself in manufacturing Pharisees. We have pointed out, if we have not demonstrated, the admirable laws by which civilisation works as regards the welfare of the poor, and we have shown the care that it takes of its sickly weeds, given to them such eminent advantages and allowing them to contaminate a whole community with their sickliness. We have acknowledged how in all respects, with the sole exception of grace and bearing, civilisation is superior to the savage state. But this much we will say, many savages we have seen who are very much more gentle in their manners; very much more honourable and even refined in their feelings, and very much more humane, than the roughs of civilisation. No doubt every civilised family has its extremely black sheep. The Buccaneer certainly had his, and compared with them, the gentle savage is a well-bred gentleman.

Then look at your pale-faced drudge of civilisation. With bent back and emaciated face and smarting eyes, her thin but nimble fingers stitch on from early morning, till after the weary sun has sunk to rest. On, on, she works with scanty food, and in an impure atmosphere. Poor soul, has civilisation done much for her? Has it buttered her bread more thickly or sweetened more her tea? Is her lot any better than that of her sister who toils and slaves out in the open, while her brave lies and basks in the sun of idleness?

But we have wandered far from that narrow strip of water that divided the Buccaneer from his neighbours on the mainland. It had been to him as a magic belt, and worth more than thousands of men. His neighbours had to look on and long and wonder perhaps how it was that such a man had been allowed to prosper. But all have heard of the row in the kitchen, between the pot and the kettle. His neighbours, however, repudiated with scorn any evil intentions and they only kept themselves armed to the teeth to keep wicked robbers and cut-throats away; but it was a wonder to many people where they could be, because, if asked, all declared that all they wished for was to be allowed to live in peace, and quietude, so that they might enjoy the reward of their honest, industrious, and highly respectable lives, and fit themselves for heaven.

CHAPTER XXIV.

ARRIVING on the shores of his nearest neighbour, Madame France, the Buccaneer landed, and as he intended to make a few calls inland, he sent his yacht round to the Golden Horn with orders to await there his arrival.

The Buccaneer took off his hat and made his politest bow; but his reception was by no means as cordial as he had expected. As is well known by all those who have experienced it, there is nothing so freezing as the cold politeness of a haughty beauty. It requires more brazen effrontery than even old Dogvane had, to carry it off with a high handed dignity as if nothing was wrong. That Madame France was beautiful there could be no doubt, and she would have made the blood quicken in the veins of the most eminent saint, and as for a sinner! well, there is no use going into particulars.

It is more than probable that the charms of this lady were not lost upon either the Buccaneer or his trusty captain William Dogvane. Then, as if the devil was in it, Madame had added to her natural beauty, by calling in the assistance of every art. Her figure was neat and most attractive, and her dress left nothing to be desired. In her display of charms she was generous without being coarse and vulgar, and her short kirtle discovered the prettiest of ankles, and just enough of a well-shaped leg to be peculiarly attractive. Even old Bill felt young again and his eyes glistened with delight, and he was no less inclined to be gallant than his master, who for the time forgot the precept taught him by his religion about coveting other people's goods.

Having coldly acknowledged the salutation she turned her back upon her visitors and pouted her pretty lips. "Master Dogvane," said the Buccaneer addressing that worthy, "there is not much cordiality here."

"It beats me altogether, sir," the captain replied, "but there is no understanding women, and, as everyone knows, Madame here is peculiarly fickle and uncertain. They all seem to go by the rule of contrary. She is an arrant coquette I'll be bound; but, Master, what a pretty foot and what a lovely leg."

"Dogvane!" cried the Buccaneer as he gazed upon the attractions alluded to, "you forget yourself." Then addressing the haughty beauty he said, "Madame, in what have I been so unfortunate as to meet with your displeasure? It is many years now since we had any cause for quarrel and all old wounds I trust are healed, and as I bear no malice, Madame, I hope you bear none. How then have I displeased you?"

"Monsieur, your memory methinks is short. Was I not set upon and beaten? Was I not hurt and bleeding? Was I not struck down until I bit the dust, and you never held out a hand to help me? Monsieur, my memory is better, I do not forget, I never shall."

"Oh! damn these violent memories!" exclaimed Dogvane aside.

"But, Madame, that is now an old old story," the Buccaneer replied. "Is it right to carry resentment so far? Is it acting up to the religion that we both profess?"

"Monsieur's reputation for piety is extremely great," said his fair neighbour, while a sneer played round her pretty mouth; she then added, "An injury, Monsieur, is never old."

"Madame!" cried the Buccaneer still wishing to appease, "you had my extreme sympathy."

"Sympathy!" cried Madame France, "sympathy! of what avail is that against battalions?"

"I dressed your wounds, I attended your sick and I sent you money, lint, and plaster."

"Sent me money!" exclaimed Madame France scornfully. Then suddenly changing her manner to a tone of polite sarcasm she said, "Pardon, Monsieur! I had forgotten, yes, you sent me money. It must have been a great sacrifice for you to part with what you love so well. The shopkeeper does not like to drain his till, even for a friend in need. I beg Monsieur's pardon a thousand times. I did not too fully appreciate his kindness. I have not sufficiently thanked my mercantile neighbour. Permit me, Monsieur," she said with a profound curtsey, " to thank you for your extravagant consideration and extreme sympathy."

The Buccaneer was going to reply; but Dogvane, fearing a storm, almost dragged his master away. " But this is not as it should be, Dogvane. It is not right."

As they went away Madame France muttered something, but the only word that reached the Buccaneer was "perfidious." This was an old retort.

" This is not right, Master Dogvane !" he cried.

" Decidedly wrong, sir. The grossest piece of ingratitude I have ever experienced. Ah ! we can plainly see, she has not forgiven you for remaining neutral in her last row with her burly neighbour inland. But a stale page of history is that."

" Master Dogvane, even a woman's resentment cannot last too long. There must be something else. Have you, Master Dogvane, been doing anything to put her out ? "

" I can tax my memory with nothing, sir ; but the other watch, who can tell what they've been up to ? Softly, my master, softly. For heaven's sake come away. Say nothing to increase her anger. The least said, soonest mended. Is she not fair to look upon ? " added Dogvane looking back as did Lot's wife. "What ripe lips !"

" What has that to do with it ? "

" Nothing, sir, nothing; what a lovely foot! what an ankle too ! what a comely leg ! "

" What the devil, I say again, has that to do with it ? " cried the Buccaneer.

" Nothing, sir, nothing. I merely ventured the remark that she was comely. No doubt that other watch have been at their handiwork. Master, you are a bit too brusque in your manner. Women don't like it ; if you had flattered more, you would have pleased more. You should have praised her beauty ; gone into

H

an ecstasy of delight over her many charms. Do you not think, sir, that the kirtle was an inch or two too long?"

The Buccaneer turned sharply upon his captain and rebuked him, told him plainly that although he was captain of his watch, he had no business to cast eyes upon his fair neighbour. Then he said, "She quarrelled with a friend of mine, and you are for ever telling me that I ought not to interfere, in things that don't concern me."

"You acted in that little affair, sir, like an upright, honest, gentleman; but do what you will you cannot please everyone. You did your best to prevent a row and you could do no more. But that is not where the shoe pinches. The other watch no doubt, the other watch. Let her alone, my master, to cool. When a woman is enraged, there is no arguing with her. No doubt some domestic trouble has disturbed her. She has always something on. Ah! I see it now," exclaimed Dogvane stopping short. "Some time ago she went in largely for old china and we all know that is an expensive luxury and probably the bill was larger than she expected. There are a thousand little things, trifles as light as air, in every household, that though hidden from the eye of the casual observer, help to ruffle the temper even of the most amiable woman. Did you notice, sir, her well turned ankle and shapely leg?" The old Buccaneer either did not hear, or did not approve of Dogvane's continued allusion to Madame France's charms. The captain, thinking he was still grieving over his cold reception, sought to console him by saying, "What though Madame France be cold and turn her back upon you, I feel confident that the island of Sark is with you to a man."

"The island of Sark!" exclaimed the Buccaneer in astonishment, "what has that to do with it?"

"Everything, sir," replied Dogvane. "For the island of Sark if not actually France is very near to it; and the moral support of such a place is not to be despised."

The Buccaneer seemed lost in meditation, from which he was only aroused by Dogvane exclaiming: "Ah! here we are, sir, at the door of your worthy German cousin, with whom you are allied by blood, by the holy bonds of wedlock, and by religion."

The mighty Von was sitting outside, in his garden overlooking the waters that divided him from his beautiful neighbour. He had a tankard by his side and a pipe in his mouth, for he was a great smoker.

The Buccaneer found that his reception here was scarcely more cordial than what it had been elsewhere. "Have I in any way done my worthy friend an injury?" the Buccaneer asked, turning to Dogvane.

"God forbid, sir, that you should do any man an injury," was the reply. "It has been my constant endeavour to keep you at peace with all men." This perhaps was true, but the result was not satisfactory.

"Give me an honest grip of thy friendly hand, neighbour," the Buccaneer exclaimed, as he held out his. The Von held out his but there was nothing hearty in the shake. "How is this, friend, thy grip used to be harder?" said the Buccaneer.

"Mein hand is mein own," replied the mighty Von.

"Tell me in what I have offended thee. If I have done thee an injury I will make amends. What, will my old friend not speak?"

"Mein counsel like mein hand is mein own, mein friend, and I keep them both."

"How do you account for this, Master Dogvane?" asked the Buccaneer, somewhat crestfallen.

"It is passing strange, sir, and I can only think that this is another piece of handiwork of the other watch. Their capacity for bungling is extremely great. But come away, sir. There is an old adage which says, 'it is ill to waken sleeping dogs.' It applies here." So saying he led his master away; but before they had gone very far Dogvane again stopped short. "Stay, I do remember there was some trivial dispute about a patch of barren land. Tut, tut, to think now that so great a friend should be affronted at such a trifle. The exact merits of the case have now escaped me; but as I was prepared to give way all round there need be no ill feeling on such a subject ; only to think now—but there, some people are that touchy that there is no pleasing them." The captain now began to sing to an old well-known song, some words of his own—

"The Von a mighty man is he with large and sinewy arms."

"Dogvane, cease ; this is no time to exercise your vocal powers. I have been a good friend to my German relations. I verily believe that I support half his army in the bands that are for ever braying out their discordant sounds in my streets. Then are not my own people constantly at me for employing my foreign relations to the prejudice of my own children? and with some show of justice too, for German bakers make my bread, German tailors make most of my clothes, and German Jews are constantly draining away my money. Do I not find royal wives for German princelets, and do I not dower them handsomely into the bargain ? and yet they give me the cold shoulder in return. No matter who dances, Master Dogvane, it seems to me it is I who have to pay the piper. To one of my worthy friend's sons, poor fellow, I begrudged nothing, for he was a king of kings and a fine manly fellow, and one who will never die."

"Marriage, my master, often severs families instead of uniting them. This only bears out what I am constantly telling you, and that is to have as little as possible to do with your relations. But, master, a good deal of what we call ingratitude in others is due to faults in ourselves. We start by expecting more than we deserve, and are disappointed when we only get our deserts ; but, of course, we never think of putting the saddle on the right back."

Our two travellers, weary, thristy, and dust-stained, now came to Austria, and were in hopes of getting a more friendly reception ; such a one, in fact, that would justify them in staying there and breaking bread and drinking a flagon of wine for the sake of good fellowship. But no, Dogvane had managed to tread upon the toes of Austria, and had got himself disliked even here. He swore it was a part of that terrible inheritance he had received over from the other watch. According to his own account, no man was ever so unfortunate.

Dogvane now entered upon a most lengthy and learned explanation upon the quality of gratitude, and what he said upon such a matter would deserve the greatest consideration, but weightier things still, attended upon their footsteps.

A messenger arrived post haste to say, that information had been received through the proper official channel, that the great Bandit of the East was behaving himself in an altogether unaccountable and strange manner. In fact, that he had broken into one Abdur's garden, and was playing, what was called in unofficial language general, Old Harry, there.

"Here is another of your confounded foreign relations cropping up," said Dogvane to himself.

"How about this, Master Dogvane?" exclaimed the Buccaneer.

"Why, this sort of thing, sir, has been going on for ages, and it is nothing more nor less than a party trick of the other watch, at the bottom of which, no doubt, is that mischievous young imp, Random Jack. I have myself frequently asked the Eastern Bandit about these unsavoury reports, and his smile was childlike and bland as he replied, that if anything was going on wrong, he knew nothing about it. He is a truthful and a Christian man and would not tell a lie, not for the whole Empire of India. At least, if he would, I have no official information upon the subject."

"Well, Master Dogvane, the readiest way to set the matter at rest is to go and see for ourselves."

"That would be a most undignified proceeding, sir. You cannot expect foreign nations to respect you if you go and poke your nose into other people's dustbins. Besides, sir, it would be a most unconstitutional thing; and before undertaking it, we at least ought to retrace our steps home and set the official mind at work to find out a precedent. Then if such a thing can be found, which I very much doubt, we will at once proceed to the scene of action, and throw the light of our official eye upon the Eastern Bandit, who, no doubt, being dazzled and frightened by such an unusual occurrence, will fear some revolution of nature, and so retire to his own ground."

"Master Dogvane, the official coach is far too slow for an occasion like this. We can walk the distance very much quicker, so set thy face to the East and march. And on our way we will pay the honest Turk a visit."

"Oh lord!" exclaimed Dogvane to himself, "here is another kettle of fish. Sir, are we not tired, hungry, and thirsty? And the weather is much too warm for such a journey. But, if go we must, gallivanting about in the East, we shall save a little, sir, if we leave this Turk on our right hand."

"Master Dogvane, the Turk is a friend of mine. We have fought side by side against the Eastern Bandit, and may be we shall have to do so again. I will therefore pay my respects to him."

"I would kick him bag and baggage out of Europe if I had my way," muttered old Dogvane.

The Buccaneer found the head of the Moslem world pensively smoking his chibouck. "Ah!" said he, "you, at least, my honest friend, will not turn your back upon me. I have at least you to fall back upon."

"Monsieur, I salute you," said the Turk with extreme politeness. "When you want to get anything out of me you call me friend and honest Turk; when you do not, I am a rogue, a vagabond, and little better than a barbarian. A while since, and your captain was for kicking me, bag and baggage, out of Europe." Dogvane was a little taken aback at having been overheard, but he soon recovered himself and was ready to argue that if his words were taken properly they could bear no such signification.

The Buccaneer was so taken by surprise that he could not speak, while Dogvane, shading his eyes with his hand, cast a look towards the beautiful Golden Horn, to see if the yacht was there, for he was weary of travelling, and had become what is called home-sick, and had he never had to consider things abroad, the chances are it would have been very much better for his reputation, and for that of his master. He said, "What is the use of your meandering in foreign parts, sir, you have a nice, snug, well-feathered little nest in the Western Ocean, where everything smiles upon you. There lies your yacht; then let us aboard: weigh anchor, and make for the rosy bed of the setting sun."

The Turk interrupted: "It suits your purpose, mon ami," he said, addressing the Buccaneer, "to seek my friendship now. But the honest Turk was not born yesterday, and he is very much more than seven, so he allies himself with those who will not cast him off when they have no further need of him."

This roused the suspicions of the Buccaneer. "Whatever you do," he cried, "do not ally yourself with the Eastern Bandit. Give him a wide berth or he will pluck you to your last feather."

"An open enemy," replied the Turk, "is better than a treacherous friend. Pat my back to-day; kick—but no matter, Allah is good! There is but one God, and Mohammed is his prophet."

"Treacherous friend," ejaculated the Buccaneer, turning to the captain. "Does the Turk call me treacherous, Master Dogvane?"

"Heaven forbid such a thing, sir! The Turk merely made a general remark, which in the abstract no doubt is true. But, master, leave the Turk alone. If you do not come speedily away he will borrow of you for a certainty."

"But he has been my friend, Master Dogvane, for these many years."

"True, sir; and you have treated him more kindly than you usually do your friends, whom you occasionally fall out with; even coming to blows at times. But the Turk's friendship, good master, is of a costly kind. He is a ready borrower, but a tardy payer. Look at the money he has spent in riotous living? Honest enough, no doubt; but as he is always out at elbows he cannot afford to indulge in such a luxury. A needy friend, good master, is a constant source of annoyance; for when poverty comes, pride goes, and your friend soon sinks into the degraded position of a most importunate and shameless beggar."

"I do not like to turn my back upon a friend just because he is down in the world, Master Dogvane."

"The feeling does you credit; it is noble; but, good sir, we must draw a line, lest at any time we give countenance to vice. We often deceive ourselves, and act as we think, generously, either out of idleness or fear, lest the babbling world should condemn us for want of kindness to those in need. God forbid that you should forsake a friend because he is down! But when a man has brought his suffering and misfortunes upon himself, then, good master, sympathy is bestowed upon a worthless object. Why should you assist one who will not help himself? Who so long as he can borrow will spend? The Turk will not live within his means, and you have found, sir, that you cannot enjoy his friendship without paying heavily for it." With reflections like these Dogvane led his master away, and the Turk watched their retreating steps with half-closed eyes; but yet he was not asleep; but the precise nature of his thoughts cannot, for obvious reasons, be disclosed.

"Oh for a sniff of the fresh sea air!" cried Dogvane, as he looked wistfully towards the ocean. "To feel yourself once more afloat, master, with your empire beneath your feet, and your good little ship dancing merrily to the music of the waves, would make a different man of you."

"Aye, aye, Master Dogvane, perhaps it would; but I have other fish to fry just at present. Those were merry days when I ploughed the seas in search of adventure, and it all comes back to me like a dream. I fancy I hear now the clack, clack of my many windlasses; the yo! heave-ho! of my merry men, as they sheeted home their sails, and mast-headed their yards. The brave sea fights; the brilliant actions of my lads; the sinking of the enemy's ships, all, all comes back upon me. I fancy I can see my merry men, pike in hand, swarming over the ship's sides, while we poured in broadsides muzzle to muzzle. I almost hear their shouts. They strike, they strike, Dogvane, while our colours still fly proudly over us, nailed to the mast. See the ocean blurred with their life's blood. Ah! it is past, Dogvane, it is past. Lend me thy shoulder, man, lend me thy shoulder, for my eyes are dim. Alas! they are clouded by memory. Are those good old days gone, never, never to return?"

Dogvane had learned from experience that when his master had on him one of these fits of despondency, the best thing to be done was to let him alone. He contented himself with saying, "Every age, my master, has its advantages. We cannot say that the spring is more beautiful than the summer, nor yet the summer than the autumn, while hoary-headed winter is not free from charms."

CHAPTER XXV.

AWAY our two friends journeyed until they came to a high eminence which commanded a good view of all the country round. At their feet was spread the garden of Abdur, and in the distance was to be seen the El Dorado of the East. The fair lands of the Buccaneer's Indian Princess. How lovely it all looked; the hot sun streaming down on plains covered with jungle and the tall cocoanut trees with their long stems and bushy heads; and the shady plaintain with its long, broad leaves. Then rivers wound through the plain like huge silver serpents making their endless way to the sea.

As may be easily imagined, the Buccaneer who was not accustomed to such lengthy and arduous journeys, was completely done up, for the ascent had been steep and difficult; often had he stopped to admire the scenery, an excuse generally made by the weary, who are too proud to admit that they are in the smallest degree overcome. Rivulets of perspiration were running down the old gentleman's face, and it took him some time to mop himself and gain his breath. Dogvane, as the saying is, had not turned a hair. Whether this was on account of the paucity of that article, or the general leanness of his condition, it is not necessary to say.

The Buccaneer sat and contemplated in silence the beauty of the scene before him, while the captain of his watch looked through the left corner of his eye towards Abdur's home. Presently a shout in that direction made the Buccaneer start from his happy reverie, and turning to his left there he saw the Eastern Bandit, apparently enjoying himself in Abdur's garden, and not keeping to the pathways either, but trampling borders and beds under foot. " Hallo! Master Dogvane," exclaimed the Buccaneer, "sure enough there he is at his handiwork, just as we were told."

"Be not too hasty, master," Dogvane replied. "Things are not always as they seem; so somebody has said, and I believe him. We are absolutely without any official information on the subject, while, on the contrary, I have the august Bandit's word for it, that he wants nothing out of Abdur's garden, and I believe him, for the fruit is of a prickly kind, and not at all enticing. In fact, more fit for asses than for human beings."

"Facts are stubborn things, Master Dogvane, and seeing surely is believing."

"Not always, sir; for how many people are deceived by their eyes? one swearing he saw one thing, another swearing the very reverse. Things are deceptive, more especially when seen through glasses dimmed by prejudice." Dogvane said nothing about the dimness of the official eye, which is well known to be as nearly blind as possible, without being absolutely so. He put his glass up and took a survey, taking good care that that part of Abdur's garden where the Bandit was should not come within his range. "For my part," he said, "I do not think the Eastern Bandit is in Abdur's garden. You may depend upon it, sir, he is merely going through the time honoured custom of beating the bounds."

"Then you go down, Master Dogvane, and see that the boundaries are fairly marked."

"It has ever been the custom to take some small boy, and by bumping him or whipping him upon the breech at certain places, to engraft the boundaries indelibly upon his memory. I am too old a man for this. It is a thousand pities that we have not young Random Jack with us. He is for ever wishing to render you some signal service, as much to make a name for himself as to do good to you. Now, this would be an excellent opportunity for him to show his zeal, and I regret extremely that the lad is not here. It would be well worth while to send for him."

Dogvane's meditations were put a stop to by the Buccaneer exclaiming, as he brought down his telescope and shut up the slides with a bang: "As I hope to be saved, Master Dogvane, the Bandit is in our friend Abdur's garden!" Here he opened his spyglass again and took another look. "And what is more," he added, "the rascal seems inclined to lay his hands upon what does not belong to him."

Fat as the Buccaneer had grown, and lazy as his prosperity and good living had made him, he did at times rouse himself, and when he did he frequently flew into the most violent fits of passion, and made use of the most terrible language, and altogether forgetting that he was a Christian he would swear like any Turk, or the proverbial trooper. Our friend was now seized with a warlike epidemic, which, as a rule, is very infectious. He was for fighting his old enemy at once, for he felt fully persuaded that he must be in the wrong. Dogvane, the man of peace, tried to calm his master down, and begged him to take things quietly; saying that it was time enough to draw the sword when diplomacy failed.

The Buccaneer when he heard that word, ripped out several oaths of such a nature, as to make Dogvane's hair stand on end. This annoyed the Buccaneer still more, and he requested Dogvane, in tones not to be disobeyed, not to do it. The captain apologized, and delared it was the "wind, and nothing more;" showing that his mind was far away. The Buccaneer, however, quickly brought him back to his senses, by commanding him to ask the Eastern Bandit, in the politest manner possible, what the devil he meant, by trespassing upon other people's property. Of course, things had to be done in a proper way, and strictly according to custom. Dogvane knew very well that it was quite useless to ask the Eastern Bandit for any information, because, whatever his intentions might be, it was not at all likely that he would disclose them. To do so, would be to act in a manner altogether undiplomatic. But obedient to his master's commands, the captain of the watch went to a small rivulet that sprang out of the mountain side close by. This tiny stream after bounding from rock to rock of its mountain bed, fell down into the plain below, and then widening and growing deeper and deeper, rolled lazily through Abdur's garden, refreshing its parched soil with its grateful waters.

Dogvane put his hand to the side of his mouth and sent down on the bosom of the rivulet a request couched in the most polite language to know what the great Bandit of the East was about. Back came a voice from the plains below, saying, "The august Bandit of the East, the master of many millions of slaves, requests the Buccaneer of the West to mind his own business."

"Tells me to mind my own business, does he? And call you that a diplomatic answer, Master Dogvane?"

"Most assuredly," replied the captain. "It would have been quite as easy for him to have told you to go to the devil. How can you find fault with him, or anyone else, for telling you to mind your own business. It is what every right-minded and honest man ought to do."

"But it is what every right-minded and honest man does not like to be told to do. This business is mine, Master Dogvane. Do you not see that he is putting his huge foot forward?"

"My eyesight in such things is somewhat dim; but be not hasty. In times past, sir, your rashness has led you into sad trouble. For all we know the Eastern Bandit does but stretch his leg, preparatory to making a backward movement. For my part, I think this must be so. I go so far as to say that it is so; for I have entered into an agreement with him; or it may be an arrangement, or even a sacred covenant."

"The devil take your covenant!" cried the Buccaneer, "I am going to see into this little matter myself," and away the old gentleman started off, with a speed that endangered his neck. Dogvane needs must follow; but he was not so good going down as up a hill on occasions like this. "Steady, my master! Steady!" he cried. "The more haste, the less speed. God forbid that we should not uphold the sacred ties of friendship; but, sir, I beg you; I beseech you, not to be rash. Remember, those who quarrels interpose, often wipe a bloody nose. Let us try the gentle force of reason first, then if that fails—"

"What then, Master Dogvane?" said the Buccaneer, stopping and turning round to confront his captain.

"Time, sir, and the course of events alone can tell. In a good cause, in a righteous cause, old Will Dogvane will be found ever ready to draw the sword."

"Damme! Dogvane, there's life in the old dog yet."

"Sir, swear not; it makes my blood curdle in my veins."

"Dogvane! Dogvane!" cried the Buccaneer, "As I live he is beating Abdur's children!"

"And why not, sir? why not? no doubt, they richly deserve it. Have you not taken the liberty of doing the self same thing yourself?"

They were now very much closer, and Dogvane put up his glass to his official eye, and declared he saw nothing out of the way going on. This so irritated the Buccaneer, that he performed something in the nature of a miracle, and he made Dogvane receive his sight. He owned that he did see something in the nature of a beating taking place. Then he said by way of excuse: "You can not expect, sir, to have a monopoly of beating other people's children. But at any rate," he continued, " the time has come for us to show the Eastern Bandit that we are not to be trifled with. We are now near enough for him to see. The man who will not stand up for a friend in need, deserves to be branded with the name of coward."

"Bravo, Dogvane!" exclaimed the Buccaneer, "I don't care for sentiment, as a rule; for it generally cloaks some infernal rascality; but damme that's a good sentiment, and one to my liking."

Dogvane felt an honest pride in having thus pleased his master. He felt also encouraged, so taking off his coat and turning up his shirt sleeves he said, " When the Eastern Bandit sees the sinews of my goodly arms, he will, no doubt, become frightened, and pause ere he provokes me to anger ; but, master, you will stand by me?"

"Through thick and thin, Dogvane!"

"It will be a costly affair, for I needs must make gigantic preparations. I shall have to go into training."

"Name but your sum, Dogvane, and it is yours," cried the fighting old Buccaneer in an ecstasy of delight.

"It cannot be done comfortably, sir, under £11,000,000," replied the captain.

"It is yours, Dogvane! It is yours, I am rich, and I am generous."

"Has the taking off of my coat in any way frightened him, my master? Your eyesight is better than mine."

"Not a bit, Dogvane. The beggar is dancing about just as if the whole place belonged to him. Go in, old man, and win. Nail your colours to the mast," the old sea king could not forget his early days, with its quaint language. "And may God defend the right!" he piously exclaimed as he took off his hat and raised his eyes devoutly to heaven. Of course there could be little doubt in the Buccaneer's own mind as to who was in the right. As has already been stated he fully believed that God was always on his side, and if he did come off second best, it was the Devil who for some good reason was allowed, for the time being, to prevail against him. This is a pardonable vanity and is shared by many other pious and devout people. With Dogvane it was different. He was blessed, or cursed according to the way it is looked at, with a most tender conscience, and though he never allowed it for any length of time to stand in his way, it caused him so to act, that people condemned him as a splitter of straws and a weigher of scruples. While he was thus occupied he generally allowed the golden opportunity to pass by and thus he frequently brought his wares to the market a day or so after the fair. And many a time the words "too late" were hung out over the gate he wished to enter at.

Scarcely had the Buccaneer finished the above pious ejaculation than Dogvane's stout right arm fell listlessly to his side. He drooped his head as he repeated, in a low tone of voice, the words of his master: "And may God defend the right! That sends a cold thrill through every vein in my body. Suppose," he said, addressing his master. "Suppose; I say suppose, my master, we are in the wrong, what a weight of blood-guiltiness will rest upon our heads? Suppose we are in the wrong, and being in the wrong we spill the blood of a fellow-creature? Good master, I have a qualm of conscience."

"Oh! damn your conscience!" cried the Buccaneer, whose blood was up. Of course such language is reprehensible in the extreme; no matter who uses it; but it is doubly so when it falls from the lips of a pious Christian gentleman. But, good people all, what is bred in the bone, will come out in the flesh. Dogvane recoiled from such language.

"Damn not my conscience, sir, nor that of any other man," he said, for his religion was unlike many a modern lady's beauty, it was even more than skin deep.

"Conscience," continued Dogvane, "is the guiding star by which we steer these frail barks of ours through life. Too many of us do not, consequently we find ourselves lost amidst shoals and quicksands. In a just cause, in a righteous cause I will fight."

"What!" cried the Buccaneer in amazement, "are you going to put your coat on again?"

"This, sir, is a matter that must receive our gravest consideration. Before we fight we must thoroughly sift the matter in the inmost recesses of the mind, until we are fully convinced of the sacredness of our cause. The man—"

"Stay, Master Dogvane! Not another word in that direction as you value the wholeness of your skin. Give me anything you like; but damme, dont't try my temper with another sentiment."

"What I was going to say, most noble master, is this. If we have in any way offended the Bandit of the East, we must make what reparation we can by craving his pardon."

"What!" cried the Buccaneer, "are you going to humble me before all the world?"

"Nay, sir; call it not by such a name. It is a noble thing, and the act of a great and generous mind to own freely that it is in the wrong. I do not humble you. I exalt you and place you upon a high pinnacle of perfection. It requires more courage to own oneself in the wrong than it does to take up the sword. It stands to reason, sir, that we both cannot be in the right; this being conceded why should not the wrong be on our side, nay, what more likely than that it is? Let us then sheathe the bloody brutalizing sword until the merits of the case are fully shown."

"And are all your mighty words to go for nothing, Master Dogvane? How about my honour? How about my honour?" said the Buccaneer sorrowfully.

"Honour, sir!" replied Dogvane. "Honour! what is honour that you should shed human blood over it? It is but a breath that comes from the mouths of other people, and the same mouth is as ready to damn as bless. This honour, what is it? It is here to-day, it is gone to-morrow, and is hunted often to death by envy, hatred, and malice, until in the end it is handed over to the tender mercies of its adversary shame. This self same honour that is so much lauded, is a picker of quarrels, a shedder of blood, a vain boaster, and a veritable swashbuckler. This honour is the veriest bubble that man ever fought for, or prated about, and it has done more mischief in the world than any other of man's vain causes of strife; because no principle has been so plentifully abused, except, perhaps, the principle of religion. For this self same honour, or its shadow, you have sacrificed countless thousands of your own sons, and slaughtered countless thousands of other people's. For the sake of this honour you have burdened yourself with a debt that you will carry with you to your grave and it will bend your back, more and more each day you live. God grant that in the end it does not crush you beneath its weight. We will place this matter in the hands of others who will arbitrate between you and the Eastern Bandit, who, I cannot but think, is grossly maligned. This, good master, will be a more humane, a more civilised, and a more Christian method of settling your dispute."

During this harangue of Dogvane's the spirits of the Buccaneer kept on falling and falling until despair sat heavily at his heart. There was something quite pathetic in his bearing as he said: "Master Dogvane, I do not wish to be better than my neighbours. They are all Christians, and yet they all fight. Madame France is armed to the teeth. My German cousin sleeps in armour always, with one eye open. Then, why should I hang up my sword, pistols and buckler and resent neither rebuke, insult, nor injury? In such a matter as this, is it wise to trust to a third party?"

"Master, what does your religion teach you? Be you the pioneer of a better state of things. God knows we have had fighting enough."

"I wish my old coxswain were here," said the Buccaneer. "This is an occasion when his advice would come in well." Perhaps, had he been present he might have told his master that he had better turn monk at once and start a monastery if he intended to follow the advice of the captain of the watch. Why, you ask, did not this fighting, hard swearing, and hard drinking old sea king whip out his hanger and go in at the Bandit himself?

Good people all, it must be remembered, that he now conducted his business on purely constitutional principles, and he would have violated some one or many of these had he so acted. So wedded was he to his constitution that it is probable he would have preferred to be utterly ruined by sticking to it, than saved by going in any way against it. He was a great stickler for routine, red tape, and custom. They, for the time, left the Eastern Bandit in the full enjoyment of his actions. Dogvane broke the silence. "Sir," he said, "I have in my mind's eye a worthy potentate who may, for a small consideration, be induced to serve you in this dispute you have with the Eastern Bandit. King Hokeepokeewonkeefum—"

"What!" exclaimed the Buccaneer, in surprise.

"Does the length of the name astonish you, sir? We have near neighbours whose names, were they all joined together, far exceed the one just mentioned. All great and illustrious people have long names; but they are all capable of contraction. King Hokee, sir, as we will for brevity call him."

"What!" exclaimed the Buccaneer again, almost breathless with amazement. "Entrust my affairs to a black?" There was an adjective used, but for various reasons it has not been recorded.

"Surely, sir," replied Dogvane, "you are above the prejudice of colour. Though black, King Hokee has no doubt a mind particularly free from prejudice. Is he not a man and a brother? Besides, sir, to borrow somewhat from perhaps a greater William than myself: Hath not King Hokee eyes? Hath he not hands, organs, dimensions, senses, affections, passions? If he has not I have no official information on the subject. Is he not fed by the same food, hurt by the same weapons, subject to the same diseases, healed by the same means, warmed and cooled by the same winter and summer as we are? If you prick King Hokee, think you he will not bleed? If you tickle him, will he not laugh? If you poison him, will he not die?"

"Cease, Master Dogvane; no more of this. You have stabbed me, and verily I bleed. To think that the old sea king should be brought so low as to ask a favour from a damned black!"

For certain weighty reasons the adjective here is not omitted.

"Have I then no friend, Master Dogvane; no great neighbour to whom I can entrust this affair?"

"It is one of the penalties attached to greatness, sir, to be without friends. The great stand upon an eminence and look down upon a gaping crowd of admirers, flatterers, and detractors; but they have no friends, at least not worth the mentioning. Besides, King Hokee would do the thing cheaper. A tin star with an appropriate appellation would satisfy him, and you could make him pay handsomely for the star."

"Am I then placed so high up on this bleak and sterile peak? I have done a great deal for Egypt; surely she will show me some little kindness? To show that my prejudice for colour is not great I will place the matter in her hands."

."People served, sir, have but short memories," was Dogvane's reply.

"We will at any rate break our journey back there, Master Dogvane, and we can mention the subject to the gipsy queen."

The captain did not seem to relish this, for he said in a disparaging manner: "Yes, you have done a good deal for the gipsy; but the man who does not wish to be disappointed will expect gratitude from no one, least of all from a woman. In Egypt, sir, our game has been, I own, a subtle one; but, like the villain in the play, we have been obliged, and still must dissemble, so as not to excite the jealousy of our neighbours."

Dogvane loved dissembling. "Sir," he added, as he shut one eye and put the forefinger of his right hand to the side of his nose in a most knowing manner, "we have not thought it wise to let the gipsy woman into our little secret. We have set up in Egypt a dummy whom we call a ruler. Behind his back we pull the strings of administration. When all goes well we come in front and make our bow to the audience, and receive our well merited applause. When anything goes wrong, we beat our dummy; he does not mind, and it would be all the same if he did; our neighbours are satisfied, and their suspicions are allayed."

"Is this honourable, Dogvane?"

"Sir, it is most diplomatic, consequently, it cannot be less than honourable."

The Buccaneer thought for awhile and then said: "It would have been better for me, Master Dogvane, to have seized the country at once. There would have been a cackling in some of my neighbours' poultry yards, but it would have saved an infinity of trouble in the end."

Dogvane was horrified at such a suggestion. This was a falling off and a going back with a vengeance. "Such a wholesale act of robbery," he said, "would perhaps have been pardonable in your old Buccaneering days, when you laid your hands on what you could, and did all you could to keep it; but in this, your age of extreme respectability, it would never do. Why! you would have had all your neighbours buzzing about your ears like a swarm of angry wasps. The act would have been most undiplomatic."

Here apparently some unpleasant thoughts entered the Buccaneer's mind, for a cloud passed over his face. "Diplomacy," he said; "that has never been a very strong point with me. I like to be open and above board, at least, at one time I did, and I loved to call a spade a spade. This diplomacy, Master Dogvane, is a genteel kind of a highwayman, who is not above insinuating his hands into the pockets of the unwary, while he distracts the attention of his victim by expressing towards him the highest esteem and regard. I would quite as soon he showed himself in his true colours and cried out boldly: 'Stand and deliver.'"

CHAPTER XXVI.

The journey homewards was a sad one, for the spirits of the old sea king were entirely broken. The captain of the watch tried all he could to cheer him up. He drew in fancy a pleasing picture of the island home they had left; of the contentment, prosperity, and happiness that reigned there, and old Dogvane did not forget to lay on the colours. As an artist in this line he was extremely good. As they left the domes and minarets of the grand Turk behind them, Dogvane turned to his master and said: "I cannot see why so good and great a man as my august master is, should not be content to rest upon the laurels he has already earned."

Flattery is at all times acceptable, and to all people; the only difference being that to suit the vulgar appetite you must lay it on thick, while to the refined the touches must be delicate and smooth. Dogvane, seeing the good effect that this kind of physic had upon his master, administered a little more. "Now take this Egyptian woman's case. See what you have done for her. You have tried to put down slavery. You have set your face against the brutal lash. You have tried at least to banish the evil-minded, blood-sucking Pasha, and in doing all this you have spent millions of money, and have sacrificed many of your bravest sons. One, even, we immolated at the shrine of the great god Necessity. We placed him in a pit even as Joseph was placed in a pit; but alas! Joseph was more fortunate; our offering was slain. Think you, sir, that in return for all this you will receive gratitude?"

"Master Dogvane, Egypt has always been of great interest to me, and through her lands I consider I have a right-of-way. Thus I have done very much for her, and if for nothing else, she ought to thank me for putting down that most barbarous of a things, the traffic in human beings."

"Sir, look rather for your reward in the righteousness of the cause. The man—"

"Stay, Master Dogvane; if you are going to give me another sentiment, spare me I beseech you."

"I was merely going to observe, sir, that the man who places the smallest faith in a woman's constancy, digs a pit for himself, into which he is sooner or later sure to fall."

Dogvane, for reasons best known to himself, was decidedly against this visit to Egypt. He seemed to be in some doubt as to the reception he would receive; but all his endeavours to dissuade his master were of no avail. The Buccaneer himself thought that Egypt must needs consider herself under the greatest obligation to him; but the best of men, and even the wisest, are often deceived, more especially as regards themselves. The poor man wanted consolation, and he was ready to go anywhere to obtain it.

There was no greater enemy in the world to the slave-dealer than was this great Buccaneer and fighting trader. He was forever going about, trying to put a stop to the degrading traffic, more especially when the wretched victims were black. His ships of war had strict orders to chase and capture all slavers found on the High Seas. His missionaries preached against the heinous trade. Both watches condemned it, and all the people of every description of belief, held up their hands in pious horror at the barter in flesh and blood. All, from the schoolboy just breeched, to the old man, whose tottering steps were leading him to the grave, were lovers of freedom, and the sworn enemies of slavery.

But, strange to say, when Jonathan attempted to put down slavery, the Buccaneer's sympathies were on the side of the slave-owner. Stranger still, though he was forever trying to put down slavery amongst other people, he allowed it to be practised to a very large extent amongst his own. Of course it was clothed in fine garments of rich words, so the sinfulness of the thing was hidden from his own eyes; but the whole of his society was little better than a huge market, where white slaves were bought and sold every day. Sold by heartless and mercenary mothers, to whom a rich equipage and a good social position was of far more consideration than any foolish and antiquated feelings of the heart, all of which are mere matters of sentiment, and weigh as light as air in comparison to the many advantages that gold can buy. It was no uncommon thing to see a fair, and perchance a blushing maiden, sold for a price to some withered piece of humanity. Their shameless mothers gave their daughters as they parted with them the kiss of Judas, and bedewed their fair young cheeks with the tears of hypocrisy, and then hastened to their churches to thank their God that they were not as others, doubters, perhaps, and unbelievers.

This inhuman traffic in human souls found its moral in one of the Buccaneer's law courts, the proceedings of which were emptied out amongst the people, and eagerly devoured by them. It must be owned that the victims of this trade bore their misfortunes with becoming fortitude. Having been well schooled by their mothers the degradation was not altogether clear to them, nor the narrow space that divided them from their less fortunate and despised sisters.

Like many other highly civilised communities the social atmosphere of the Buccaneer's island was largely impregnated with sham. Everything lay upon the surface, there was no depth. There was not only a greed for money, but there was a great greed for excitement, and a passionate desire on the part of the rich and vulgar nobodies to scramble up into a position higher than that to which they were either entitled, or fit for, and not unfrequently people who had the entry into what was called good society, let themselves out for a consideration to these upstarts, who would consider it a great condescension to be kicked down-stairs by one of noble birth. It was all this that perhaps gave a colouring to the sayings of those who declared that our bold Buccaneer was about the biggest humbug and hypocrite that ever walked upon the face of the earth.

Our two travellers occupied themselves with many pious speculations on their way to the land of the Pharaohs, for Dogvane for a sailor, was well up in the Scriptures, and his knowledge of the Old Testament was considerable. They compared the past with the present, and wandered through many flowery fields of thought, until the land they sought came up out of the sea before them.

CHAPTER XXVII.

As they approached the Buccaneer swept the shores with his glass, "She seems to be going in for repairs, Master Dogvane." Dogvane remained silent, as his eyes rested upon the land in front. He knew more about things than he wished to say. "I told you, sir," he said, "that we had knocked down a few forts."

As they approached nearer they saw the Egyptian Queen sitting upon a heap of ruins; her right elbow on her knee, her head resting upon her hand. Her flashing eyes showed there was anger in her heart; that something was wrong. Dogvane evidently did not like the look of things, for when his master landed he hung back; but the Buccaneer, not knowing the cause of Egypt's sorrow, went boldly forward. When he spoke Egypt turned so fiercely upon him, that he was taken completely aback. "Hence fiend!" she cried, as she pointed to the sea. The Buccaneer looked for his captain, but that worthy was keeping out of the way and was pretending to look for shell fish. His master hailed him and he arrived just in time to hear Egypt say, "The Ten Plagues with which God smote me in days of old were as blessings compared with thy accursed friendship."

"Dogvane!" exclaimed the Buccaneer, "how's this?"

"'Tis passing strange, sir! all official information is dumb upon the subject." Then turning aside he said: "How the hag raves."

Egypt rose up from her throne of crumbled stones and stood majestic. Extending her right arm towards her afflicted country and looking at the Buccaneer, with eyes filled with hatred, she exclaimed, "You have slain my children and their blood has flowed out like water upon the sands of the desert. Their bones lie bleaching in the sun; a witness to thy barbarity and cruelty

You have burnt my children's homes; driven off their flocks, laid waste their lands and destroyed their wells; but with parched throats and blistered tongues they curse you."

"Dear me!" was all the Buccaneer could say. Egypt continued: "You have set my children at each other's throats, and yet you dare stand before me." The Buccaneer turned to go away and Dogvane prepared to follow and showed considerable alacrity in getting to the boat. The parting words of Egypt fell upon the ears of the old Sea King and dwelt long in his memory; being very unwelcome guests there; making their voices heard when all else was wrapped in slumber. "Hence thou blighting plague!" she cried, or rather hissed. "Begone thou hypocrite! thou Christian masquerader! for in thy footsteps follow poverty, ruin, and misery. May the curses of the widow and the fatherless attend thee!"

"Tut, tut!" ejaculated Dogvane, "how the hussy raves!"

"God bless me!" exclaimed the Buccaneer, when they were well away. "What say you to that, Master Dogvane?"

"As a curse, sir, it is undoubtedly good, and as a specimen of female anger it is by no means bad. The baggage! Here is ingratitude for you. But I told you how it would be, sir. I had a kind of a presentiment that the other watch had been at their handiwork even here."

"If you, Master Dogvane, were as ready to keep out of difficulties as you are to saddle them upon other people's backs it would be the better for you."

"It is enough to make a saint swear," replied the captain. "I feel inclined to register a vow to heaven never again to do a good turn to a living soul. What language the vixen used!"

"She called me a hypocrite! a Christian masquerader! I, who pride myself upon my righteousness. I, who have held my head so high, to be called a Christian masquerader!"

"Sir," said Dogvane with extreme respect, "if one so humble, may dare offer an opinion, I should say that pride is not a Christian virtue, and sooner or later it must have its fall."

"Yes, fellow! but I do not want the fall to come from thy

hands. Is this what you call being respected abroad? Is th
your pinnacle of greatness?"

"I am not to blame, my master. It is the other watch. Wh
though the Egyptian gipsy raves; what though our cousin Ge
many and fickle France be cold, and Austria and Turkey aggrieve
by some idle words, say if you like, of mine, you have with yo
my master, the whole Calf of Man."

"Out upon thee for a blatant windbag!" cried the Buccanee
now out of all patience with Dogvane. "Out of my sight,"]
exclaimed, "keep clear of me, or, by Heaven, you will have wi
you the whole toe of my broad boot." They took to their boa
and the Buccaneer ordered his men to bend their backs to the
oars. Dogvane, who knew his master too well to trifle with hi
in his present mood, doubled himself up in the bows, and takii
out of his pocket his Bible, he was soon lost in the Mosa
Cosmogony.

CHAPTER XXVIII.

THE captain of the watch thought it would never do for his master to arrive home in his present frame of mind, for if he did, there would be, as sailors say, "The devil to pay, and no pitch hot." The other watch, too, would be sure to take advantage of the cloudy state of the weather to stir up strife and discord, and no stone ought to be left unturned to prevent this; so old Dogvane thought. He fully believed with that clever, funny little fellow, the cook, that the other watch were a greedy lot of office grabbers. Their hunger, perhaps, might be in a measure accounted for by the small amount of food they received of that particular kind.

The bold Buccaneer paced the deck in moody silence, and ever and anon turned a look back to the land of ruin he had left behind him. The words of the gipsy were still ringing in his ears. Old Dogvane was at the wheel, and he anxiously watched the old rover's face. The Buccaneer when in anger was not unlike a thunder storm. He made almost as much noise, he was quite as destructive, and nearly as uncontrollable; but if left alone he in time worked himself out, and after the storm, came the proverbial calm.

The canny old captain having waited a while, watched his opportunity, and he made bold to speak, couching his language in the most respectful terms; but first of all to attract attention he muttered something to himself.

"What is that thou sayest?" asked the Buccaneer, stopping short in his walk.

"Nothing sir, nothing," was Dogvane's reply; "I was merely thinking as it were, to myself, of the land we have just left behind us, and I was saying to myself, sir, only to myself, that needs must when the devil drives." It would be difficult to know to what the captain's words had reference. In all probability he did not know himself, but an old saying is generally a safe one, for it may mean much or little, or even nothing at all.

"In what way are you heading now, Master Dogvane?" asked the Buccaneer.

This gave the old captain the opportunity he had been looking for.

"You see, sir," he replied, "it is all very well for this Egyptian hag to curse; but I was driven by necessity to do what I did, and indirectly, if not directly, the other watch are responsible for the blood that has been shed."

"Still on the old tack, Master Dogvane; still on the old tack? Will you be for ever putting the saddle upon other backs but your own?"

"Heaven forbid that I should accuse any body of men wrongfully; but the other watch have, or seem to have an especial aptitude for getting into scrapes. They are a quarrelsome lot and their captain has a proud stomach. But look you, master, at this Egyptian baggage. See what a disorderly house she kept; I will not say disreputable, for God forbid that I should take away any woman's character. But her house was such a disgrace to all concerned, that we had to interfere. The Arab is a brave man; but he is a heathen, and full of atrocity; a follower of an impostor, what then if we slew a few of them; if by doing so we saved, as the saying is, our own bacon? For the same reason we, as I have already said, put your beloved son into a pit, and no doubt, he would have been saved even as Joseph was, only a little thing prevented it, he was slain in the meantime. Had it not been for this little accident, I have every reason to believe that he would have risen far higher than ever Joseph did in the Egyptian household." The Buccaneer was now sitting upon the after-skylight, and became an attentive listener to the captain, who continued:

"Even as Joshua discomfited Amalek and his people with the edge of the sword, so have we the black population of the

Soudan. The heathen furiously raged, and we smote them hip and thigh. The cross has again triumphed over the crescent."

This allusion to the Buccaneer's religion was a happy one, but who knew the master better than Dogvane? Was Dogvane then a humbug? Good people all, upon this subject there will be a diversity of opinion, for his enemies accused him of many worse things than being a humbug, while his friends and admirers were ready to canonize him as a saint. The true course, perhaps, lay in the middle of the stream. Dogvane continued, "Have you so little love for your religion, sir, that the slaughtering of a few thousands of infidels causes you remorse, and sorrow? Why in olden days you slew thousands of Christians without the smallest compunction; why then cry over the spilling of a little infidel blood? Time was, sir, when you would have regarded the affair otherwise. For every one of your sons killed, I dare swear a thousand Arabs have fallen, leaving the balance largely in favour of Christianity, and so clearing the ground ready for a purer faith. The weeds have been torn up by the roots, so that flowers may be sown. What though we did kill a few thousands of people, did not Pekah, king of Israel, slay in Judea, one hundred and twenty thousand persons in one day? Would any one say Pekah did wrong?" The Buccaneer was mollified. It no doubt flattered his vanity being compared to the ancient king of Israel.

"But she called me a hypocrite; a Christian masquerader, Dogvane," he said.

"Who, sir, would ever think of paying the slightest attention to what an angry woman says? Why ten to one if we were to return there now, you would find there had been a heavy fall of rain and all was sunshine again, and if you taxed her with her words, she would swear she had never used them."

"I would even now retrace my way to yonder land, that is just sinking below the horizon, if I thought it would be as you say."

"Counting upon the extreme uncertainty of a woman's mind, I have no doubt it would be so, and if my master wishes it, about we go. But stay, second thoughts they say are best. This Mediterranean is a treacherous sea. Storms often rising beneath the serenest sky. Besides, it would ill become one in my master's position of high respectability to dally away his time as Mark Antony did in this self-same land. A woman, sir, is far more dangerous in her softer moods than in her anger. It is under the mellowing influence of a smile that the hardest men fall. We had better keep our head pointed homewards. Then, sir, we can retrace our steps at our own convenience, and receive from the Egyptian gipsy's cooler mind the thanks we deserve. These Easterns are a prolific race, and multiply as fast as flies. To lop off the surplus population with the sword is a benefit. A tree is all the better for the occasional application of the knife."

Thus did Dogvane clear away the anger from his master's mind. He played upon all his weaknesses, and he approached him above all on the side of his religion, and, as will appear hereafter, on the side also of his trade which touched him more nearly even than his religion. Perhaps one side of religion is not, nor has it been in the past, fully appreciated. It has always proved an instrument to work off the surplus population. Even that gentlest and most peaceful of all, that religion which was breathed out over the world, near two thousand years ago, has often and often, been dragged in to sanction, and sanctify, the bloodiest and, at times, the most unholy of wars. As people will bring forth and multiply, in obedience to Divine command, it is fortunate that pestilence and famine have so able an ally to keep in check the flood of human nature.

Dogvane, finding he was master of the situation, said: "I had in Egypt, sir, as I told you, a deep and subtle game, but of that, no matter. If your old servant has displeased you, shift watches, say I, and joy to those who come after us."

Of course there was no better way to obtain a hearing than to excite the Buccaneer's curiosity and then stop short. The trick succeeded, for Dogvane was at first asked and then entreated, or rather commanded, to disclose his policy Having stowed away his quid in the lining of his hat, and expectorated freely over the ship's side, as every honest sailor should, before commencing a lengthy yarn, the captain thus began. It has been mentioned that at a yarn he could not be beaten.

"Day and night, sir," he said, "my thoughts dwell upon your affairs, and we often sit up late on board the old Ship of State discussing them. Often, and often has broad-faced day looked in upon our counsels."

"I am sorry to hear, Master Dogvane, that the Ojabberaways indulge at times in rebellion, and even indecent conduct on board the old ship. If they are not very careful I shall punish them. I shall stop their grog; but proceed."

"The Ojabberaways do at times, sir, make use of unseemly language; but it is their bringings up. I cannot deny between ourselves that our trade has been falling off. Our neighbours have learnt very much; they have in a measure overtaken us, and unless we are careful, sir, they will beat us on our own ground."

"But when the other watch said this, Master Dogvane, you stoutly denied it."

"That was done, sir, as a matter of principle. Of course we could not conscientiously admit anything to be right that the other watch said. But there are other grounds, sir, for silence; for to use a homely proverb, it is never wise to cry stinking fish. That holds good all the world over. In the management of one's private affairs silence is golden. Our trade is undoubtedly depressed. Boots, shoes and woollen stuffs may be up, as our doughty carpenter said, but other things are sadly down. It cannot be denied, for instance, that the demand for heathen gods has sadly fallen off in recent years."

"Have the labours then of my missionaries been crowned with such success? Are infidels turning from the errors of their ways, Master Dogvane?"

"Heaven only knows, sir! the fact remains the same; whether it is that the endeavours of your missionaries have been blessed; or whether it is that the gods made at your great idol manufactory of Brummagem are not up to the usual standard of perfection I know not; but there it is, heathen gods are a drug in the market."

"Dogvane, this is a most weighty matter, and it must be looked to. Idolatry is a dreadful thing; most degraded and very much to be condemned; but it is better than nothing, and until the heathen become converted it would not be well, nay it would be cruel to take from them whatever little comfort they may find in their brazen images. To counteract any evil influence that may arise from the worship of these things, Dogvane, order my State Church to purify the idols before they leave our shores. Give instructions, Dogvane, directly we arrive home, to our High Priest to this effect. Command him to have solemn prayers and fastings, so that they may, all of them, be the better able to wrestle with the devil. It would be as well also, Dogvane, to bid the rich amongst them to share what they have with their poorer brethren, who will be the better able to pray when their minds are not distracted by the emptiness of their stomachs, for we hear there are poor amongst them. Let all my divines of every denomination humble themselves before their God. Why that troubled look, Master Dogvane?"

"This is a delicate matter, sir. I have noticed the ecclesiastical temper does not brook much interference. It does not appear to me that they care very much about humbling themselves. Had that young rascal, Random Jack, belonged to our watch this would have been again a favourable opportunity for him to show his zeal and courage."

"Dogvane, I notice a disposition in you at times to shirk your duty," the Buccaneer said.

"Master, not another word. I will brave the displeasure of all your many religious denominations rather than you should harbour such a thought about old Bill Dogvane."

"Bid, then, my priest pray over these idols, sprinkling them well with holy water. Who knows, Dogvane, but that some good may thus be done? These brazen images being blessed by our pious divines may carry into the midst of the heathen some subtle influence, and by some mysterious agency they may be converted even at the very time they are praying to their false gods. Dogvane, it is worth the trial, and at any cost we must prevent the trade from falling into the hands of our unscrupulous and unconscientious neighbours." The Buccaneer was silent for a few moments, then he said : "Dogvane, I am fully convinced that even in this world sin brings its own punishment; and this falling off in our trade in idols may be due entirely to a falling off in the article. Have you received any information of a confidential nature that either France or Germany or our cousin Jonathan have gone in for this industry?"

"No, sir, I have no official communication on the subject; though Jonathan has that turn for business that he would manufacture anything from a tin pin to a brazen image; while, if it would only pay, he would turn out devils by the thousand."

"You may depend upon it, Dogvane, that this depression in our trade is owing either to the inferiority or costliness of the article. Here lies the keystone of our mercantile failures."

"Then, sir, there are other things. Our cotton stuffs hang heavy upon our hands. In fact, we want fresh fields for all our industries."

"Ah! say you so; where, Master Dogvane, is your remedy for this evil?"

"Sir, the eye of your faithful servant has rested upon the naked population of the Soudan. To clothe this people in our fabrics would take many millions of yards of your cotton stuffs."

"The idea, Dogvane, is certainly a good one, and it pleases me. Let us hasten to put it to the trial lest our neighbours be beforehand with us. Say not a word, Dogvane, of this when we get home, for if the idea gets wind some of our many cheap-Jacks will take possession of it and turn it to account; for, as you say, that fellow Jonathan has a keen eye for business, and if he could he would try to get to windward of his own father. The selfishness of our friends, Dogvane, is always to me a fruitful source of regret. But let us not forget that our primary object is not the selling of our goods at a remunerative price—no, Heaven forbid!— it is the converting of the heathen. The base motive of gain would not make me stir hand or foot in this matter; but to bring these poor benighted savages into our fold, Dogvane, is a worthy ambition. To make them Christians like ourselves, good Dogvane, would be a glorious thing. This, I say, must be our very first consideration. Into our cotton stuffs let there be worked some moral precept; or better still, some prayer. A waistcloth, Dogvane, if used fore and aft would be a suitable table for the Ten Commandments, which would thus be conveniently placed before the eyes of all. In time the seed thus sown on the outside of the black soil may take root inwardly and bring forth much good fruit. By degrees the whole population may become converted, and putting away the habit of barbarism may put on the garb of civilisation, thus opening out for us a wide field whereto to send our industries. Our ales will moisten their parched lips, increase their stamina, and strengthen their inward man. Our spirits, too, will supplant the vile concoctions they at present drink. Being thus strengthened in body and soul, their intellect likewise will become stronger. Their eyes will be opened, and a new and more beautiful world will dawn upon them. It is a grand idea, Dogvane, and well worthy of you. Commence at once. By converting this people we shall reap the reward of millions of fresh consumers. Stop slaughtering, Dogvane; stop at once. It is inhuman, it is cruel; besides they are only fighting for their hearth and home, and what people so base as not to shed their blood in so good a cause? Stay, then, our hand, for by cutting their throats, Master Dogvane, you are contracting the field for our home industries. There is undoubtedly a bright future in front of us, and you, Dogvane, have done much to re-establish yourself in my good opinion."

The Buccaneer was quite elated. His step became buoyant again. The dark cloud that had rested upon his brow passed away. "Soon," he said, "we shall again hear the merry rattle of our looms. Our stills will have fresh life thrown into them. The heavy scent of the hop shall weight our atmosphere; and rest like a grateful fragrance over our island home. Our friend and helpmate, old John Barleycorn, shall lift again his cheery head, and in his train will come, dancing merrily, his hand-maidens, Colombia root, camomile, quassia and cheretta."

The Buccaneer was in such excellent spirits that he began singing an old drinking song of his, to the merits of John Barleycorn, and he made Dogvane join in the chorus. Thus they merrily passed the time, until the look-out man aloft cried out: "Land ho!" and soon the bold coast of the Buccaneer's stronghold loomed out in the distance.

CHAPTER XXIX.

It is necessary now to shift our scene and to retrace our steps.

Opposite the old Ship of State there stood on the land, a little back from the river, an ancient and old-fashioned public-house. It had a picturesque appearance, with its quaint gable ends and mullioned windows. Its different styles of architecture and its patched walls led you step by step from the present to the remote past, for it was an antique hostelry. It was two storied and had two large chambers, and if the walls of these could speak, they could many a tale unfold. What scenes too they had seen and what noble personages. The old clock that stood sentinel there had ticked many a brave man to his grave. In that old public-house the greatness of the old Sea King had been built up, and the spirit of many a brave lad still haunted the place. A large sign-board swung heavily on a beam, projecting from the wall in front, just above the door. The name of the public-house was written in large letters. It was called the CONSTITUTION; under this there was a scroll, on which was written the Buccaneer's motto, "DIEU ET MON DROIT," and the whole was surmounted by a crown. This was the favourite resort of both watches, and, in fact, of the whole crew of the Ship of State, Upper Chamber and all. No more respectable, or better conducted house could be found the whole world over. Many thought the Beggar Woman ought to have been the landlady of this ancient establishment, but she was not.

Though well on in the night the Port Watch were still sitting in the snug parlour of the Constitution, sipping their grog, smoking their pipes and yarning over things in general; at the head of the table was the captain, Bob Mainstay, and by his side his first lieutenant, honest Ben Backstay. Many of the other officers were also there, and they were trying to keep their spirits up by pouring spirits down, but they could not do it. Things looked gloomy, and they seemed to see no break in the clouds ahead. But it is said that the longest lane has its turning, and to those that wait all things come. Of one thing they all felt assured, if Bill Dogvane was allowed to keep the helm of the Ship of State much longer the Buccaneer would find things at pretty sixes and sevens. But how was the helm to be taken out of his hands? That was the question.

Their meditations were interrupted by a gentle knock at the door, and on permission being given to come in, the door was gently opened, as if the intruder was not certain of the reception. It was the Beggar Woman. "Kind gentlemen," she said, "will you assist a poor woman? With weary steps I have begged from door to door, but no one will assist me or let me in. A crust of bread, good gentlemen, for the love you bear your country, for I am cold and starved with hunger."

"Come in," cried a dozen voices at once. "It is a shame," one added, "that you should be thus neglected; but what can we do, my lass? So long as the Starboard Watch is aboard the old ship there, things will be as they are."

"Let us have a shift of watches, and then you will see what you will see," said another.

"Cannot you help us, madam," asked the captain, "to oust old Dogvane and his lot? He made up to you, courted you, chucked you under the chin, and then the rascal jilted you. The Port Watch would not have served you so scurvily, you may swear."

"Good gentlemen," replied Patriotism, "the people on shore all turn a deaf ear to my entreaties, or say, anon, anon, good woman, and then hasten away about other business, or to pay their addresses to my rival, Party."

The Port Watch now took the Beggar Woman in tow, for they hoped that she would help them. They all set to discussing the state of affairs, and turned over in their minds different plans of action. What they wanted was a good watchword and a safe cry.

When they had been for some time talking over the matter without any satisfactory results; for they had passed in review all their old tactics without deriving very much satisfaction, because, as they all said, they had failed before to dish Dogvane with them, and in all probability they would fail again.

Just as things seemed to look at their worst, the door burst open, and in rushed Random Jack. He was breathless, dripping wet, and his teeth were chattering with cold.

"Hallo!" cried the captain. "What ducking pool have you fallen foul of, my little lad?"

"Mates!" cried Random Jack as he sank down on one of the seats, first of all having carefully removed the crimson cushion for fear of wetting it. "Give me a tot of grog, and make it hot and strong, for I am drenched to the skin, and the very marrow in my bones is frozen. Pretty things I have to tell."

The landlady of the old Constitution public-house was quite distressed to see the poor little middy in such a sorry plight. She was a buxom motherly woman, and nothing would do but she must get him a shift of things, or, as she said, the boy would catch his death of cold. Having brought him a suit of clothes which Billy Cheeks, the burly butcher, had left behind, Random Jack got into them, and though, as he said, they were miles too large, they were better than nothing. He tied the trousers round his neck, thrust his arms through the pockets, and thus saved the necessity of a waistcoat.

"Well, my little man," said the captain. "What is in the wind now?"

Random Jack took a deep draught, and then said: "That is good, and warms the cockles of my heart. Mother," he cried, turning to the landlady, "fill me another glass. Now, my mates, the likes of what I have to tell, you've never heard before. It will make your very hair stand on end, that is, of course, those who have any, and for those who haven't, no matter. Better to follow my example and fortify yourselves with good stiff glasses, three fingers deep, if you take my advice, and little water. No doubt, my mates, you have all read of mutinies, conspiracies, and such like; I have one to tell you about, that will surprise you."

"My goodness!" cried the landlady, as she busied about her orders. "Just hear how the little man talks!"

"Your news, my lad! your news!" came from many, as they one and all eagerly crowded round the little middy.

"Lend all of you, your ears, my mates. Knowing that the governor was from home and that the cunning old fox was with him, I thought I would just stow myself away on board the old ship there, just to see how they passed the watches of the night. Just to see, mates, if I could catch any of the weasels sleeping. Some of them are wide enough awake, I can tell you." Here he winked at the company.

"Throw it off, my lad!" cried the captain. "Don't go beating about the bush, but come to the point at once. So you were a stowaway." They contemplated the little middy with wonder, for most of them had never seen a stowaway before.

Random Jack, being thus exhorted and encouraged to make a clean breast of it, disclosed the whole of the diabolical conspiracy of the cook's caboose, and how it was that he had so frightened Billy Cheeks, the butcher. This part of the proceedings caused no little merriment. Bob Mainstay, having listened to the story from beginning to end, exclaimed, as he slapped his leg: "Mates, I see land ahead. It strikes me we have old Bill on the hip at last. Madam!" he said, turning to the Beggar Woman, who had remained a silent listener to the midshipman's story. "Madam, with your help I think we shall be able to dish old Dogvane. What with the Church Hulk in danger and old Squire Broadacre on the war path, and general discontent all round, the devil must be in it if we cannot clear the ship of its present vermin." The Beggar Woman promised to do her best, for her sympathies were for the most part with the Port Watch; perhaps, because on the whole, they treated her best. She was given an order to get a spic and span new outfit of silks and satins, and she received invitations to many feasts, but frequent adversity made her bear this turn of fortune with becoming modesty.

The Port Watch were now in high spirits and began talking of what they would do when they took charge of the ship. The little middy was highly complimented; and the captain promised to reward his courage and virtue with a good billet. He was pretty well sure now of promotion.

"Who laughs now?" cried Random Jack. "I owe one to Master Dogvane and to Billy Cheeks. The cook, he is a Jack-pudding, and I will baste him well with his own dripping." These were bold words; but the cook did not hear them.

"Now, my lads!" exclaimed the captain, "we must work with a will. Would that our master had returned; but we must make things ready for him when he does. Away some of you on board the old Church Hulk. Wake her crew up, and let your cry be Church in danger. Others of you hasten to the Squire and tell him there are robbers about."

"A toast before we part," cried Random Jack.

"Here is general damnation to old Bill Dogvane, and all his crew!" All laughed, and the toast was drunk with enthusiasm, and they were all just about to separate when some one fired a shell amidst them by saying, "How about the Ojabberaways?"

"To make any compact with them," said the captain, "would be an unholy thing."

"Any port in a storm," cried Random Jack, who was now, what with the grog and the flattery he had received, in high feather. "They have their price; are they worth it? If we don't buy them old Dogvane will. There's the rub."

Here the noise outside of two women wrangling claimed their attention, and one and all ran out to see what was the matter. They found Liberty and the Beggar Woman in angry altercation about a lout of a boy. Indeed, boy he could scarcely be called, for he was approaching nearer to manhood. It was Demos. "Indeed, madam!" cried Liberty with a sneer, "it does not appear from your dress that you are held in very great estimation amongst my master's people." Patriotism had not yet received her new clothing. Then Liberty continued in the same tone: "You are somewhat old-fashioned methinks! What would you have me do with my boy? Would you have me clap a gag in his mouth, or muzzle him as if he were a dog in the dog-days?"

"You need not pamper and pet him," exclaimed the Beggar Woman, "until he becomes a perfect nuisance to every one. Why don't you teach him to work for an honest living?"

"Because the boy is not strong; besides, he does not like work, do you, dear?"

"Why should I work," cried Demos, "when others play? Others live and fatten in idleness, why not I?"

"Bread that is buttered too thickly is not wholesome food," was the Beggar Woman's reply.

"The boy is a clever boy," exclaimed Madam Liberty. "He is wonderfully good at speaking; and he is good at figures; and he shall not be kept back; shall you, dear?"

"Mind he does not turn and bite the hand that has fed and petted him," replied the Beggar Woman, and the two parted.

The old coxswain, as he watched the retreating steps of Liberty and her boy, said: "There you go with that spoilt brat of yours. A wilful woman never yet wanted for woe, and to spoil a child is to put a rod in pickle for your own back."

A quaint sound was now heard, like the wailing of a pig in pain. Some thought it must be the cook playing a tune in the early morning upon his barrel organ; but the sound did not come from the direction of the old ship. It turned out to be the national music of the Ojabberaways, and presently a voice by no means untuneful, sang, "Come back to Erin, Mavourneen, Mavourneen."

The Ojabberaways were serenading both Liberty and Patriotism, while in the back ground was the cheap-Jack Jonathan, who provided the dollars for the serenade, also for other entertainments which the Ojabberaways got up to please themselves and annoy the old Buccaneer.

Opinions varied very much as to whether the Port Watch did, or did not, make a treaty with these people. Such a thing could scarcely be conceivable; but for party purposes either watch, it was said, would sell themselves to the devil. Some went so far as to say that Random Jack had had something to do with it; but then, when anyone comes out of obscurity, there is scarcely a thing that he is not supposed to be capable of doing; and a place is found for his finger in every pie. Happy is the man who never leaves the smooth, broad, and well-beaten path of mediocrity! He will escape many evils, and even slander will pass him by for the most part with contempt; for her sport is with bigger game. "This only grant me, that my means may lie too low for envy, for contempt too high." So sang a poet long years ago.

It was generally believed that old Bill Dogvane had a secret understanding with these Ojabberaways. There can be no doubt that he smiled upon the boy Demos, who was showing signs of giving trouble. He was becoming intoxicated with the very worst of all things, namely, his own self-conceit, and the old hands shook their wise heads, and said that if the Buccaneer was not very careful this boy would break out and disturb the peace. This child of Madam Liberty was a difficulty; and how to treat him became a matter of the gravest consideration. Be kind to him and he would mistake it for weakness, and take advantage of it at once. Kick him, beat him, or try to drive him, and he became as stubborn as an ass. All agreed that he required a very strong hand, and yet not too rough a one. The conspirators of the cook's caboose were one and all on the boy's side; and the cook himself acted the part of an indulgent foster father to him. Buttering the boy's bread as thick as he possibly could, and giving him constantly cakes and other sweetmeats; some said this was done out of pure contrariness, because Pepper could not be happy if he were as others; but while the cook told the boy that he was being kept out of his just dues by an idle lot of rich drones, and hinting to him that it would be no great crime to put his hand into the pockets of these people, he said not a word about sharing his own worldly goods with the boy; and the cook had laid up for himself riches upon earth, but he was a wise man, and took good care that no thief should break into his house and steal.

CHAPTER XXX.

THE Port Watch mingled about amongst the people and told them of all the wonderful things that had happened, and of the many more wonderful things that would be sure to happen if they did not at once combine together and get their master, the old Sea King, to change the watches. Of course the doings of the Port Watch could not be concealed from the Starboard Watch, who went about contradicting, and swearing there was not a word of truth in the whole thing.

The cook took under his especial care the Buccaneer's Upper Chamber, and it is tolerably certain that happiness would not come to Pepper on his death-bed, unless that lumber room with all its antiquated furniture was cleared out of the old ship, and replaced by some assemblage of men as clever as what the cook was himself; but to get the modest number of only twelve such men, in a whole kingdom, would be almost impossible, and this is providential.

The butcher was not idle. He did not speak much; but when he did, it was to the purpose, and no one could say more cutting things than could Billy Cheeks. He also thought a good deal; he was driven to this extremity because most people, and most things, were beneath his notice. The carpenter took under his care the family of Hodge; the members of which were generally accredited with a full share of stupidity and ignorance; but it is wonderful how the aspect of things changes when you want to get anything out of people. Then we find virtues that were never seen before, and that the individuals themselves never even dreamt of. Then in the distance was the large family of Sikes. No one as yet had found much virtue in them; but they were ready for anything that might turn up, outside of it.

"Honest Hodge," cried the carpenter from the top of a barrel, "for generations you have been oppressed."

"'Ave I now?" exclaimed Hodge, scratching his honest head. "I thought summut was wrong."

The boy Demos who had been playing pitch and toss with the cook, left the game to attend to what looked to him more like business.

"For generations," cried the carpenter, "you have been ignored and defrauded by one whose rights are arbitrary, and almost absolute, for they extend from the heavens above, to the earth beneath, and to the waters under the earth." Demos became a most attentive listener and he liked the tack the carpenter was on.

Chips continued, "The minerals are his. The timber is his, and so are the birds of the air, and the fish that swim in the streams, and I suppose that the greater part of all that the industry and toil of man has added to the original value of that property, is now practically subject to the land owner's sole consideration and good. Now I want to see you, honest Hodge, replaced upon the old squire's land, at a fair compensaticn, of course."

Upon hearing this Demos winked at Hodge, but the latter being very slow of intellect, and moreover honest, did not take the wink in.

"But," said Hodge, "if the squire won't part, maister; what be we to do then?"

"If the squire will not do his duty," replied the carpenter, "he must be made to."

"And what be we to get out of it?" Hodge asked.

"The least you can expect, will be three acres and a cow," was the carpenter's reply; or the reply of a friend of his.

Here one of the Sike's family pushed his way to the front, and addressing himself to the carpenter, said, "Master, what are we to get out of this crib you're agoing to crack?"

The question being an extremely awkward one to answer, the carpenter pretended not to hear it. This is always a safe way out of such a difficulty if the questioner be not persevering.

The Port Watch struck a more popular, and at the same time, a more honest chord. "Look!" they cried, "at our market places! They are full of the cheap produce of our neighbours, who do a thriving business while our own people are starving. They bring their goods here without let or hindrance; but they shut their own doors against us, or make us pay toll. Look at the river there! that used to be crowded with our own craft. Now you see the flag of every nation floating upon its bosom, while our own ships are rotting for the want of something to do. Foreign competition is ousting you from your markets as the marten ousts the squirrel from her nest. If you want a coat, or a pair of trousers made, in comes your foreign tailor who will sew and stitch for sixteen hours a day for what is barely sufficient to keep body and soul together. If you, my lads, come down, he will come down lower."

At this speech loud cries of indignation rose up from a multitude of listeners, and the spokesman of a crowd of sailors, jumping up on a tar barrel, exclaimed, "Damme, my mates! (It is a bad habit, but sailors will swear.) The gentlemen of the Port Watch says true. We are being weathered by these lubberly furriners, who visit our shores in shoals like mackerel; and thus take all the wind out of our sails. Damme, mates! they are that mean that a well worn quid won't escape them, can we work against such varmint as these?"

"No!" came from a thousand hoarse throats.

"Is it right, my hearties," continued the speaker, "that the old man should treat us like this?"

"It ain't right," came from all sides.

"Where would our master be now without us?" cried the sailor, "where will he be if he allows these furrin chaps to put us down below hatches? Who then will he have to trim and shorten his sails when the stormy winds do blow? Will these fellows club-haul him off a lee-shore in the teeth of a gale of difficulties; or fight for him his battles? Not they, I'll swear."

The old sailor's yarn met with very great approval, and as is the custom with all sailors they freely damned their own eyes, and hitched up their trousers and swore that things were not as they ought to be; but the cheap-Jacks still went about amongst them and sold their goods, and people bought. Up too spoke many others, and there was scarcely a man to be found, or woman either, that was contented.

There was a movement amongst the crowd and the old cox'sn came forward, and getting up on the place vacated by the sailor, cried out: "Heave to, my hearties, whilst you hear to a brother sailor spin you a yarn." There was a feeling now pretty prevalent that they were in for a good thing. "No doubt," he said, "many of you here know me by name."

"Aye, aye, Jack, we know you," came from many; "you are as long-winded as a sky pilot, or as old Bill Dogvane, and any one knows he has wind enough to fill the sails of a line o' battle-ship."

The old cox'sn, nothing daunted, continued: "Belay talking, my lads. No doubt many of you know me by name, but many of you have no other acquaintance with me, more is the pity say I. Long-winded I may be; but I don't go about emptying myself like a wind-bag; but let that fly stick to the wall. Many a voyage I have taken with my old master, and when on the Spanish main together, looking out for the Don, we learnt a thing or two. The Spaniards say, my lads, that it is always a good, and safe thing, to search well yourself when anything goes wrong with you, and that is what old Jack Commonsense tells you now. You want our master to do this, and to do that, to protect this trade and that; but damme, shipmates, legislation never yet stopped a leak in a cask, nor made a stale egg into a fresh one. My mates! you are all of you heading in the wrong direction. There are breakers ahead, so put your helm down and go about as soon as you can. Don't you listen to those wiseacres who are going to put everybody and everything right. The cook, he is a clever lad, and can spin a cheerful yarn, but let him stick to his trade, and the same I say to the carpenter and the butcher. You can never put an injury right by committing a wrong, and if the carpenter or anyone else wants to put his hand into the squire's pocket, he is only inviting a thief into his own house. Let the cook then keep to his galley and cater for the general public. His dishes are spicy, and then when he treats us to a tune in his leisure hours upon his barrel organ, well, so much the better, for there is no harm done."

The crowd began to show signs of impatience, and old Jack was made painfully aware that he was not a popular orator, for the lovers of freedom hooted him; but he was not easily put down. "Here, lads!" he cried, "is where my Spanish proverb comes in. Search well yourselves, and see if any fault lies at home. It is no use anchoring yourselves by your starns, and crying out that trade is going, and that the cheap-Jacks are taking the wind out of your sails. You ain't obliged to buy from them, and who brought them over, pray? If trade is gone from amongst you; it is yourselves that you have to blame. In years gone by you combined against your employers; I don't say you were at all times wrong, but evil counsel sat at your boards, and with your bushel of good came a sackful of bad, you drove your trade out of doors and now you cry out: 'Help us or we starve!' If your platter and your pewter pot be empty, you have yourselves to thank. No song, no supper, is a good old saying. If you, my hearties, won't work your fair time for your fair wage, there are others who will. When you combined against capital, messmates, you frightened, if you did not kill, the goose that was laying your golden eggs. She is a timid bird and will only lay where she gets peace and quiet. Having done all this, you are now crying out to be protected, and think that all will be well again if this thing and that thing are only legislated for; but legislation, my lads, as I've said before, never yet bolstered up either a rotten state or a decaying trade. You may stop for a time the footstep of the one or the other, but the fall will surely come again unless you tap the part affected and stop the hole with good, sound, solid material. Look at you servants! Why, you are always on the move; some of you even are idle and insolent. Do you not see the gaunt form of Poverty in front of you? Away then will go your airs and graces, your flaunting ribbons and your finery

Beware how you listen to the teaching of Demos. He is a dangerous companion and generally turns and rends those who have housed and fed him. A bridle for the mouth of an ass, and a rod for the back of a spoilt child."

There was here some good-natured bandying of words, and old Jack was recommended to try the bridle himself, just to see, as they said, how it felt and how it fitted. Jack being a good-tempered fellow, continued his harangue: "My advice, my hearties, to you is this. Turn to and live thrifty lives. Take your hands out of your pockets. Do away with the quart pot and you will increase the amount of stuff upon your platter. If you cannot do away with the pewter altogether—and I am no teetotaller myself—then reduce its size to at least a half. By a strict regard to economy, and by practising self-denial and by cultivating your understanding in a proper direction, try to turn out a better and a cheaper article than your neighbours and so beat them on their own ground. Do this, my hearties, and you will win back trade and regain your place in the markets of the world."

The old coxswain had been listened to for some time with a respectful attention; but the doctrine he preached was not at all in keeping with the general sentiments of the disaffected, who were stirred up and incited to violence by Demos and his disciples, and very shortly there was a disturbance of a serious nature. It was commenced by Demos, who having gathered a crowd of followers round him, began to speak to them in language peculiarly his own. The consequence of this was that some one from amongst the crowd, aimed a brickbat, with too true an aim, at the Buccaneer's old coxswain, who amidst the delighted yells of the mob was knocked over. The excitement now was intense, for though old Jack was not killed, he was severely bruised, and shaken, and taken very much by surprise. Those who have never heard the angry howl of an infuriated mob of Buccaneers can have no conception of the savageness of its sound. The war whoop of the wildest Indians is soft compared to it, and the roar of hungry wild beasts is less terrifying. Demos with what he called "the people" now rushed to an open space, beautifully situated, but called the Place of Discord, where four grim lions watch night and day, but they never interfere, and nobody minds them. Here Demos harangued the multitude; told them they were being starved and trodden under foot, by the drones of the island. His language was violent in the extreme. He called upon them to break their chain of slavery and to elect as their ruler King Mob. This was but natural, so up on their shoulders they hoisted the bloody tyrant and cried out: " Havoc and robbery; now shall the gilded thieves disgorge their ill-gotten wealth." Away they made for the rich quarters of the Buccaneer's fair city, intent upon plunder if not murder; but they were met by the guardians of the peace, behind whom came the old coxswain with a chosen band, cutlass in hand. He called upon his men to rally round him. Now commenced a battle between the two factions. The partisans of King Mob nerved on and excited by the hope of plunder fell upon the champions of law and order. Heads were broken and the combatants fell struggling to the ground, and the crowd swayed backwards and forwards in fierce strife. At first the old coxswain and his side seemed to be getting the worst of it, but he fought like a veritable demon, laying about him in a fashion well worthy of the Buccaneer's best fighting days.

What seemed most strange was, that the watchword was the same on both sides, namely Liberty. Step by step, the old Coxswain was beaten back through a narrow gorge which opened on to a small square in the centre of which was a statue representing Victory in her idle hours, playing at quoits. This open space was flanked on one side by a museum of Naval and Military antiquities, glorious relics of a glorious past. On the other side of the square and away from the narrow gorge was another museum, which was filled with a most valuable collection of ancient fossils, and other scientific remains. Back into this open space the old coxswain and his men were forced. Inch by inch they disputed the narrow way. Old Jack every now and again let fly a quaint oath or two; but as he afterwards said, the occasion justified the deed. In a voice of thunder he kept cheering his men on, crying out, "Rally, men! Rally!" Just as King Mob was pushing old Jack extremely hard, assistance came from an unexpected quarter.

The uncrowned queen had shut herself up indoors; but Madam Liberty upon whom both sides had called, came now to the front and allied herself with the coxswain. Knowing full well that if she allowed the ugly faced monarch to gain the day, she herself would, in all probability, be bound hand and foot, and cast into prison, with a gag in her mouth, she threw all her weight on the side of the coxswain, and brought up just in time her numerous followers to the rescue. Demos when he saw his mother against him, made use of most disrespectful language, calling her all kinds of bad names, which will not bear repeating. Just as Liberty reinforced the coxswain in front, the Beggar Woman who was now mounted on horseback, attacked King Mob with a strong force on his flank. Thus assailed, and without either drill or discipline the would-be monarch wavered, then turned and fled through the Place of Discord. The retreat was disastrous, and his followers were driven back well within their own quarters. As they went they did what damage they could; smashed windows and laid their hands upon everything of value that came in their way.

Thus was Demos and his father for the time at least defeated, and the old coxswain and his allies were hailed as the saviours of the people. In olden days, no doubt, he would have been accorded by universal acclamation a triumph, when he would have made a public entry into the Buccaneer's great city, mounted on a magnificent horse richly caparisoned; with his two lieutenants, Liberty and Patriotism, riding one on either side of him. Such things, however, have long ceased to be, and now we can only read of them in the pages of history.

The Buccaneer's people celebrated the victory in a manner more in keeping with their character and disposition. When the noise and turmoil of the battle were over and the fighting men had left off swearing; when their passions had cooled down a little, the bells upon the old Church Hulk rang out a summons to prayers. The joyful sound was taken up by every belfry on shore, and soon the clang of the iron tongues vibrated all over the island. The many idlers took their last sip at the cup of pleasure. The churches filled; the people prayed, the priests all preached and the great Hat was sent round. That was never forgotten, no matter what was going on. Many consciences were eased and all were strengthened and made more ready for the wear and tear of everyday life; while the cheap-Jacks took advantage of the pious moments of the Buccaneer's people to push their trade.

It is not to be supposed that the Buccaneer's Press gang were idle on such an occasion. But to their credit it must be said that they all, with about one exception, forgot their little differences and took the side of law and order against the followers of King Mob.

But now the big mouthed cannon belched forth the joyful tidings of the Buccaneer's return. Loud cries of welcome greeted his ears as he stepped ashore. " Hail! all hail! to the old sea king; to the mighty trader! Hail to the Defender of the Faith, the ruler of the sea; to him on whose vast dominions the sun never sets! Hail! all hail," so cried the people.

CHAPTER XXXI.

THE first thing that saluted the Buccaneer's ears after all the rejoicings at his safe return were over, was a low, dull, rumbling sound as if distant thunder.

"What is that?" he asked of Dogvane.

"I know not, sir; but the atmosphere is heavy, and there may be a storm abrewing; but I hear nothing." This was an official statement on the part of Dogvane that was wide of the truth.

The art of lying has already been touched upon; but there are many kinds of lies which have not been enumerated. There is the oblique lie, the lie direct. The lie by implication and insinuation; and passing by the various kinds of social lie there is the official and the diplomatic lie. The latter is very much superior to the "lie vulgaris" or common lie, and it moves in the very best society. It is a most polished courtier. The official and diplomatic lie require very great skill and study so as not to betray their owner. They require also a natural aptitude, a schooled countenance, so that neither the eye, the voice, nor the mouth discloses their secret. Your diplomatist especially, to be successful, should be indeed a most refined and accomplished liar.

Dogvane knew very well what the rumbling sound was. It was the Drum Ecclesiastic. He thought for a moment and then muttered to himself, "Who the devil has set that old instrument going?" Then after a pause he said: "The handiwork, I'll be bound, of that young rascal Random Jack. Drat his little skin! He's always in mischief."

But louder and louder grew the sound, and in a short time there could be no disguising the fact that the Church was sounding the alarm. Dogvane thought it best to take at once the bull by the horns. "It's a bold party stroke, sir," he said, "a very bold party stroke and well worthy of the other watch. Knowing your love for the old craft, God bless her ! they have tried to frighten you. Their goings on are really shameful." But now a most imposing procession formed up on board the Church Hulk, and headed by the High Priest, proceeded on board the Ship of State and discovered to the Buccaneer and his trusty captain the vile and sinful plot of the cook's caboose.

No doubt in olden times the cook, the butcher and the carpenter, with his mate, would have been cursed with bell and book, when the devil would have put in an appearance and have carried the conspirators away with him bodily to his infernal regions ; but cursings have gone out of fashion. In fact they seem to have lost their power, like drugs that have been too long kept. The High Priest told the Buccaneer that his cherished Church was in danger. That in fact there was a conspiracy afloat, to board and rob her, and then to cast her adrift, when Heaven alone knew what would become of her. Of one thing he felt certain ; the many flocks would wander about without shepherds, or would be tended by those of inferior learning and understanding. The High Priest then began to lecture the Buccaneer, thinking no doubt that he was the same pliant and penitent gentleman as of old, when he was ever ready to fall upon his knees and cry, " I have sinned." But now when the High Priest told him that the danger to his Church was brought about by his selfishness, worldliness, and general religious indifference, and that to counteract all this accumulation of evil he ought to humble himself and scourge himself inwardly by prayers and fastings, the bold Buccaneer opened out in an altogether unexpected manner, and said : " Should not all this be done by my State Church ? At least," he added, " set me the example, and where you lead there will I follow; but it is no use your pointing up the steep hill which leads to heaven and bidding me walk, while you and all your followers drive there in a well cushioned carriage and pair. If my Church is in danger, the danger comes from within, and you have no one to blame but yourselves. Let the crew of your ship, my lord, cease squabbling amongst themselves about trifles. Let them set their face against the pomps and vanities of the world, and let them look well within to see if by chance any worldliness has got possession of their own hearts."

This cruel language shocked the Buccaneer's High Priest, and he was about to reply; but the Buccaneer stopped him, saying; "Stay, stay a minute, in the past you have lectured me a good deal and told me, no doubt, many a home truth, and I thank you. I now return you the compliment, for it may be of service to you, as you say your Church is in danger. All things on board that old Hulk there are not as they should be; for while some of her crew lead the life of Dives, too many have to walk in the footsteps of Lazarus. The labour and the hire are not equally divided. I am going now to look a little more into my affairs, and I shall soon call upon you to render a just account of your stewardship. Many of you do not act as if you believed in what you preach: the salt having lost in many cases its flavour.

"How have the mighty fallen?" exclaimed the High Priest. The Buccaneer, misunderstanding the words of the head of his Church, replied, "And pray, whose fault is that? Perhaps there are hypocrites and even Pharisees amongst you; those who seek the highest places in the synagogues and at the social table, and who are worshippers of forms and ceremonies." What wickedness was here! But this bold, bad man continued in the same strain, or stay, it may have been the wicked devil who was making this eminently respectable and pious old Buccaneer, his mouthpiece. "Has pride, arrogance, and self-sufficiency any place in your hearts?" he asked. "Has my priesthood fallen and been led captive by mammon and selfishness, and while they fix one eye constantly upon heaven, do they not with the other look too lovingly upon the earth? Fast then and pray yourselves, for thy faith may be weak, and as the Israelites of old fell away and worshipped more gods than one, so too may my priests have set up some graven image or images, and here may lie the danger. Search well yourselves and put your ship in order. It is no use preaching to the world abstinence if you do not practise it yourselves. Our religion was placed in poor soil, tended and cared for by mendicant labourers, and it flourished. The workers now are of a different caste, the spirit of the first teachers has passed away, and the flower fades."

This was not a bad specimen of pulpit oratory, coming as it did from an old gentleman who had commenced life as a pirate; but it is well known that the greater the sinner the greater the saint. The language of the bold Buccaneer was fully discussed and fully condemned, and the great Church drum still kept beating. The sound went out all over the land; was heard upon many a hearth, and put fear into many a breast, for the old Church Hulk was dearly loved, with all her faults, more especially by the Buccaneer's women, in whose eyes a priest was little less than a god clothed in a decent suit of black.

But what was going on on board the Church Hulk all this time? The burning question of Church in danger was pushed aside, and high above everything else the voice of controversy could be heard arguing upon a matter of the deepest import to all the world. It was the question of eternal punishment, which, alas! can never be satisfactorily settled; as to whether the soul that dies in sin is surely for ever damned. The adventurous spirits who had started this rank and soul-destroying heresy of hope even beyond the grave were few in number. These seemed to have a beautiful faith, if an erroneous one, in God's unbounded mercy, which, overtaking the poor lost soul before it entered the gates of hell, might in some cases bring it back to the bright realms of eternal bliss. For so rank a heresy there was perhaps neither authority nor justification, and it did more honour to the hearts of the schismatics than it did credit to their understanding or learning; so it was thought. The majority of the disputants stuck, however, to the penal clause, which says that the soul that dies in sin shall surely perish. These fortified themselves behind ramparts built up of dogma and bound together with the strong and lasting cement of human passions. Over the battlements they hung out their banner, on which was emblazoned the words, " No Surrender." The little band were driven back and had to seek consolation in the thought that no matter what is said and done, God is the God of Mercy.

Poor, poor soul, how heavily you are weighted. Given passions, and desires, and all kinds of forbidden fruit placed well within your reach, with a longing to taste. Pluck, and you are straightway handed over to the devil, to be flagellated, tortured, and burned everlastingly. So it is said. Ye priests, in the past, what a heaven and what a hell have ye made for human beings! See the father torn away from his fair-haired child and hurled headlong to the bottomless pit, where there is nothing but weeping and gnashing of teeth, and a fire that is never quenched. See the mother taken away from her erring son, and winged up to heaven with a bleeding, broken heart. See the sister with her loving arms twined round some lost brother's neck, and crying out in her anguish, "Lord! Lord! let me share his lot; let his misery be mine. Let me moisten his parched lips with my tears. Where he lies let me lie also." But the bitter parting has to come, and while one sobbing is taken to Heaven, the other is sent to Hell. In the dark clouds that superstition has hung over trembling humanity we see a little rift, as vivid in brightness as when the Heavens are cleft with lightning, and through the rent we see pale-faced Pity weeping for the loss of her children.

CHAPTER XXXII.

A DAY having been set apart by the Buccaneer's High Priest for solemn fasts, prayers, and humiliations, to counteract as far as possible the evil effects which might be expected to arise from the impious conduct of the Buccaneer, and devilish machinations of the conspirators of the cook's caboose; and all the wise men in the island having been set to work to find out the exact pressure that the ecclesiastical wrath had upon the square inch of the social atmosphere, things sank down again to their usual level; for no storm lasts forever.

The captain of the watch, old Bill Dogvane, now summoned all the conspirators before him, and rated them well for their folly and want of forethought in setting the big drum of the church going. "Don't you see, my lads," he said, "that things aren't ripe yet for such a sweeping measure? All in good time; all in good time. But first and foremost see which way the wind is blowing, and which way the current sets, and then, my hearties, steer your course accordingly."

The conspirators affected very great surprise; said that the whole thing was a gross misrepresentation; a mere game got up entirely by Random Jack, who, having stowed himself away, had listened to a private conversation they had had in the cook's caboose.

"Well, my lads, I think the storm is over, and the dust this time is laid; but Chips, my man, where is your mate?" It now came out that Chisel was ashore in tow of a lass, and when a sailor is so situated he is never fit for duty.

Just as old Dogvane was congratulating himself upon having got, as he thought, into smooth water again, there come a hail from the shore of "Ship of State, ahoy!"

"What the devil is in the wind now?" cried Dogvane, as he took a look over the ship's side. At the same time the Buccaneer, who was below, called up to know who it was that was calling. "Ah!" said Dogvane to himself, "I ought to have known that that old coach was a slow one to travel."

"Ship ahoy!" came again. "Who is that?" demanded the Buccaneer.

"It looks uncommonly like old Squire Broadacre, sir," was Dogvane's reply. Now this old gentleman had at one time been extremely well off, and had kept up great state and open house; keeping many retainers, feeding many mouths, but hard times had overtaken him, and he was now sorely pinched, and even poverty was seen on the outskirts of his property, and was drawing nearer to his door every day. The Buccaneer ordered a boat to be sent ashore.

"Send a boat ashore!" muttered Dogvane. "Why, a line of battle ships would not hold him and his cargo of grievances, I know." However, a boat was sent, and the old gentleman was ferried on board. The captain of the Starboard Watch seeing the conspirators together abreast of the cook's galley went up to them, saying, "A pretty kettle of fish you fellows have put upon the fire. Here is some more of your handiwork."

The butcher chuckled to himself, and said, "If you fellows had nipped round and caught Random Jack, all this bother would have been saved." The butcher was always criticising.

"Ah! Billy," replied the carpenter, "like many another clever fellow, you are extremely wise after the event; you see, it is not for you to talk; if you hadn't had a nervous attack you might have caught him yourself."

All further discussion was put a stop to by the appearance on board of the old squire, who seemed to be completely overcome with excitement. He told the Buccaneer that he had it on the very best authority that he was to be attacked and robbed, and he came to demand protection. Of course in the abstract being a member of the Buccaneer's family he had a right to protection. Things, he said, had come to a pretty pass if honest folk were to be deprived of their property without people saying with your leave or by your leave.

The squire, following so closely upon the heels of the church, aroused the anger of the old Sea King, who always on such occasions, made a scapegoat of some one, and he now tried to make Dogvane perform that most necessary but disagreeable office, but the captain was much too old a bird to be caught either by chaff, or to have salt put upon his tail.

Then no sooner had the fears of the old squire been somewhat allayed by Dogvane declaring that it was all a party trick, than fresh trouble arose; for the Ojabberaways taking advantage of the state of affairs, so acted as to stop all business, and played on board the ship their old game of "Mag's diversions," or the "devil's delight." But amidst all this confusion there was one bright spot, and that was the noble way in which the old coxswain had acted. When the Buccaneer heard of it he was delighted and determined to reward him by elevating him to some high position on board the Ship of State. Indeed, so impressed was he with old Jack's abilities, that he was for sending him at once to the Upper Chamber; but Jack said he would rather decline the honour, for the members were proud, standing very much upon their dignity, and he feared they might give him the cold shoulder. Besides which, he feared that as the cook had taken a dislike to that establishment it could not last long. Then the Buccaneer called to him Dogvane, and ordered him to find honest Jack some post of distinction in the after part of the ship.

The captain of the watch demurred to this, saying it would be a most unconstitutional thing, and he contended that to raise so ordinary a personage as Jack Commonsense from a position that was humble to one that was exalted, and make all at once an officer of State of him, would be fraught with extreme danger. In all probability everybody would resign, for such an honest, straightforward fellow as the cox'sn was, would be sure to rub the whole crew up the wrong way, which everyone knew was a most dangerous thing to do; putting the fat in every way upon the fire. He plainly intimated that to promote Jack Commonsense would probably bring about discord, which might end even in revolution. "Heaven only knows, sir!" he exclaimed, "we have wrangling enough as it is on board the old ship."

The Buccaneer thought the matter over, and said that he was considerably disappointed, as he felt sure that Jack would not disgrace himself at the council board. A thought seemed suddenly to strike him. "As you will not have him here, Master Dogvane, I will make a bishop of him. His presence on board the old Church Hulk will be an advantage to every one, more especially in these critical times." He at once hailed the old ship alongside, and expressed his wishes. There was a solemn conclave at once held, and all the divines who were conspicuous for their learning and piety were called together to consider so grave a matter, and after a careful discussion, which lasted many hours, they arrived at the conclusion that the old cox'sn could not on any account be made a bishop or given even a place of any importance on board the Church Hulk. They intimated that it would be more in keeping with a modest demeanour if he contented himself with his present lot in life, and they pointed out that pride which had turned satan himself out of Heaven was altogether to be condemned. Besides, they said, they feared that if they gave the old cox'sn a permanent place on board their ship he would in time undermine the whole of their authority, and bring down the sacred edifice about their ears, and that the High Priest and other ecclesiastical dignitaries would be buried in the ruins, and forever lost to the cause of religion. The members of the Solemn Conclave admitted that Jack Commonsense was an inestimable and even religious fellow, and that in the Buccaneer's realms he had nobly done his duty; but as virtue was at all times its own reward, the old cox'sn could not want any further recompense. Besides, they added, he had received no ecclesiastical education; knew little or nothing of the Levitical Law, or of the Fathers of Theology, and could not therefore be expected to wrestle against the Devil's first lieutenant, Heresy.

Thus poor old Jack's doom was sealed; but when he heard that neither ship would have him at any price he was not downhearted, but went on his quiet way as before; giving himself neither airs nor graces like so many people do. Old Jack was not one of those ambitious, self-confident, self-seeking fellows whose only virtue is unbounded impudence, and who are forever thrusting themselves forward, not caring two straws who falls, or who is thrust to the wall, so long as they can struggle and keep to the front; holding up before the eyes of the people their farthing dip, and swearing its light is equal to ever so many candles, or even oil lamps.

"Well," said old Jack, as he trudged away, "if I do not rise, neither shall I fall. Let those who like soar up on the butterfly wings of ambition, I'll have none of it myself. Sooner or later old Dame Fortune turns round her wheel and up comes her eldest daughter and pins your butterfly to the earth with the sharp-pointed pin of adversity. Then where are you?"

CHAPTER XXXIII.

So far so well. The storm had been avoided. The cook and burly butcher bowed their heads humbly before their captain; for no matter where he led they were prepared to follow. Some said that the cook could only expect promotion by sticking through thick and thin to the coat-tails of old Dogvane; but the carpenter's spirit was mutinous, and he showed no disposition to dance either to the cook's organ, or to be monkey-led by the captain of the Starboard Watch.

Although the Buccaneer was somewhat pacified, he determined to look into things a little more himself, for, as he said, there could not be so much smoke without a certain amount of fire. To begin with, he told the captain of his watch that he intended interviewing the heads of some of his departments. Dogvane tried to dissuade his master. He said it would be unconstitutional and all sort of things. That the officials would not like it. They could not bear meddling; it hurt their dignity. But it was of no use, the Buccaneer was determined.

The high State officials who had the management of the affairs on board of the old ship thought, like most other servants, that they could best serve their master by squandering his money; and they did it right royally. Perhaps royally is not the proper word, for royalty is often careful, if not close, with its own money, whatever it may be with other people's.

The lavish manner in which the Buccaneer's servants spent his money was conspicuously shown in the administration of his army and navy, and in fact in all his public works. The one great principle being to spend a pound in laying out a penny, no matter whether it was a ship of war that had to be built or the mouth of a poor starving person that had to be filled Whether this waste was due to carelessness, stupidity, or ignorance, or to a combination of all three, matters little. The result was the same.

Finding his master was not to be put off, Dogvane began to cry up his wares like the long shore cheap-Jacks.

"Your Navy, sir," he said, "is in excellent condition, though of course, the watch on shore deny this; but that is according to custom. We have placed your navy in the hands of those who have been chosen on purely constitutional principles. Here again, we show that we are not the revolutionist that our enemies would make us out to be. Your first lord of the Admiralty we have selected from amongst those who are distinguished for their ignorance in all maritime matters. Men who do not know a ship's head from a ship's tail. I believe I should, to be quite correct, call it stern. It is of course a difficult thing to find amongst an insular, and seafaring people, any man absolutely ignorant, but we do our best, and no man can do more. One thus selected, sir, on purely constitutional principles, is more likely to be free from prejudice than your professional man, and he is likely to exercise a healthy check upon your sea lords, whose predisposition is to drift into bloated armaments and bloody wars. This, of course, means money, and your expenditure is already more than any of your neighbours, and if we have not as many ships, sailors, and soldiers, as we ought to have, or than what your neighbours have, we at least spend ever so much more money, which must be to you an extreme satisfaction. If they say, look at our armies! we say, look at our expenditure! Your fellows do not cost a quarter, or a fraction as much, man for man, as our fellows do, or ship for ship. Cheap things, it is well known, are not only not good, but they are frequently nasty. Although your first lord may be totally ignorant of all things pertaining to the sea, he is ably assisted by distinguished sailors, and your first sea lord is ever ready and willing to set your first lord right when he goes wrong, which he seldom if ever does, or if he does we never receive any official information on the subject. They all support their party. They see nothing they ought not to see, and are at all times ready to swear that whatever is, is right, as far their watch is concerned, and that whatever is, is wrong, as far as the other watch is concerned. Honest sailors can do no more."

"Master Dogvane, is this as it should be?" the Buccaneer asked.

"Most assuredly, sir. It is most constitutional, and according to your general custom."

"Master Dogvane, I have found you to be of a sanguine temperament. You told me my people were prosperous and contented. I have my doubts, and I shall satisfy myself. But of that anon. Let my first lord of the Admiralty be called."

The first lord was down below listening to the first sea lord spinning a yarn, and he was trying to learn how to do it; because at times he was called upon to spin yarns with reference to his department. As has been already stated in this most truthful history, there was a time when the Buccaneer ruled the stormy ocean. He was then one of the finest sailors that ever trod a plank or made use of a strange sea oath; but times had changed, and many thought that modern innovation had taken the wind out of his sails, and that he at present traded upon his past reputation. But people must say something.

The first lord of the Admiralty appeared. "Now, sir," said the Buccaneer, "take charge, and let me see what you can do." The whole seafaring world had been so changed and modernized since the old Buccaneer had commanded in person, that he really knew very little about things; but ignorance can always be concealed by a discreet silence.

The first lord being thus called upon to show his professional knowledge, cried out, "Ease her! backer! stopper!" This was addressed through a speaking trumpet to the old Church Hulk alongside; but as she had never been known to move for years past, what the first lord said was without effect. Indeed the crew of the old Church ship were busily occupied in trying a rebellious priest who would neither mend his ways, nor leave his pulpit, but breathed defiance against the High Priest and all his ecclesiastical big guns.

"What is all that about?" exclaimed the Buccaneer, addressing his first lord.

"Those, sir, are nautical expressions I have picked up on the river," replied the first lord, "and I believe they are technically correct. If they are not, I have no official information on the subject.'

The old Buccaneer not willing to display his ignorance, said, "I want, sir, to know what state your department is in. What have you been doing; and how are my ships?"

"I have spent your money, sir, right well. I have bought some very fine and fast new cruisers, and I gave as much for them as I decently could."

"How is this?" cried the Buccaneer, "I used to be the first shipwright in the world."

"Rest easy, sir," Dogvane said. "These goods are of home manufacture. It is your custom in times of peace to let your shipyards lie idle; but when a scare comes, as come they will, in the best regulated nation, then we buy your ships from private firms, and having husbanded your wealth, you can the more readily give high prices in cases of necessity."

"But is this wise, Master Dogvane?"

"It is constitutional, sir," was the captain's reply. He might have added that it was also a customary thing to sell these ships, for which so much had been given, for a mere song after the panic was over.

The first lord continued, "Then as to what I have done, sir, I have had the Admiral Superintendent's house at your principal naval station thoroughly repaired, cleaned, and re-decorated. All your ships that float are in a serviceable condition, and as they have no enemy to contend against, except the elements, they occasionally run into one another, just to keep their hands in, and occasionally a ship is sunk or disabled. Although we have a due regard for your great wealth, we do not encourage a too frequent repetition of this, as it is extremely costly. There is still 'a sweet little cherub that sits up aloft and looks out for the life of poor Jack.' That is, he would no doubt sit up aloft if he had anything to sit upon or any place to put it."

"You see, sir," exclaimed Dogvane with delight, "what excellent hands your navy is in. Your first lord can also tip you a stave, as they say at sea. He can sing you 'Oh! Pilot, 'tis a fearful night,' or 'All in the Downs,' he is also exceptionally good at a break down."

This high praise quite pleased the first lord, and wishing to advance himself still more in the good graces of his master, he said, " I can take an observation. I can use the strangest of sea oaths, and I can at all times make it eight bells."

"A man, sir, who can at all times make it eight bells, must needs be a good sailor," Dogvane said.

"But let me see him work the ship, Master Dogvane."

The first lord being thus called upon to show his professional skill, told the sea lord to stand by and look out for squalls, which he accordingly did.

"Close by fours—" cried the first lord; but the sea lord stopped him at once by saying, "Steady there, shipmate! you are getting mixed."

There was now a long discussion between the two lords of the Buccaneer's Admiralty. The first lord declaring he never mixed, the first sea lord declaring that he did. "Anyhow," cried the latter, "put your helm down and go about."

"Aye, aye," cried the first lord. "Helm's a lee; raise tacks and sheet. All hands splice the main brace!"

"Capital! capital!" exclaimed Dogvane, "your first lord, sir, is indeed an excellent sailor. He can actually splice the main brace and I feel sure that must be a most arduous undertaking; requiring much skill and intelligence. He seems, indeed, to be gaining so much knowledge of his profession that I shall have to move him to some other department, probably the army; he has some slight knowledge of military matters, but not enough to render him unfit for the post of secretary of State for war. Fortunately the heads of your different departments are all interchangeable."

"How about his accounts, Dogvane?" the Buccaneer asked.

"Ah! there, sir, I think you will find his ignorance most

creditable. Accounts are a sort of thing that no high official could possibly be expected to understand."

"What does my sea lord say?" asked the Buccaneer.

"Rivet my bolts and split my plates! what do I say."

"Note, sir, the change," Dogvane exclaimed. "It used to be shiver my timbers, you see, sir, your first sea lord is quite in keeping with the progress of the age. These changes of course have not been brought about without much trouble and at great expense."

"What do I say, your honour!" cried the first sea lord, "why clear the decks for action and strike up the band."

"What!" exclaimed the Buccaneer, as the blood mounted to his face, "are we going to have a naval engagement? I have not seen such a thing, Dogvane, for these many years past."

The Buccaneer now looked on with surprise at the first sea lord, who, having thrown aside his cocked hat, folded his arms and danced round the deck on the circumference of a circle.

"What is all this, Master Dogvane?" the Buccaneer asked.

"He is going to dance you a hornpipe, sir. Your people are particularly fond of such things and they would come in crowds from miles away to see your first sea lord do the double shuffle."

"But I don't want to see it, so stop him. I want to know something about my ships."

With very great difficulty the first sea lord was stopped, for he was well under weigh and it was some little time before they brought him up by hanging on to the swallow tails of his coat.

"What do I say?" he cried. "That must depend very much upon what I am expected to say. How's your head, captain?" This was addressed to Dogvane and was meant as a signal of distress, and not as an expression of solicitude for Dogvane's cranium. The hint was taken and the captain said that their master wanted to know if his ships were well found and whether he still ruled the sea.

To this the sea lord replied, "Every ship, sir, that is not in Davy Jones' locker, has the sea well under her, and, therefore, it may be asserted that she has complete control of the sea."

"Davy Jones' locker!" cried the Buccaneer in amazement, "why I sent very few of my ships there in olden days and my enemies sent still fewer."

Dogvane explained to his master that rapid strides had taken place in all things naval and that great changes had been brought about. "We have been so pressed for room, sir," he exclaimed, "that we have been obliged to turn Davy Jones' locker into one of your principal dockyards, where we keep many of your ships which are not required for immediate use."

The first sea lord doused, as sailors says, his starboard glim, and contemplated old Dogvane with the other, while a look of admiration and a jovial smile played over his weather-beaten face as he answered:

"Aye, aye, sir, and every year we send a ship or two there to be repaired. The remainder we tinker up ourselves." The old Buccaneer made no answer. Things had evidently changed very much indeed since he was himself afloat, but it never does for a master to display a want of knowledge before his servants. As to whether the Buccaneer had lost his skill in seamanship and shipbuilding was merely a matter of opinion. But there could be no doubt that anything he had lost in one direction was amply made up by what he had gained in the tinkering line. Here he could not be surpassed.

"All your guns," continued the first sea lord, "that are neither cracked nor burst are in excellent condition. Every ship that does not want for anything is particularly well found, and your sailors, sir, are as jolly and rollicking a lot of devils as ever turned a quid or drained a tot of grog."

"Capital! capital!" cried Dogvane, as he clapped his hands with delight, "such skill and knowledge must be rewarded. We must bestow some high distinctions upon these two officials. We must ennoble them and send round your Hat of maintenance." The lords of the Admiralty were then dismissed.

In passing, it may be said that the old Buccaneer had navigated the world in ships that, beside his present monsters, were but as cockle shells, and all his great victories had been gained on board his old wooden walls; but now his seamen were incased in iron or steel and had to live and fight almost under water, and it was a matter of constant dispute as to whether the Buccaneer had ships enough even to defend his own shores. Some people going so far as to say that not only had he not enough ships, but that he had no guns for what he had.

CHAPTER XXXIV.

THE Buccaneer's War Minister now received his summons, as in naval matters, so in military. The high official who had charge of his army, and was responsible for the safety of the Buccaneer's vast empire, was totally ignorant, or nearly so, of all things connected with the military profession. When Dogvane descanted upon his ignorance of all things military, the Buccaneer exclaimed: "Stay, Master Dogvane! if my body is ailing should I not send for a physician, one skilled in disease? If my mind is disturbed upon some spiritual matter should I not send for my spiritual adviser? And if I want a legal opinion should I not go to my lawyer?"

"If you did, sir, I do not hesitate to tell you that you would be acting in an altogether unconstitutional manner."

"What! then if I want a coat made I should not go to my tailor? If I want a pair of boots I should seek some other than my shoemaker to make them?"

"Undoubtedly, sir, for such ever has been your custom, and who will say that it has not worked well; for you are both wealthy and great. Your plan ever has been to put the roundest of men into the squarest of holes. It is a fortunate thing, sir, that human nature is so pliable that it can adapt itself to any condition."

The War Minister was in his particular part of the ship, occupied, together with the most eminent of the Buccaneer's military officers, in testing and trying which of all the advertised food for infants was best adapted to the requirements of the Buccaneer's military babes. They had not settled this weighty matter when the War Minister received his summons. Not being a soldier he was completely taken by surprise, of course no soldier would allow himself to fall into such a perilous position; but to show his comrades that he had not lost his self possession he altered somewhat an old song of the Buccaneer's to suit present purposes, and went away merrily singing :

> " I'm afloat, I'm afloat
> In the old Ship of State,
> The sailor's profession
> I cordially hate."

No doubt his thoughts were wandering back to the time when he himself had been at sea. In all probability he had had charge of the Buccaneer's navy and becoming too full of knowledge had been removed to the army. When he appeared before his master he became quite flustered. The official mind does at times, it is well known, play sad tricks, and displays upon occasions the most wonderful oblivion. When asked as to the state his department was in, he replied : " Quite ship-shape, sir, and ready for sea."

" It appears to me, sir," said the Buccaneer, "that you are at sea."

"Am I ? Then let me go below. Like many others, I suffer until I get accustomed to the up and down motion. The lee lurches and weather rolls disturb me. The smell of the oil and tar is offensive, and the result is painful. Then the sailor's quaint oaths I cannot understand. I dare not chew, I cannot smoke, and I do not care to drink, so I feel convinced I was never meant for the sea."

The War Minister was brought sternly back to his senses by Captain Dogvane, who told him in a severe tone to "wake up," and remember that he was at present in charge of the Buccaneer's Land Forces.

The War Minister was profuse in his apologies, and said : " In my time, sir, I have filled so many posts that I occasionally get confused. Your Army, sir, is most efficient, and I am proud to be able to tell you that you pay more for your food, for powder, than any other nation under the sun. This to one of your vast wealth must be a source of the greatest satisfaction; indeed, it must be a glorious thing to contemplate. We have recently made vast prepartions, which of course have been costly."

" This, sir, is as I told you, and will account for the money you advanced me, over that little affair in the East.'

" Ah! Master Dogvane, how is that going on?"

" Excellently well, sir," was Dogvane's reply; "at least I have no official information to the contrary. At present, sir, things nearer home claim our attention."

The War Minister continued: " We have laid in an immense amount of warlike stores, and these, as every one knows, are most costly articles, and it takes far more to kill a man in the present state of military science than it would take to keep him alive and in comparative comfort to the crack of doom. On paper, sir, I can mobilize an army, on paper I could place it in the field and on paper I could feed and clothe it. I could, if called upon, club either a battalion, a brigade or even a division."

Dogvane was not a soldier, but he thought it right to encourage his subordinates whether they were right or wrong, so he exclaimed: " Capital, capital!" Then turning to his master, he said: " Beyond this, sir, you could not expect your War Minister to go. For a general deficiency in professional knowledge I feel sure it would be hard to find his equal. For your practical information you must go to your Field Marshal Commanding-in-Chief, than whom I am told you have no better soldier, and no one has done more to stamp out from amongst your soldiers the pernicious habit of using bad language; and this has not been done by any brutal exercise of power, but all by kindness and the force of good example."

" Then my Field Marshal never swears?" the Buccaneer asked.

" Never, sir; at least," he said aside, "hardly ever."

The Buccaneer, being a very religious man, was very pleased to hear this. " But what is all this I hear," he said, " about my poor fellows who are fighting for me not having proper food?"

" The campaign in which you are at present engaged in the East."

Dogvane stopped the War Minister abruptly, and went into a long explanation. He drew many subtle distinctions as before, between different kinds of warlike operations some of which he said, though offensive in form were purely defensive in essence. In fact, if looked at from a proper point of view were no operations at all. Dogvane's reasoning was of such an obscure nature that nobody could understand it, and there were doubts in the minds of some as to whether Dogvane himself understood what he was talking about.

The Buccaneer, fearing he might get out of his depth if he followed his captain too far, came back to the main charge, and said to his War Minister: "I am told my soldiers' food was so bad that they could scarcely eat it. That their tea and coffee was mere filth, and that even the water they had to drink was of the vilest description, and this too, when I am surrounded by the newest inventions which will make the muddiest stream as pure as crystal, and I spare no expense?"

"None whatever, sir," was the War Minister's reply. "I can assure you we pay the highest price for everything, and we can do no more. We have heard no complaints, and vague rumours we never heed." The official ear on the Buccaneer's island was quite as deaf as what the official eye was blind. Dogvane said he should not be at all surprised if all these reports were put about by the other watch, or as likely as not by that busy little devil, Random Jack. "All about your War Office, sir," he said, addressing the Buccaneer, "look particularly well fed, and are well clothed. I have not seen a crack in either coat or trouser. They seem to want for nothing, and they are, I presume, a fair sample of the whole; but satisfy yourself, sir. Ask your Field Marshal if he is well fed and well clothed, and as the fountain-head, so, no doubt, is the stream that flows from it. No expense has been spared, I can assure you."

"And so, Master Dogvane, you all think to serve best my interests by squandering my money, which goes into the capacious pockets of the money grabbing rascally contractors."

"We have it, sir, on the authority of your only general, who, though an Ojabberaway, is worthy of credence, that, at no time in your whole history has your army been in so excellent a condition."

"Have I then only one general?" the Buccaneer asked in surprise.

"Only one that we have officially any knowledge of; for further information on that subject, sir, I must refer you to your Commander-in-chief. Your military administration is distinguished for its very great zeal and energy. For long and weary hours—in fact, from 10 o'clock in the morning till 4, or even 5 o'clock in the dewy evening, the busy brains of your War Office officials are constantly at work grinding up all military ideas to a common level of official pulp, and it says a very great deal for the quality of the official brain that it has never yet broken down under the severe strain that has been put upon it. There has not been, as far as I know, a single instance of well authenticated madness inside your War Office. Go to your arsenals, and you will find them a busy hive of industry. The hive is occasionally blown up by an explosion, but the operatives, as a class, are happy and contented. Your military nurseries are full of the most promising children, who will, should they survive the many ills that childish flesh is heir too, develop, no doubt, into most excellent soldiers. Is it not so?" This latter was addressed to the War Minister, who said that it was, and added: "They have all been vaccinated, and most of them have had the measles, and not a few the hooping-cough. In olden days, sir, your battles were fought by the scum of your populations. This great blot in your military system we are eradicating, and in the future, sir, moral force, which, it has been estimated, is equal to about three to one of physical force, will play no mean part in all your military undertakings. Therefor, multiplying your units by three gives you a first fighting line of over 500,000 men, with a total fighting power of about one million and a half."

"Take care, sir," said the Buccaneer, "that you do not make my soldiers too thin skinned. A pampered dog won't fight, and a hound too finely bred will not face the prickles of a gorse bush. Whatever my soldiers were in the past they fought well, and have built up for me a reputation, that I hope my soldiers of to-day and those who lead them and those who guide them will know how to keep. The deeds, Master Dogvane, of the brave lads that are gone are written on tablets placed on the walls of the Temple of Fame. Let no foul breath of calumny be breathed over them, for whatever sins they have committed have been washed out with their own blood. One thing, Master Dogvane, they at least had, and that was, good trusty steel."

Dogvane took the hint, and thought that a little candour would best serve his purpose. "It has come to my ears, sir, that our modern steel is not quite up to the mark, so to test it I have ordered a Royal Commission to sit upon our bayonets and cutlasses, and if they can support without bending or breaking so severe a strain, their temper must be good indeed. It has been said too, amongst other things, that your machine guns occasionally jam and I will not deny that it is so, when they are in the hands of your sailors, but, then, they are such merry devils that they would jam almost anything."

The War Minister now being called upon to continue his report, said : " Your militia, sir, which has always been considered the backbone of your army gives us little or no consideration, and it seems to get on very well without our interference. Whatever care, attention, and patronage we have to spare we bestow it upon your volunteers—a most worthy body of men, costing you but little ; not encumbered with too much equipment, and fed and nourished almost entirely upon official butter, which is the cheapest of all articles of food, on a recent occasion, sir, when you were engaged in operations in Egypt."

"In Egypt!" the Buccaneer exclaimed, and the hot words of the gipsy came back upon him, and he was lost for a while in his own moody thoughts.

For a time the War Minister spoke to deaf ears. "You bought thousands of camels, and mules, and pack-saddles innumerable. After the purchase was completed we were delighted to find that these saddles were for the most part perfectly useless, as they would not fit any animal in your possession, so we were enabled to sell them at a considerable loss."

"Is this right, Master Dogvane?" the Buccaneer asked, waking up.

"It is quite constitutional, sir, and is the result of your peculiar and long cherished system. I do not say that things would not work better under a round hole for a round man plan; but you are so accustomed to the other that to change might be dangerous. It would certainly be revolutionary."

The War Minister continued. "In purchasing your stores, sir, we also acted upon principle and custom. We gave as few orders as possible to your own people; but distributed them as evenly as we could amongst your neighbours."

The Buccaneer was about to make a reply; but Dogvane nipped it in the bud by saying: "It is quite constitutional, sir." If this was so of course the old Sea King had nothing to say, for he loved his constitution.

"Our beef and pork," said the War Minister, "we get from our cousin, the cheap-Jack Jonathan. Our sauce we get from your neighbour, Madame France."

"Do you remember what a neatly turned ankle she had, sir?" said Dogvane, who, like all sailors and not a few landsmen, had a great admiration for the ladies.

"Our pickles," the War Minister continued, "we get from Germany, and are of a well known brand, high flavoured and satisfying. As we are the very best tinkers in the world, our pots, pans, and camp kettles we make and mend at home. We feed your full-grown soldiers on worn-out draught-bullocks brought over from Holland, and on the most delicious messes. We give them a highly flavoured stew peculiar to the Ojabberaways. They have had an abundance of Egyptian hash. This again has been varied by a goodly supply of Indian curry, Afghan ragoût, and a very savoury mess peculiar to Burmah. I may just mention in passing, that through the most creditable carelessness on the part of one of your generals we got rid of a very large number of camels, which were slaughtered by the enemy; thus saving us the trouble and expense of their keep. For any other information I must refer you to your Field Marshal."

Dogvane dismissed this official, praising him very much for the state of his department.

When the distinguished soldier appeared, who was at the executive head of the army, he stood in the attitude peculiar to soldiers. His head was erect and every limb was rigid, and the arms were extended by the side of the body, fingers straight and closed on the thumbs, which were in a line with the seams of his trousers. This is the easy and graceful attitude of military respect as laid down by regulation.

" How, sir, is it that you have allowed my army so to deteriorate that I have only one general ? " asked the Buccaneer, as he cast upon his Field Marshal a look of pride. "At one time I could count them by the scores."

" Sir, two kings cannot sit on one throne, and at present your island is not sufficiently large to hold more than your only general."

The Buccaneer showed extreme solicitude for the well being of his only general, whose life was, of course, extremely precious, so he exclaimed: " Field Marshal ! I command you on all occasions to protect the life of my only general. Form yourself into a rampart round him and save him from the bullets of my enemies. Even as David in the days of old sent Uriah the Hittite to the front of the battle, so send I you, should I be engaged in any military operation either of an offensive or defensive nature."

The Field Marshal, commanding in chief, no doubt felt keenly the very great confidence thus placed in him, though of course it would not have been in keeping with the tradition of his profession to show any outward signs of exultation.

The captain of the watch, seeing the great concern that the Buccaneer had on account of the dearth of generals, and knowing his love for the Bible, tried to console him by saying : " Fear not sir ! that Providence which shapes our ends, rough hew them as we may, will find you with other generals, even as Abraham was provided by Heaven with a ram in the bush."

Sometimes the most trivial circumstance will ward off the most serious catastrophe, and the remark of Dogvane gave the old Sea

King an opportunity to indulge in a little pleasantry. "A general in the hand, Master Dogvane," he said, "is worth two in the bush." Now, however small a joke may be, or indeed however heavy and obscure, it is the duty of all subordinates to see it at once, and to laugh at it immoderately. This was shown to an eminent degree even in the Buccaneer's Courts of Justice, the atmosphere of which was so charged with judicial gravity that the slightest possible humour on the part of a judge was quite sufficient to convulse the whole court and bar with laughter. The Commander-in-chief being in uniform could not laugh as much as he would have done, had he not been so buttoned up. It was his duty to appreciate the joke of the Buccaneer, and in a matter of duty the Field Marshal was never found wanting. Dogvane laughed as immoderately as if the joke had been his own. The clouds having been dispelled by merry peals of laughter the Buccaneer asked if his soldiers were as good as those who fought at Ramillies and Waterloo; these being two of the Buccaneer's most famous battles. The Field Marshal was obliged to answer this officially. He said that as far as brute strength and physical force were concerned, that perhaps the soldier of to-day was not quite equal to the soldier of the past; "but," he added, "what he has lost in stature and chest measurement he has gained in morality and sobriety. The men of Ramillies drank deeply, and those of Flanders swore terribly hard, so we are told; no doubt on account of some peculiarity in the climate; but now, sir, by the force of my own good example I have done very much towards stamping out the pernicious habit of making use of bad language from amongst your soldiers."

"So I have heard," replied the Buccaneer, "and it does you extreme credit." What a gross iniquity to call so good a man as our Buccaneer a psalm-singing, old humbug! It only shows what a hold envy, hatred, uncharitableness, and even malice, have upon the human mind.

"Field Marshal!" said the Buccaneer, addressing the Commander-in-chief, "you have done well, and it is my intention to reward you. I can bestow upon you no greater title than you at present possess, and of income you have ample, so I cannot increase that; but knowing how much you have at heart the welfare of the profession which you yourself so much adorn, I wish to give you some mark of my high esteem and favour. I therefore command Dogvane, that my army be at once increased by one man and two boys."

Hearing this the Commander-in-Chief was overcome with emotion, and Dogvane said, " My master is indeed generous. I am myself much against bloated armaments ; but still it is as well to strike at times a little awe into our neighbours, who are always peacocking about Europe, and they will respect us all the more. With this increase, and the aid of our reserves, and our brave auxiliaries, our army will be placed on a war-footing. No doubt all this will not be without its effect upon the Eastern Bandit, and will assist King Hokee in his undertaking."

CHAPTER XXXV.

In spite of what Will Dogvane had said to the contrary there was discontent in the Buccaneer's island. Now the sound was far away; now it surged up and dashed against the old gentleman's ears like the angry surf upon the sea-shore. It is necessary to make some little mention yet of the cause of this disaffection. His toilers and his moilers were undoubtedly very much better off than what they had been, and considerably better off than those of many of his neighbours. They earned more wages, and worked less hours, and in recent years wages had increased nearly twofold; but it must be owned that they were less thrifty, and loved too well their pewter pot. His population, however, had increased to such an extent, and other nations had entered into such competition with him, producing many things as good and as cheap, and even very much cheaper, that he had lost the control over the markets of the world, consequently many even of the skilled hands were idle, and for the unskilled, the weakly, and the sick, their case was still harder, yet every mouth had to be fed, and every body clothed. All kinds of medicines were prescribed by the multitude of doctors, who were forever trying to treat the disease. Then behind those above alluded to there came a gang who would only work at cutting throats and picking pockets, and who were always ready to join in any cry, or any movement, that might tend to advance their particular calling.

The carpenter had addressed the family of Hodge on more occasions than one, and he had told them that they were the most pathetic figure in the whole of the Buccaneer's social system, for that they were condemned to unremitting toil, with only the poor-house before them. Alas! that the cry should ever come from honest Hodge that all he asked for was work. This poor fellow does commend himself to the sympathy and compassion of all; for the sunniest side of his life is to work with bent back and horny hands from sun-rise to sun-down. But he was not the most pathetic figure in the Buccaneer's island. Behind him Poverty came struggling along, and with barely food enough to keep body and soul together, brought forth and increased without the slightest thought for the morrow. Pity was forever trying to help her, and over her sad lot she shed an abundance of tears. The old coxswain tried to reason with her; but all to no purpose, she clung to her wretched hovels and held on her own way. Nature took her in hand occasionally, and taught her a lesson in a rough and ready fashion. Our universal mother is not soft-hearted, and she never spoils her children by sparing the rod, so when Poverty's family becomes overcrowded, she works off the surplus by disease, when the guilty and the innocent suffer alike. Is not Mercy to be seen standing in the back ground?

The old Buccaneer thought to find some healing power in the fruit taken from the tree of knowledge, so that Poverty's children partaking thereof might learn somewhat of the blessings of thrift, temperance, industry, and self-denial. But is not the fruit of this tree somewhat like that flower of which a celebrated friar once said:

"Within the infant rind of this small flower,
Poison hath residence, and medicine power."

In the above nature of things lay the root of very much of the discontent. The tools lay ready for the worker's hands. The worker being that human wind bag, called an agitator; one who would find fault with the order of things even in heaven itself.

This wind bag is forever holding up before the eyes of his dupes a picture painted in the most gorgeous colours; plenty without labour, and a general basking in the sunshine of idleness. He points the finger at wealth, and cries out with a loud voice, "There lies the cure for all your suffering; see how high above your heads the rich man looks. Go take, eat and be merry, to-day live, for to-morrow you die." To the empty stomach, and the ragged back this doctrine has a pleasant sound. Neither is it without its effect upon that large multitude who have to earn a scanty living by the sweat of their brow. The uncertainty of the daily bread; the fear of sickness, and the cry of hungry children open the ears sometimes even of the well disposed. Then amongst many other things, man is by nature a lazy animal, and will not work except in rare instances, unless necessity compels him. Take the noble savage of whom honourable mention has already been made. He only hunts by compulsion; for want of food in fact, which, having found, he lies down and sleeps, and idles his time away until necessity prods him in the stomach again, and sends him off to his happy hunting grounds. Man is the same wherever found, and if anybody will provide him with food and clothes, without any exertion on his part he will not say him nay, nor will he show much gratitude. He will soon learn to look upon it as a right.

There were a good many kind-hearted people in the Buccaneer's island who were doing all they could to develop and foster this innate love of idleness. Already the people had their food for the mind given to them free of charge in the shape of free libraries, and soon the cry for free food for the body might be expected to rise up all over the land, to be followed in due course by a demand for community of property. This, indeed, was already being whispered about. It is an unmitigated evil to take from the individual the responsibility of keeping himself, and bringing up his family. He will not work if you do, and the train of poverty becomes increased, and there is no limit to the extension. As the Devil even is supposed at times to quote Scripture, so do the wind bags, who play upon the wants of the people, frequently base their doctrine of universal plunder upon the teachings of Christ. But did not a small band of early Christians try this share and share alike principle? But it did not answer, and see what has come of it. The pomp, magnificence, splendour and wealth of the Roman Catholic Hierarchy with its Priest-King. Who too would think that the pride and majesty of the Buccaneer's State Church with its High Priest clothed in temporal as well as spiritual power took its rise from the teachings of Him, who gathered on the shores of the sea of Galilee a few simple and faithful disciples to whom He preached the doctrine of humility, chastity, poverty, and love, and a charity as bountiful as the rain which falls from heaven on flowers and weeds alike. Did He not say to them "Provide neither gold nor silver, nor brass in your purses, nor scrip for your journey, neither two coats, neither shoes, nor yet staves; for the workman is worthy of his meat?" Ah! the meat, sometimes called hire; there lies the rock upon which so many run, and their frail barks are shivered to pieces; allured to their destruction by the songs of a siren called Mammon.

But the priest he has a stomach as well as the layman. He has a back too which must be covered, and he has his many other wants that must be attended to. One has taken to himself a wife, and he would fain have his Lord excuse him, on her account. Another has many children who have to be fed, clothed, and taught, and put out into the world. Then things have changed since the days even of St. Paul. Wages have very much increased, and around religion there has grown surroundings that must be attended to for the sake of the uncrowned queen Respectability. Ask not how all these mighty things have been brought about. Without doubt, the Buccaneer's High Priest or anyone of his learned ecclesiastics could explain all to you in a most satisfactory manner. They would tell you how the Scriptures have to be construed to suit the needs of modern Christians. The mighty "*This*" has he contracted and the small "*That*" has to be stretched; but so long as an orthodox priest sits upon the box of your coach and four, it matters little where, and through what he drives.

Briefly, it may be said, that community of property has no charm except for that class of a community known by the name of rogues and vagabonds. Then, as if the very Devil was in it, the Buccaneer's women were beginning to cry out for more liberty, and disaffection seemed to have taken a strong hold upon the female breast. The advanced portion of these wanted to overturn the present order of things, and to put up in its place, a sort of Hen

Convention in which women were to have equal rights and apparently man's privileges as well as their own. To tell these women that they had a sphere, was merely to excite their ridicule, and court their contempt. But the strangeness of the thing was, that while the men were crying out because they had not work sufficient to keep them in many cases from starving, the women wanted to increase the difficulty still more by entering the same fields of labour. Of course poor women must live, and if men are so selfish that they will not keep them in the Holy bonds of matrimony, why, the women must keep themselves. It is true that the men did show an indisposition to set upon their hearth a rival, who instead of attending to domestic duties, might give them a political lecture or a discourse upon either ethics, philosophy, or science. The women too out-numbered the men; spinsters growing more numerous every day, and as it is well-known that the mortality amongst the males of all species is far greater than that amongst the females, on account of the greater risk they run, the above evil might be expected to increase rather than diminish, unless nature took the matter in hand and balanced matters by an epidemic amongst the women. But as matters now stood, the conspiracy amongst the Buccaneer's female sex bid fair to be far more serious than that of the cook's caboose.

It has been said that the man who allows a woman to usurp his authority is in a pitiful condition, for that it shows he has lost somewhat of his manhood. One thing is certain, the woman he has to live with will not respect him, and it is more than probable that she will take the earliest opportunity to show her contempt. It is still worse when this applies not to an individual here and there, but to the majority of a people.

What voice is that crying out that we insult the whole of womanhood? Good lady, if you cast aside your bodkin, and take up the weapons that have hitherto been considered as peculiar to man, you must not cry out when you feel yourself injured. You cannot have your cake and eat it too. "A foolish woman is clamorous; but a good woman retaineth honour." So said one, who is accounted the wisest man that ever lived,

It does not appear that the true position of woman in the world's economy has yet been clearly defined. She was once man's slave. She is now supposed, in all civilised countries, to be his helpmate and companion, and in the Buccaneer's island she showed a strong disposition to become his rival. Poetry has assigned to her a place amongst the angels; reality, on the other hand, has frequently given her a place amongst the devils. Then again she is supposed to be weak and fragile, but though she may not be able to walk a mile in pure fresh air, she will dance many, and several nights a week in the fetid atmosphere of a ball-room. Although she takes little or no healthy exercise, the general woman's appetite is good if not absolutely robust, and although they are all more or less invalids, they generally outlive man. A recent philosopher amongst the Buccaneer's people had said, when speaking of woman, that though eminently adapted to that position for which God apparently intended her, she is not from her constitution and make, adapted to take man's place in the world, and by attempting such a thing all concerned must lose. Unfortunately, the Buccaneer's advanced women did not seem to see this, and they seemed disposed to quarrel with the work of our Creator. The woman's character is conflicting. When she is drawn by her sister, she does not at times appear in too beautiful colours; for she is frequently depicted as vain, silly, jealous, weak, cruel and revengeful, often kissing the sister she intends to stab, and in this resembling somewhat those reptiles which slobber over the victim they intend to devour. But is it the model or the artist who is at fault?

From history we learn that the presence of woman upon the earth has not been an unmixed blessing, for she seems to have caused as much sorrow as ever she has joy, and the estimation in which she was held in ancient Biblical times is pretty well manifested by the author of the Mosaic Cosmogony, who attributes to her the damnation of the whole human race. Through her first act of disobedience man first tasted of the cup of misery, and she has been holding the cup to his lips ever since. Constituted as woman is, was it not cruel to place an injunction on that fatal tree? for, tell a woman not to do a thing and she is pretty certain to do it. Of course our first father did not act over honourably. If he had been imbued with the principles of modern chivalry he would have screened Eve; have sworn, perhaps, that she was not at all to blame, and finished up by flinging the apple at the tempter's head. But man ever had, and always will have an ungodly stomach, and so Adam took the apple and did eat. Notwithstanding the chivalry aforesaid it is generally believed that there are more Adams in the world now than what there are Josephs, and if the trial of the apple came over again, man would fall even as he fell before, though he were to be ten times more damned. It is a thousand and one pities that the arch Fiend did not wait until Eve had become a little old and ugly, for then Adam might have refused the apple and the whole human race might have been saved.

The Essenes would not marry, not because they denied the validity of the institution or its necessity, but because they were convinced of the artfulness and fickleness of the female sex. Then again, the Buddhist believed, if he does not believe, that no woman could attain a state of supreme perfection. The accomplished woman becomes man.

Read where we will, and what we will, and let us bend our steps whither we like, and we find that woman is generally believed to be at the bottom of everything. We are told that Metellus Numidicus, the censor, acknowledged to the Roman people in a public oration that had kind nature allowed us to exist without the help of women, we should be delivered from a very troublesome companion. But, though man still growls, poets still sing about woman, lovely woman, and though man sometimes finds her a devil, painters still depict her in the form of an angel, and man's imagination fills heaven with beings in her shape and likeness.

To be just; has not woman somewhat to complain of? Was she not made after man, and, as some think, of the refuse material? Then again has she not been sent into the world with, on an average, five ounces less brains than the allowance given to man? And has she not, from the very beginning, been obliged to bear patiently, and for the most part with meekness, all these slights and insults? And to finish, was she not made as a meet and fitting companion for man? Who will be so impious as to say that she was spoilt in the making? Alas! we cannot do without her; no matter how uncomfortable we may at times be with her; and a smile, or a tear, on a pretty face will blot out and efface all the splutterings that fall from the pen of ill nature.

What man is there who has not created in his mind some womanly idol, and here often lies the misfortune; for idols will fall and break into thousands of pieces; but until the catastrophe happens, we worship at our shrine and look upon fair forms with heavenly faces; bright radiance is shed over every feature, and we are in an atmosphere free from all impurity. We look up to and adore a being whose soul is never clouded by a base thought; whose chaste and cherry lips never give utterance to a tainted word. One who can be pure without being a prude; gentle and charitable without there being a suspicion even of foolishness; one who can be sensible without being masculine, and innocent without being a vain and frivolous idiot.

Do I dream? Hush then! do not wake me. Let me wander on, if only for a brief space in the realms of fancy. I will build for myself castles, and will people them with fair fantasies. What lovely faces do I see! fit indexes for pure and intelligent minds. Complexions never touched by the paint soiled fingers of Art, but as delicate as the petals of a lily, with the faint blush of the setting sun resting upon them, the whole crowned with a woman's glory dipped in sunshine and not in dye. What lovely forms, clothed in silver sheen and girdled with golden belts made in the armoury of the King of Day!

CHAPTER XXXVI.

THE Buccaneer not being able to obtain any reliable information, for reasons already mentioned, and the voice of the disaffected becoming louder and louder every day, he determined to hold a grand court, when all grievances could be made known, and all wrongs if possible redressed.

When old Dogvane heard of this fresh departure of his master from the beaten paths of custom, he was very much disturbed. "What, my master!" he said, "take the muzzle off people's mouths? Rest assured, sir, that wherever there are human beings, there will be discord and discontent, which, if encouraged, will soon break through the bounds of moderation and flood the whole country. Think you, sir, there is a single one in all your realms who looks upon himself as well treated, though for many of them hanging would be too good? Say but the word and every molehill of discontent will be turned into a mountain of no mean size."

It was of no use, the Buccaneer had made up his mind, so the proclamation was sent out and vast preparations were made. There was soon great commotion all along the hard. People busy, and a constant running to and fro. Loads of timber were brought and placed all ready for the carpenter's hands. There was very much sawing, chiselling and hammering from early morning until late at night. Bit by bit a huge structure was built up just in front of the old Constitution public house, which was, for the time, quite hidden from view by the tiers of seats, which commencing from a low dais or platform, rose up to a considerable height behind, being as high indeed as the roofs of the tallest houses. On the dais and in the centre, there was placed a chair of State, and the seats immediately behind this were of superior make and were draped with crimson cloth of superior quality. The awning overhead was of cloth of gold, and banners were fixed in every suitable place, while tall flag poles reared their heads and displayed a cloud of different coloured bunting. Flags of every nation were to be seen, and altogether it was a noble sight. Then all the windows along the hard were dressed out gaily, and festoons of natural and unnatural flowers were hung about from poles, windows, and roofs. The old Ship of State was decked in holiday attire, and flags fluttered in the breeze from her mast heads down to the very water's edge. It was indeed a noble sight to see the Buccaneer's two ships, and his chief city thus arrayed.

The day at length dawned that was to witness this wonderful pageantry. Almost as soon as the first ray of light peeped over the head of departing night crowds of people began to assemble. The old Ship of State fired her morning gun, and the ship alongside of her called all the pious Buccaneers to prayer, and hymns rose up on the morning dew.

The leaders of the disaffected began to marshal their respective bands. There was the sound of music, for on such occasions, people can not get on without it. It soothes the savage beast, so it is said, and it other ways does good. Curious idlers with open mouths, full of wonder, passed to and fro, for such a sight had never been seen before.

The hour came for the great march past to begin, and Liberty, who was the mistress of the ceremonies, was trying with very great difficulty to keep her motley crowd in order. The brazen-throated trumpets now brayed out the notice of the approach of the great Buccaneer, or fighting trader. How he now styled himself will be shortly seen. With slow and stately step the great man walked, preceded by his lion and followed immediately by his trusty coxswain old Jack Commonsense, who was got up, regardless of expense, for the occasion. The Buccaneer walked between walls of his subjects, and listened, no doubt, with extreme pleasure to their shouts of welcome and delight. To see the great is at all times a gratifying spectacle, when the treat is not repeated too often. After the Buccaneer had passed his people and had taken his place in the chair of state, they began to make their comments. "Ah!" said some, "he is not the man he was." "Yes, yes," cried others, "he is indeed sorely changed. See how gingerly he treads; how fat he has grown; he is terribly out of condition. Did you notice, too, that his lion has lost most of his teeth?" It could not be denied that the bold Buccaneer's step was not as elastic as it used to be. He was not the gay, rollicking, hard hitting old sailor that he was in days of yore. Luxury had begun to mark him as her own, and much energy of action is never found in her train. He looked puffy and bloated, and altogether, as some of his people said, out of condition. A voice from the crowd exclaimed that a good healthy skunk would be far more serviceable than that old lion. It was the cheap-Jack Jonathan. It was wonderful how he tried to pass off that skunk of his upon other people; all of whom had no doubt plenty of skunks of their own. But Jonathan was such a boastful fellow that he would not be beaten even in a matter of skunks.

Behind the Buccaneer came a numerous retinue of priests, ministers, soldiers, sailors, statesmen, officials of every degree and parasites of all kinds and descriptions, for, of course, so great a man could not be without his fair share of these human insects to feed upon him. The Buccaneer having taken his seat, with his coxswain standing behind his chair, the numerous and splendid retinue filed on to the platform and took up their respective places behind. First of all came the Lords Spiritual and then the Lords Temporal, and then the rest of the goodly company, according to their rank and condition. Just as everything was ready there was a slight confusion caused by an angry discussion between a pimp and a parasite about the order of precedence; but the dispute was happily settled without bloodshed. Both watches were, of course, present on so great an occasion, and amongst the rest were the conspirators of the cook's caboose. The magnificence of the assemblage was gorgeous in the extreme, and dazzling, for all wore their robes of state. Jonathan thought he saw a favourable opportunity of doing a little business, so he began to offer blue spectacles of a cheap make, and at a seductively moderate price to the assembled multitude.

Many shouts rose up as some well-known personage passed to his place, and to save trouble Dogvane kept on bowing acknowledgments for all. Pepper, the cook, who sat between Billy Cheeks and Chips, with the man who had been thrown overboard on one occasion, just behind him, tried very hard to make himself big enough to attract public notice; but he was only partially successful. Just in front of the platform, but off it, there was a railed-in space for the Press, to the members of which the Buccaneer was obliged, as has been already stated, to be particularly civil, for if affronted, not only would they turn upon him and lecture him, but they would abuse him plentifully into the bargain. They all had in front of them their pots of ink, coloured according to the party they served. Better kill a plenipotentiary than hurt one of these gentlemen by an unguarded expression. The Beggar Woman, though no doubt somewhere amongst the crowd, was not conspicuous on this occasion.

Silence was ordered, and prayer was said, and hymns of praise were sung. The greatness and the goodness of the Buccaneer were set to sacred music, and the singers also glorified themselves while they glorified their master. The High Priest then asked the Ruler of all things to take this most respectable and pious Buccaneer under His especial protection, and through His priesthood to bless him; to confound his enemies; to make him happy, prosperous and glorious, and a few other things scarcely worth the mentioning, but which would materially increase his joy in this world. In the end, he asked that the Buccaneer might, through his Church, obtain a good inheritance in the Kingdom of Heaven. After this light spiritual refection the Buccaneer experienced that gentle calm which piety and respectability alone can give, and that inner consciousness, which at all times so gratified him, namely, that he was so much better than any of his neighbours, and all those who did not walk along his road to heaven. He was now quite ready for business.

A very high state official, who was robed in cloth of gold of superior quality and make, and whose back and front were covered with heraldic devices, now blew a long and loud blast upon a brazen trumpet, he then cried out in a loud voice: " Listen all ye whom it may concern. Know ye then that the most illustrious, potent, and powerful Sea King (thus he was styled in all official documents), the mighty ruler of an empire, upon which the sun never sets, the keeper of the keys of Heaven, the defender of the only true Faith, having heard that some few of his liege subjects, consider themselves in some trifling matters aggrieved, has been most graciously pleased to hold this grand court at this time assembled, so that grievances may be heard and wrongs redressed. May God bless our great Sea King!" The last few words were merely a matter of form, because it was well known that the Buccaneer and all his people were the Lord's anointed. The trumpets again sounded and the procession, or march past, of the disaffected was ordered to begin; but now another grave difficulty arose; who was to lead? The mistress of the ceremonies, following a time-honoured custom, was for bringing on the ladies first, but a noisy lot of Ojabberaways declared that their burden of oppression was so great as to do away with all traditions, and that unless they were allowed to have their own way, no business should be done.

Nothing, perhaps, showed the unfortunate state into which things had been allowed to pass, than the extreme licence which the Ojabberaways were allowed to have. They had been given an inch and they had taken the proverbial ell. A small tribe of people, headed by a small band of paid patriots, who reaped a rich harvest out of the disaffection of their countrymen, was allowed to obstruct all business and dictate to the great Sea King or Buccaneer, what he was to do, and how and at what time he was to do it. All this was the handiwork of Madam Liberty, who used Dogvane and a few of his watch, to carry out her designs.

Even Dogvane had said that he must be clothed with sufficient authority to enable him to rule this obstreperous people, but Dogvane had veered round a little; and under his protection the

Ojabberaways had become a perfect nuisance, doing very much as they liked.

They gained their point, and with a wild yell, peculiar to their country, and as blood curdling as the cry of the savage when his hand grasps the scalp of an enemy, they came on. Some had on masks; some carried blunderbusses, while others, under their coats, concealed the dagger of the assassin, and the cartridge of the dynamitard. On they came, dragging, with ropes round their necks, a lot of unfortunates whose general bearing and appearance showed that they had seen better days. These poor gentlemen—for gentlemen they were—had the misfortune to own land in the green and fertile isle of the Ojabberaways, some indeed had Ojabberaway blood in their veins; but they belonged to the hated class called landlords, and their chief crime was, that owning land, they expected their tenants to pay rents.

No doubt, in the past, injuries had been done and very much injustice. They may have been hard and even grinding, and even now there might be some amongst them who were not a credit to their class; but that scarcely justified a refusal to fulfil all legal contracts. Their fathers no doubt did many wrongs, lived beyond their means, and ground, in many cases, their tenants down, for there never was an Ojabberaway who could live within his means.

"What is our crime?" cried the captives; "what sins have we committed?"

"What sins have ye committed?" cried the Ojabberaways, in turn. "It's mighty short memories ye have, and eyesight too, for the matter of that. What are your crimes? Have ye not ground the finest peasantry in the world down under your feet? And if it was not you, then it was your fathers, or your grandfathers, or your great grandfathers." They then turned to the Buccaneer: "We want to be rid of these land-grabbers, these blood-suckers."

"What is your grievance against them?" the Buccaneer asked.

"Our grievance! Grievance is it?" they replied. "By the Holy Powers, our country is thick with them. Are we not a down-trodden race? Has not the foot of the conqueror been upon our necks for ages past? It's a forgetful memory that perhaps ye have?"

"In the past," the Buccaneer said, "injury may have been done to you, but ample amends have now been made; and I rule you with the same laws as I do my other people. What more, in reason, can you ask?"

"We want no laws of your making. We ask that the last link of the chain that binds us to you may be broken. We demand our independence."

Now one of the victims spoke: "We have our rights too," he said, addressing the Buccaneer, "and we claim your protection. For many years we have been your garrison and we are a law-abiding people. We have been faithful and loyal to you; will you then see us dragged before you with ropes round our necks, and with hands tied behind our backs? Is this to be the reward of our loyalty? We ask for what is the birthright of the meanest of your citizens, protection for our lives and for our own property."

Thus it went on, and ground that had been trodden over often and often before, was trodden over again. The difficulty was now to get rid of this section of the disaffected, for the members showed a disposition to become squatters and take entire possession of the situation. But some divinely-inspired individual raised the cry that there was a free fight going on in an adjacent neighbourhood and so the difficulty was overcome and the Ojabberaways disappeared as if by magic.

The ladies now were ushered in, but again there was a slight delay arising out of a dispute about a matter of precedence. A woman will suffer almost any indignity rather than that of being put in a position lower than that to which she thinks herself entitled, and it is probable that in many cases a woman would rather go to the devil in her proper place than to Heaven out of it. The matter was settled and Madam Liberty ushered in Miss Progress. She was by no means attractive, and in her dress she aped somewhat the man. She prided herself upon her intelligence and looked with disdain upon things usually considered to belong peculiarly to the female sex. This advanced lady showed none of the modesty or timidity usually found in women. In a voice loud and clear she said : " I claim for women equal rights with men. By brute force we have been kept under and we now demand our freedom. Man has made us his hewers of wood and his drawers of water ; the cookers of his food and the sewer on of his buttons and the nurser of his squalling brats. Is woman never to rise superior to such a base position ? Is she for ever to be a slave, at man's beck and call ? Away with such a thought ! We demand equal rights and equal voice in all matters, for we are man's equals, and no longer will we live under laws made by man for the benefit of man. We will board yonder ships. Our voice shall be heard in your councils, and our voice shall ring out from your pulpits."

This language was comprehensive and bold. Some amongst the grand company gave signs of approval. Then a dead silence followed, which was broken by the old cox'sn, who having first of all hitched up his trousers, exclaimed : " Mates, I thank my stars that my lower rigging keeps up without buttons." Just as Miss Progress was again going to begin, old Jack cried out : " Vast heaving, my hearty ! " This familiar language on the part of a common sailor very much annoyed the lady, who, fixing her spectacles full upon the cox'sn, asked him who he was. " I am not surprised, miss, at your asking the question. Now, it's no use beating about the bush, and as, miss, you wish to be on an equal footing with man and to rub shoulder to shoulder with him in your daily life, you must not be too tender-skinned, and you will not mind the plain language of an honest sailor. You ask me who I am ? I am Jack Commonsense, very much at your service, miss, and with your permission I will return the compliment and ask you a question. How about your lower rigging ? "

" My lower rigging," cried Miss Progress, " what does the vulgar fellow mean ? "

" Well, miss," Jack replied, " petticoats are all very well in their way, and many a brave and honest lad has run ashore on 'em before now and become a total wreck ; but petticoats do

O

hamper a person a bit, and they ain't the sort of things to go aloft in, in a gale of wind."

"Who want's to go aloft, pray?" Miss Progress asked.

"Well, miss," Jack answered; "you must take the rough with the smooth, and if you are going to be man's equal, you must do your fair share of man's work, and must not cry out if you lose your place in the social order and in man's estimation. Some of you are even now crying out that man does not treat you with the consideration that he used to. The fault lies at your own door. Who is going to take all the blows and hard knocks; and who is going to do all the fighting?"

"Man, of course," replied Miss Progress, "it it his province, his sphere."

"But has not woman her sphere? But let that fly stick to the wall; duty first and pleasure after. As to the fighting, miss; many people think that that spirit is not altogether absent from the female breast. Many go so far as to think that the apple which Eve gave to Adam was flavoured strongly with discord. Never a row yet, so some say, that a woman was not at the bottom of it. Put your helm down, miss, and go about; you and your likes are on the wrong tack. No good ever came yet from a crowing hen; and a maid that whistles ain't likely to be a credit to her family."

The Buccaneer complimented the cox'sn very much and hoped that his language would find favour amongst the ladies. Many of the grand company had dropped off to slumber; others were eagerly engaged in discussions amongst themselves as to whether it would be a good party stroke to take up the ladies. Many were for it and old Dogvane, it was thought, was amongst the number. Miss Progress was by no means satisfied and declared that woman's sphere was very much too narrow. The cox'sn, being encouraged by his master's approval, attacked Miss Progress again in good earnest. "Look'e here, miss," he cried, "your sphere is large enough if you will only do your duty in it; but as is well-known a bad workman always finds fault with his tools. If you try to be man's rival in the world you will come off second best." Many thought that old Jack would before long be in troubled waters; but he marched boldly on. "Woman," he cried out, "has a noble sphere. Let her study to be a good companion for man. Let her aim in life be to make his home comfortable, and his children happy, useful, and good. That, my hearty, is a woman's sphere."

Miss Progress explained to the deaf ears of the grand company that she was single, and the Buccaneer, by way of enlivening the proceedings, asked his cox'sn if he would not take Miss Progress in marriage; but old Jack declined with many thanks, and he told the lady in brutally plain language that spinsters were likely to increase if many women followed in her wake. Then speaking at the whole sex, through the lady before him, he exclaimed: "Too many of you are gadders about, and are to be found everywhere but in your own homes. A good, thrifty, cheerful, and pleasant housewife is a thing of the past. Too many women in the lower walks of life by neglecting their first duty, drive their husbands to the fireside of the pot-house, and their children to their workhouse."

Other of the Buccaneer's women now came forward. One wanted to banish vice from the streets by the strong arm of the law. She drew attention to what she called the gross immorality of the age, and had she had her way she would have shut up half the theatres, or turned them into churches; and have burned most of the light literature of the day. Perhaps this would have been no disadvantage. She also would have dressed all the nude figures in the Buccaneer's several academies, leaving nothing but her own bare shoulders of an evening to offend the eyes of modesty. The female mind does at times go to strange extremes. Another peculiarity of the Buccaneer's people was that most of the racy light literature in his tight little island was written by the women, and how they became so well acquainted with the shady side of human nature was a mystery. But genius can explain all things. There is only one thing to be said against driving vice from the streets by the strong arm of the law. She is so very likely to find shelter in private houses, when the purity of the domestic hearth would probably suffer.

After this lady came another who wanted the Buccaneer to banish from his realms all violent death. She said: "To furnish your idle sons with sport, birds are slaughtered, and hares and foxes are cruelly chased to death."

"Young hounds must be blooded," the Buccaneer said.

"Under the cloak of science," the lady continued, "animals are cruelly tortured, under the inhuman plea that man is to benefit. Then men love to see cocks spur each other to death, while dogs are allowed to fight amongst themselves and worry cats in the public streets, without any interference on the part of the brutal police." The lady finished up by asking the Buccaneer to banish all violent death from the island, and thus set a good example to the rest of the world. "Let the butcher die," she cried, "rather than his innocent unoffending victims."

All eyes were turned upon Billy Cheeks, the burly butcher of the Starboard Watch, and many pitied him, and the cook who was a merry man, said to his friend in a jesting manner: "Billy! old fellow, it was not for nothing that you had that nervous attack in my galley, but cheer up, you are not dead yet."

The Buccaneer now began to talk the matter over with his trusty friend, who said, "Well, yer honour, only speaking for myself, I don't like meat that dies a natural death, though no doubt your butchers will be glad enough to sell it. Indeed, some of them will do it now when they can."

Here a pale-faced, solemn, and even miserable-looking man exclaimed: "Why partake of animal food which brutalizes, when a bountiful Providence has placed at your hand a vegetable kingdom? Eat, I would say, of the crumbs that fall from the celestial pantry."

Both the Buccaneer and his cox'sn declared that they did not see how they were going to make a good square meal out of such a diet, upon which the last speaker said: "If you must nourish your unrighteous stomachs, you will find that lentils and even peacods are both pleasant and sustaining.'

"What say you to this, Jack?" asked the Buccaneer.

"Give him rope, yer honour, and before long he will come to the thistles, and then we had better write ourselves down asses at once. If we go on, on this tack, sir, there will be no such thing as getting a chop, or a steak, or even a homely rasher for either love or money, and the best thing for me to do is to turn to and dig my own grave. But master, there is another thing that troubles me, though I scarcely like to give vent to my thoughts before so goodly a company." Jack upon being earnestly solicited to unburden himself by his master, said: "Well, sir, it's this way. If we are to banish all violent death from this fair isle of ours, what about the flea?"

The allusion to this vulgar insect caused no little confusion in so goodly an assembly, and a wave of irritation seemed to pass through the whole crowd, affecting even the Lords Spiritual, and Miss Progress was so put about by being kept in the back-ground, whilst so much good time was being wasted upon so trivial a matter, that she exclaimed with considerable warmth, "Perish the flea!" Upon this old Jack cried out to the amusement of all, "There I am with you, miss; but first of all you've got to catch him."

The bold Buccaneer was extremely tickled, and his sides shook with merriment, and of course every one joined in. So great was the mirth that the whole noble structure was shaken to its very foundation, so much so, that the old lion got up from his recumbent position, and looked round in a terrified manner, and the cox'sn cried out as he turned towards the company, "Vast heaving, my hearties! Clap a stopper upon your laughing gear, and make all merriment fast."

The shrill blast of a herald's trumpet now claimed the attention of all, and the aggrieved women were dismissed with a promise that their case should receive the consideration it deserved, and the probability of a Royal Commission was hinted at, and with this they were obliged to be satisfied. Again the shrill notes of a brazen trumpet pierced the air, and silence unfolded her wings and hovered over the company. Now a herald, gorgeously apparelled in cloth of gold, emblazoned back and front in the customary fashion, entered upon the scene, and expectation was all on tip-toe.

"A messenger, a messenger, no doubt," cried Dogvane, "from his august and most sable Majesty King Hokee with dispatches from the most noble Bandit of the East."

With much pomp and ceremony the herald advanced, carrying over his left shoulder a spear, and in his right hand what looked like a battered beaver hat, with the crown knocked out. Halting in front of the Buccaneer, he exclaimed, after having made the usual obeisance, "Most noble and illustrious Sea King, ruler of the universe, the holder of the only key to Heaven, the redresser of wrongs, the chastiser of the evil doer, and the terror of the oppressor, know that a little while since, while yet the day was but a few hours old, two friendly factions of the Ojabberaways met, and entered upon an argument apparently from opposite premises, and this is the conclusion that they arrived at." With this he stuck his spear into the battered beaver, for such it was, and raised it up on high, for an admiring crowd to gaze upon. When curiosity was satisfied a very high state official took charge of the interesting relic, and it was conveyed with much ceremony to one of the Buccaneer's principal museums.

It must be owned that to sit and listen to the complaints of so many people was trying to the patience of all; but the Buccaneer and his family were well trained to this sort of thing, and even liked it. Sunday after Sunday the uncrowned queen, Respectability, sent them all to church, sometimes even twice. There they sat quietly under their favourite pulpit, and listened without a murmur to their pastor, who frequently either chided them as children, treated them as fools, or eternally damned them all as incorrigible sinners.

The upper ranks of the Buccaneer's people now came on and complained that their heels were being kicked by those who came after them, and that the respect that once was given to rank and social position was now grudgingly bestowed, if indeed it was bestowed at all. The deputation was presented with the proverb which the Buccaneer and his cox'sn had picked up in their roving days on the Spanish Main, and they were recommended to have it framed and hung up in some convenient place, where their children might be able to look upon it.

The Squire followed, and he again laid bare his numerous complaints; said he could never remember the time when he was in such low water, for he could get little or nothing out of his tenants, whilst his burdens were more than he could bear. Scarcely had he finished speaking, when his tenants appeared in a body, and declared, that owing to the foreign cheap-Jacks underselling them, they could not get enough out of the land to keep body and soul together, let alone money enough to pay their landlord rents. Some of these tenants complained too, that the clergy were too exacting, and made no abatement in their tithe charge; but demanded the pound of flesh that was in their bond.

This brought the clergy forward, and they declared that their claim was the first charge upon the land, which was taken subject to the burden. The pulpit produces the speaker, if it does nothing else. "Is it not in our bond," they said, "that we shall have the tenth part of the yearly increase arising from the profits of the land, the stock upon the land, and the personal industry of those living upon the land, or a just equivalent for these?"

There was now a most learned discussion upon the origin and nature of the tithe charge, all of which did little less than breed confusion. The argument was taken up amongst the company. Some said that it began first as a purely voluntary offering, but that long since a crafty priesthood had fossilized it into a hard and fast legal right, which weighed heavily upon the land in such hard times. The clergy said that it was on account of the hardness of men's hearts that the offering had to be legalized into a right. "If," they said, "the charge were left to the free will of man, we should soon starve, for man would give nothing in so selfish, degenerate, and worldly an age. The custom is sanctioned by age and by Divine authority, for did not Abraham, when he spoiled the five kings, give a tenth part of the spoils to Melchisedek?" No one seemed bold enough to deny this, and the clergy finished up by saying that as they were called upon to fulfil their obligations, so they must call upon other people to fulfil theirs.

This seemed but reasonable; but just as the Buccaneer was going to deliver judgment, the poor clergy took the opportunity to come forward and present their grievance, which was to the effect that they, and their families, were in many cases in want. Upon being appealed to, the High Priest and Lords Spiritual declared that it was so, and that it reflected the greatest discredit upon the Buccaneer and all his people, for it betokened a selfish hardness of heart that was most unchristian-like.

The poorer clergy were treated to a most excellent discourse upon the beauties of poverty, which beauties, it would appear, that even the clergy love best to contemplate at a distance, which in this, as in most things else, lends enchantment to the view. It was pointed out to this section of the disaffected, by those in spiritual authority, that Christ Himself was a great advocate for poverty and condemned in no measured terms the greed after riches; that all His early disciples were poor and lowly, and that His religion was propagated by a band of holy, but shoeless beggars. The poor clergy were bid to find comfort in this, and walk in the path to which they had been called with a sanctified humility.

The old cox'sn now got himself into disgrace, for he turned round and asked the preacher how he could reconcile the precept with the general practice. How, if poverty was such a fine thing, the clergy did not practise it themselves. The high ecclesiastics to whom Jack addressed himself did not condescend to answer so impertinent a remark, but all chance of Church preferment was for ever gone from the old cox'sn, and it is even possible that if he then had died he would not have been allowed Christian burial.

"This difficulty," cried the Buccaneer, "can be easily overcome." Then turning to his Lords Spiritual and other high church dignitaries, he said, "While some on board of your ship, my lords, have too much, others have too little of this world's wealth. A little while since some amongst you preached a homily upon the beauties of poverty. All of you follow the Master who said that it is easier for a camel to go through the eye of a needle than for a rich man to enter the Kingdom of Heaven, and when that rich man is a priest, how doubly hard must be the task. Therefore, I say to you, as I have said before, and in the language of Him whom you profess to follow, 'sell all that you have and give it to the poor,' or at least, share your riches amongst your poorer brethren."

Now, when those in authority on board the old Church Hulk heard this they were extremely sorrowful and sorely grieved, for many of them had large incomes and other worldly possessions, while some had fashionable and ambitious wives, and many had large families, and, as everyone knows, it is hard enough to serve two masters, and next to impossible when the masters are increased to many.

The old cox'sn, who was of a pious turn, wondered what would happen if Christ were to appear again upon earth and enter some one of the Buccaneer's many temples where the perfumed flowers of his fashionable society worshipped God, or, perhaps many gods, in all their pride and splendour. Jack, however, kept his counsel. He was an humble individual and it was not for him to meddle in such weighty matters.

Close upon the heels of the Church came the Buccaneer's lawyers, and true chips were these of the ancient block. The members of the Devil's own, as they were called, complained that an interfering fellow on board of the old Ship of State had called them brigands and other offensive names. This they did not so much mind, but what they did object to was, that busy bodies, instead of paying attention to their own business, wanted to meddle with theirs, and by so doing, to curtail their perquisites and cut down their fees. Of all the Buccaneer's trades and professions, in no one was the principle of the parable before alluded to more conspicuous than in his legal profession, the members of which not only fleeced their sheep, but flayed them, whenever they had the smallest opportunity. The estimation they were held in, even amongst the Buccaneer's people, was shown by the fact that in all his works of fiction, either on the stage or in novels, almost all the rogues were provided by the legal profession.

But the spirit of robbery to which allusion has been so frequently made, was to be found even where it ought not to have existed. Many of the Buccaneer's schools were presided over by members of his State Church and many of his teachers were drawn from the same source. Now some of these, in an underhand way, robbed the parents of the boys intrusted to their charge, for they were paid extremely well, if not exorbitantly, to educate their pupils, but in too many cases they taught them little or nothing, and sent them home, into the bargain, to live a good portion of the time at their parents' expense. Then at the end of what was by courtesy called their academical career, the young birds were sent out into the world veritable fledgelings as regards their knowledge, with not feathers sufficient to cover the nakedness of their ignorance or to fly in search of food. This is at the top of that scale at the bottom of which lies the vulgar thief who breaks through and steals.

After the lawyers came the doctors, who complained that people apparently had little or no inclination to get ill. They declared there seemed to be a selfish desire on the part of every one to keep the time-honoured and much-trusted family doctor out in the cold, and if it were not for the love which still kept a strong hold upon the people, to over-eat and over-drink themselves, their profession would be but a poor one, though in young children they still found some little support. Whether the doctors robbed the people or not, could not very easily be told as they rendered no details with their accounts.

The next lot to appear, showed by their double chests and double chins that they were no strangers to good living, and no doubt beneath their capacious waistcoats lay the tail end of many a bottle of their master's wine. These men complained that their masters had become so niggardly and looked after things so closely themselves, that perquisites (by some called plunder) were quite things of the glorious past, so that the modest independence with the public house, the lodging house, or the green-grocer's shop, was put so far away into the future as to come too late, if it ever came at all.

These much ill-used individuals had the same sad story to tell about foreign competition. They declared people came over in crowds from their neighbours and took the bread out of their mouths. Now came the women servants, resplendent in their cheap finery, and with airs and graces aped from their betters. Some of these quarrelled with some thing, some with another, and one and all seemed considerably above their position, being much too proud to work.

Before dealing with these the Buccaneer ordered on the masters and mistresses so that by hearing their side of the story he might be the better able to judge. It was a sign of the times that the servants came on first, and many believed that this merely was the finger post which pointed to a state of things, when all would be changed and the classes would be the humble and obedient slaves of the masses, when King Mob would wield the sceptre over the Buccaneer's people. It, therefore, behoved those interested to see that their future masters were properly educated.

The employers now declared that it was almost impossible to get good servants. Not one would bear correction. They demanded high pay for doing very little work, and grumbled at all times both at the quality and the quantity of their food. They declared that the lower orders were now so educated that all the girls preferred either to go into shops, or into the school-room, and then the suffering upper classes were called upon to support institutions to keep these spoilt children off the streets. There was a general complaint too, that the stomachs of the serving classes had become so dainty, that they turned up their noses at what their betters were very well contented with, and there was a general concurrence of opinion that, rather than put up with the insolence, ignorance, and idleness of the Buccaneer's own people, masters and mistresses would either do without servants altogether, or employ foreigners, who were more industrious, very much more sober, and quite as honest as the Buccaneer's people, while they did not go to their local clubs or pot houses, and talk over their master's affairs, and disclose to the vigilant burglar the whereabouts of their master's silver. Nor were they in league with the local tradesmen to rob their masters.

"Away with you all," cried the Buccaneer, addressing the servants. He was always ready to condemn peculation on such a scale as this. "Away with you," he cried, "for you are all robbers in disguise. Speak to them, Jack, and trounce them well with thy tongue."

"Aye, aye, yer honour. 'Bout ship, my lads and lasses, before shame and misfortune throw their grappling irons on board of you. You're heading for the jail and the work-house, and before you lie poverty and misery. 'Bout ship, I say, before you find that hunger is the best sauce for a proud stomach."

This batch went away more dissatisfied than ever, and they declared that the old coxswain's language was brutal in the extreme, and they swore they would have nothing to do with such a fellow as that. They determined to get some one of the ship's crew, who wanted some opportunity to bring himself before the public, to take their case up, and by putting a heavy tax upon foreign labour, give them greater opportunities to be independent, more idle, and insolent.

CHAPTER XXXVII.

THE Buccaneer thought that for a contented and prosperous people he had his fair share of disaffection; but Liberty now ushered in a pale-faced and solemn looking batch, who declared that drink was sending the Buccaneer's people to the dogs and the devil. They carried in front of them a banner on which was depicted a drunkard beating his wife, and ill-using his starved children. On the reverse, there was the besotted mother and the sober but miserable husband. This cheerless-looking lot, upon whose features laughter-loving mirth never seemed to dwell, were the total abstainers, who declared that nothing would save the Buccaneer and his people, except they were all made sober by law.

"Why, Jack!" cried the Buccaneer, turning to his friend, "one lot wants to feed me on peacods, while another wants to drench me with water."

But now a portly lot of red-faced, pimply-nosed publicans, whose stomachs were as round as one of their own beer barrels, pushed their way to the front, and swore that water was being the ruin of them. They told the Buccaneer in plain and unmistakable language, that if his people continued to walk in the paths of sobriety at the same rate at which they were at present going, the source from which he derived no little of his revenue would be completely dried up, and he would lose millions of his yearly income, when his upper classes would have to bear the burden of increased taxation.

The Buccaneer always taxed his upper classes as much as ever he could. Perhaps this was right. Besides, what was called the people, that mighty, but barely defined force, did not like taxation, and therefore they were exempted; but they had no prejudice otherwise against the principle.

The Buccaneer was touched, and after a moment's consideration he said, "Why can't my subjects drink in moderation, and not make beasts of themselves?"

"Why not, indeed, sir?" answered the publicans. "A man in moderation can take a good quantity of liquor and not hurt himself, and yet benefit the trade and his country. We set our face against your habitual drunkard. He is our enemy, because he gives in too soon. It is the steady drinker; the man who is always at it, and yet who never gets himself into difficulties, that is our friend."

To lose millions a year. This was indeed a serious affair, and the Buccaneer feared that those muddling water drinkers would do him considerable harm. But there was a bright spot looming in the distance, for had not his trusty Captain Dogvane told him that there was a heathen nation with an immense population to be civilised? Of course it was against his religious principles that he should place drunkenness within easy reach of this people; but then, if at the same time he gave them his Book, and rescued them from the devil, that would be a fair exchange, and in all things human, there must be shortcomings; things that one would willingly prevent if one could, but we cannot expect perfection in this world, and we must therefore have recourse to that most useful and necessary custom of winking at things we cannot help. It is much to be regretted, that the heathen with civilisation will take to strong liquors, as naturally apparently as a duck takes to water. But he does, so there is an end of it. The Buccaneer now eased his conscience by being extremely severe upon his publicans whom he read a sharp lecture. He treated them in a most haughty manner, said they were a demoralizing agency; a blot, a blemish, and a disgrace; but still he took their money. He told them they had better take care of themselves.

The publicans said that was the very thing of all others they would try to do; but they added that the officers of the Buccaneer's Revenue were so precious sharp, and were so much against them, and were down upon them with such heavy penalties if they attempted to help their friends the teetotallers, by watering their ales, and other strong drinks, that virtue had no chance to be over-virtuous. They declared that the licentious Revenue officers hovered over them like a lot of hungry vultures; and with their meddlesome ways were doing an infinity of mischief.

The publicans were a mighty power in the Buccaneer's kingdom, and it is to his credit that he rebuked them even as he did. He read them a lecture, and having in his mind's eye the banner of the teetotallers he pointed out to the delinquents the frightful consequences of drink. The publicans were quite equal to the occasion, they said that there were two sides to every question, and that the devil himself was not half as black as he was painted. To this the Lords Spiritual took exception, and they rose in a body and entered their protest against such a blasphemous assertion. Of course this weighty matter could not be argued out at such a time, or in such a place; but it was taken up on board the old Church Hulk, and received there all the attention it deserved, and no doubt it was the means of adding still more to the Buccaneer's numerous sects.

Some were inclined to subject the devil to the fashionable process known as white-washing. As every eminent blackguard in ancient, and up to a certain time even in modern history, has undergone this treatment, there is no reason why his satanic majesty should be left out in the cold. It seems hard that the blackguard Judas should not have been favoured, but perhaps some champion will yet arise to take up his cause. Does not the Christian world owe him something? Would it have been saved from the torments of hell, if Judas had not played the betrayer's part? The publicans said there was a good deal of prejudice about drink. That party feeling here, as elsewhere, ran extremely high, engendering very much animosity, and thus a good deal of obloquy and unjust reproach was heaped upon the head of the poor drunkard. They begged that the subject might be approached in no mean or narrow spirit. They maintained that the drunkard, if only a steady going drunkard, and a man of regular habits, was a public benefactor. One who did his best through the means of indirect taxation to swell the revenues of the State, and as a vast number of the Buccaneer's people paid no direct taxes, the only way they helped to keep up the dignity, the honour, the welfare, and the safety of the empire was by getting as drunk as they could, as often as they could. Indeed, looking at it from their point of view, the greater the drunkard, the greater the benefactor he was to the community; he being a man who sacrificed himself, and frequently his family, for the sake of his country, as every good citizen should. If he broke down occasionally under the burden of indirect taxation, he was an object more of pity than of contempt. And if he beat his wife, and starved his children, what then? The individual must at all times be sacrificed for the sake of the general public. So eloquent were the publicans, and there was so much force in what they said, that the Buccaneer began to waver. The publicans seeing the good impression they had made, continued on in the same direction, and pointed out that if the teetotallers set up the pump and pulled down the pot-house, that not only would the great Buccaneer lose his revenue, but that his people would assuredly become gourmands, for that there never was a total abstainer who was not a large if not a coarse feeder, and of the two, a drunkard, they declared, bad as he was, was infinitely to be preferred to a glutton.

The case was undoubtedly a serious one. Not one amongst the grand company—not even Dogvane himself—would dare to give an opinion directly against the publicans, such was their power in the island. The Buccaneer was obliged to admit that the drunkard was a despicable rascal, and the cause of very great misery; but then the public-houses brought in such a very large revenue.

There appeared to be only one way out of the difficulty and that was to have recourse to a Royal Commission. This institution which has before been mentioned, requires to be explained, for it was extremely useful to the Buccaneer and got him out of many difficulties. It was a wonderful institution and had many and various virtues. It was supposed to contain a cure for every evil under the sun and to possess wonderful powers of finding out ills and their several remedies; and it was supposed to have a microscopic eye, and a bright intelligence, that shed a light into the darkest holes and corners. At least, it was supposed to do all this. It was a mysterious institution, having, indeed, some of the attributes of the Inquisition. There was one thing about it that was evident to all. It was extremely slow in its working, and perhaps in this lay no little of its virtue, for anything that it took under its consideration faded away from public view long before any conclusion was arrived at, and thus it may be said that it squeezed all the life out of whatever it sat upon, and then buried its victim in some official pigeon-hole, or other tomb belonging to oblivion.

What the publicans had said brought forward the butchers; but Billy Cheeks had nothing to do with these. They declared they were doing scarcely any business. They said that however true it might be, as a general rule, about water-drinkers being large eaters, they saw no signs of total abstinence in this respect amongst the people. They added that what with foreign competition and the growing carefulness of housekeepers, who kept far too sharp an eye upon their allies the cooks, their profits were falling off every day. Then they pointed out that their trade was being threatened by the vegetarians, who could stuff themselves to repletion for about sixpence, or even less. Now a farmer, who having heard what the butchers had said, declared butchers ought to be making large fortunes, for that they charged the people quite double, and sometimes more, than what they gave for the meat. This was quite true, but then the butchers only acted upon that principle of robbery which was to be detected in the breast of most of the trading Buccaneers, and was all due, no doubt, to an old Sea King, or pirate, having taken to business in his latter years, and the principle on which he traded, namely, of turning his five talents into ten.

The dispute between the burly farmer and the burly butcher

seemed likely to end in blows; but the vegetarians stepped in and acted as a buffer. They declared that animal food was not at all necessary, and that if men would only feed upon vegetables there would be no wars and they would live longer and more intellectual lives.

"If that comes to pass," said old Jack, "farewell to the lowing herds and the bleating flocks, for man isn't going to keep these things to look at, and a pretty flabby weak-kneed lot we shall be. Give me my chop and toothsome steak, say I."

Jack was told that he was very much behind the time and that science was dead against him. This discussion was put an end to by the appearance of the milkmen who complained that they had suffered considerably since they had been stopped manufacturing their own cream, adulterating their milk with water, and mixing fat with their butter. In fact, all the tradesmen had the same story to tell, and cried out against the stringent laws which ground them down to a rigid line of honesty. Perquisites and peculation, they declared, were almost things of the past, and they added that all this was strictly against the interests of trade, and was not according to precedent. They wanted to know where the Buccaneer would have been if, in his fine old Buccaneering days, he had been so hampered. In conclusion they declared that a too rigid honesty was not compatible with prosperity, and that though "honesty is the best policy" is a capital text to put over your door, it is a bad principle to practise behind the counter. They added that "*caveat emptor*" ought to be the motive power between man and man in all his mercantile transactions, and that idiots should be left to take care of themselves.

This unprincipled language horrified the Buccaneer, who having long since become wealthy, could now afford to be honest, virtuous, and respectable. So he condemned, in no measured terms, these nefarious adulterators, and would-be peculators. It is true that these tradesmen were but chips of the ancient block; but that block had now been laid aside, and was only produced on very great and state occasions, when the magnitude of it quite overshadowed all the small chips that had been cut from it, and the block was so highly polished that it looked altogether beautiful and quite virtuous.

But who are these men, who look like whitened sepulchres, that are treading so closely upon the heels of the milkmen?

These are the Buccaneer's bakers, who declared that nearly all the Buccaneer's bread was made by foreign hands, who were literally taking the very bread out of the mouths of the Buccaneer's own sons.

The Buccaneer knew there was very great truth in this. But how was he to remedy the evil? His was a free land and people ever had been allowed to come and to go at their own pleasure; and to buy and sell, and to make their money as best they could. Then the bakers had the same complaint about the severity of the law, which kept so strict an eye upon them all to the detriment of trade, that it was not safe to use any of the substances so useful in adulterating bread, such as bean meal, rice flour, potatoes and peas, indian corn, salt, and alum. Of course they admitted that too much alum was not good for the human stomach, but that was no business of theirs, and the human stomach could adapt itself to all things, so wonderfully and marvellously was it made.

The brewers next had their say, and declared that their ales and stouts stood a chance of being washed out of the market by the light beverages from the other side of the water, and that these and wishy-washy wines were ruining their trade, and undermining the constitution of the people. These malcontents declared that this was but the thin end of the wedge which was eventually to cleave the Buccaneer's prosperity asunder. It was by good strong brewed ales and beef that he had made himself what he was, and unless John Barleycorn was reinstated they fully believed that the Buccaneer would dwindle down to the mere shadow of his former self.

This oration met with general approval; for there were many who thought that beer and beef produced good muscle, sound bodies, and healthy and courageous minds; but a sickly smile played upon the features of the teetotallers and vegetarians, who pitied all those whose minds were so much clouded by ignorance.

Now a general cry rose up from amongst the traders against the buyers, who, it was said, were ruining trade by their co-operation, which, it was declared, had taken all the gilt off their gingerbread. The strange part of the thing was, that while the shopkeepers claimed the privilege of combining together to fleece their customers they denied the latter the right of combining together for their own protection. "How," they asked, " were poor people to maintain their families, make a modest competence, and support their public burdens, if the consumers patronized co-operative stores?" They all declared that in days, unhappily long since past, people lived quite as long as they did now, if not longer. This they considered a conclusive proof that adulteration, if conducted upon the principles of moderation, was not detrimental to the coatings of the human stomach, which, they said, was being ruined by the extreme care that was being taken of it, until indeed there was a good chance of that pampered and petted member ruling the whole body in a most tyrannical manner. The stomach had been made to do certain work; then why relieve it of its responsibility?

The tailors now advanced, and they also had their grievance; for they declared that the atmosphere was so impregnated with honesty that their cabbages were nothing like as fine as what they used to be; and they made the same cry out against foreign competition. The shoemakers had the same tale to tell. Behind these came the handmaids to fashion and folly, who declared that their field of operation was becoming more and more contracted, not on account of any falling off in the vanity of the female sex, but on account of the cruel laws that had been passed to guard the husbands against the extravagance of their wives. All this they declared was extremely unjust and entirely against the interest of trade.

The honest Hodge family now came lumbering along, and each member carried in his hands a halter of rope. The Buccaneer beheld them with amazement, for he feared they were going to take a leaf out of the Ojabberaways' book and make a prisoner of the poor old Squire. He was relieved to find they had no such intention. The Hodge family were one and all agriculturalists, but they declared that times were sadly out of joint with them. They said they wished to make a prisoner of no one; but they each of them had been promised a cow and a bit of land, by a gentleman they saw amongst the grand company, and they had brought the bit of rope to lead their beast back. "Hodge," cried the Buccaneer, "your bed may not be one of roses; but your condition has wonderfully improved. Your wages in the last fifty years have been doubled, and so have your comforts. You ever have had the reputation of being an honest fellow, willing to earn by the sweat of your brow a living; keep in the same track. Remember promises are made of pie crust, and take care, my honest fellow, that designing people neither make a tool nor a fool of you." Hodge scratched his head to try by gentle irritation to conjure his brain into such a state of activity that he might understand the situation, but he found no relief, and had to go away muttering to himself that "summut must be wrong somewhere."

A complete damper was now put upon the whole of the proceedings, by the appearance of a most melancholy and miserable-looking body of men. On their faces woe, deep woe, sat enthroned, and their dress bore testimony to the depth of their sorrow. This mournful section of the disaffected could scarcely speak for emotion. It was a deputation from the undertakers, who declared that unless something was done to revive and encourage their drooping trade, they would all have to throw themselves upon the community by entering the workhouse. They said their business was not what it had been or what it ought to be. Though perhaps they did not suffer as much as other traders from foreign competition, people still having sufficient respect for themselves to wish to be buried in home-made coffins, yet the general depression, but more especially that which bore so heavily upon their worthy friends, the publicans, bid fair to ruin them. Indeed, they saw little before them but their own tenantless coffins. Then they said that buryings had so fallen off that little or no margin for profit was left, for not only had they decreased in number, but also considerably in quality. People, they declared, seemed to take more care of themselves than they used to; eating less, and drinking less; consequently living longer. Then when they died they generally left behind them strictly economical and even niggardly instructions, and worse still, relations who were mean enough to carry them out. They said all this was against the interests of trade, and ought to be put a stop to. All hired grief, they declared, was a drug upon the market. The nodding funereal plumes were fast vanishing. The pensive, sorrow-faced, and red-nosed mute, they declared, would soon be a being of the past, and would only live in the pages of history, unless some fresh life was put into him by more frequent deaths, and more decent and expensive funerals. They said that the money now spent upon floral decorations, which in a few hours were crushed under the earth, if they did not find their way to the grave-digger's cottage, would keep a mute in drink and his wife and family in bread for many weeks, and they declared that such sinful waste ought to be put down by the strong arm of the law. It was a pity, they said, that such a hardness of heart had seized upon the Buccaneer's people, for that now the circumstances of the deceased could no longer be told by the funeral obsequies, and that now many a great, and even rich man, went to his last resting-place with no more pomp, than if he had been one of mean degree. A few widows perhaps, whose hearts were stricken with remorse for the lives they had led their husbands, and out of gratitude for the comfortable circumstances they had been left in, still showed liberality, but the number, though respectable, was not more than sufficient to give a small flicker to the dying lamp of their prosperity.

With eyes brimful of tears, they declared that their old friends, the doctors, were deserting them, for they did not now kill half the people they used to, and there seemed to be a selfish desire on all sides to cheat the grave, and consequently to injure the undertakers.

Then they declared that science was doing an infinity of harm by poking its nose into every offensive smell it came across, by trapping drains, emptying, and forbidding cesspools, and finding sanitary preventions for nearly every disease. This, they declared, was violating one of the Buccaneer's most cherished principles, namely, the liberty of the subject. They further said that their trade now, owing to the doctors, science, and the spread of education, which was an enemy to dirt and drains, seldom, if ever, received a fillip from the friendly hand of an epidemic. As the absence of outdoor, and indoor, parish relief was an index to the prosperity of the country, so they declared that the falling off even in pauper funerals bore ample testimony to their languishing trade.

Thus ended this funeral oration, and it had such an effect upon the Buccaneer that what little spirits he commenced the day with had completely vanished. It seemed to him that each hour brought before him a sadder picture, and he called for the captain of his watch, for he wanted to ask him how he could reconcile what he had said about the general happiness, and prosperity of his people, with this long list of disaffection. But old Dogvane was not to be found. Some said he had only just gone round the corner for a few minutes, while others said he was on duty on board of the old Ship of State.

After a little consideration the Buccaneer made known to the undertakers how deeply he was grieved at their sad story, "But," he added, "in such things it is not well to act with indecent haste, lest some greater injury should be done. So grave do I consider the matter you have brought before me that I promise you a Royal Commission."

With voices quivering with emotion the undertakers thanked their august master for his extreme consideration, and most gracious condescension, and they said they felt sure that if their case was only laid before a Royal Commission it would certainly not be prejudiced by any undue, or indecent haste.

But now there was a great commotion going on in the crowd, and two angry women were heard abusing each other like the proverbial fish-fags. The one was called Fair Trade, the other Free Trade. These two had had a quarrel of long standing, and they never met that they did not exchange compliments. Each carried baskets, in which were various articles of merchandise. They seemed now to have a strong inclination to tear each other to pieces, and their shrill voices were heard for a considerable distance, and forced themselves upon the ears of the grand company.

"If I had my way," cried the one known as Fair Trade, "I would tear all that cheap finery of yours off your back."

"Yes," exclaimed the other, "and stick it upon your own. That costly, but sober looking homespun of yours needs something to set it off," so said Free Trade, who held up before the eyes of the people her cheap wares.

"Buy my home-made loaf," cried Fair Trade.

"Buy mine at half the price," cried Free Trade.

"Better give me double for mine," exclaimed Fair Trade, "than deal with that woman. She is bringing ruin upon us with her cheap trash. Through her our cornfields lie fallow. Through her our industries languish, and some even have passed away from us. Through her our country has been filled with idle hands, and the wolf of want has been brought to many a door."

"They don't seem to have settled their dispute yet, Jack," the Buccaneer said.

"No, sir. A few years since and nothing would do but you must lie the old bluff-bowed ship Protection up, and now some of them are always casting longing eyes at her, and their sighs of regret would fill the sails of a Seventy-Four."

"What!" cried the Buccaneer, in dismay, as he saw Poverty with her large family of ragged and half-starved children now come on to the scene. "You here again. Why I am constantly doing something for you, and my Great Hat is forever being sent round."

"And still I want," said Poverty.

"I have built you model dwellings. I have ordered all your drains to be trapped; your cesspools cleaned, and your dustbins emptied; and all your children I insist upon being sent to school, so that they may learn the efficacy of comfort and cleanliness, and learn to bear with patience their many sufferings."

"But I ask for food," persisted Poverty.

The Buccaneer now said, "I give you, my good woman, the very best of all food, namely, food for the mind."

But Poverty answered, "Why turn the lamp of knowledge into my hovel? Why teach me that while others have plenty, I am in rags, cold, and hungry. Knowledge on an empty stomach is a dangerous thing. To open my eyes is the refinement of cruelty, for ignorance, at least, dulls the edge of misery. If you cannot fill my stomach and patch up the rents in my clothes, then in pity kill me. Send me to a lethal chamber and let me revel for a brief moment in the luxury of one good meal, and let me pass into eternity without the pinching pangs of hunger."

This language shocked every one, and the feeling was still more increased, when Pity, who was standing not far off weeping, said, "Mother, if you cannot feed this poor woman and her many children; if you have no room for them, then for my sake take them to thy bosom, close their eyes, and hush them to sleep in everlasting slumber."

Poverty was chided in a gentle tone by the Buccaneer's High Church dignitaries there assembled, and prayers were said for her, and she was told that though she received stripes and lashes here, in the next world she would be rewarded, and she was bid to fix her gaze upon that region which lies beyond the grave, where the bright star of Hope is forever shining, and where there is neither hunger, cold, nor thirst.

Just as all sympathy was enlisted on the side of this poor woman a circumstance happened that changed the whole current of feeling. Suddenly a cry rose up of "Stop, thief." It was now found that while all interests were centred upon Poverty, one of her children, seeing the opportunity, slipped round, and getting unobserved upon the platform, had crawled along, in a most irreverent manner, under the legs of the Lords Spiritual, and being totally uninfluenced by the atmosphere of sanctity in which he moved, the young rascal had slipped his hand into the capacious pocket of the Buccaneer, and had taken therefrom ever so much gold and silver, while the old coxswain was found to have lost his best silk bandana

This bold act of robbery caused a great commotion, and extreme indignation, and in trying to catch the thief, Poverty was entirely forgotten, for, of course, crime in a community is a much more serious thing than any amount of want, though one is frequently but the offspring of the other.

So indignant was the Buccaneer at this gross act of ingratitude, that directly he regained his composure, he read Poverty a lecture and told her she ought to be ashamed of herself, and that unless she took better care of her children they would be sure to fall into either the jailer's or the hangman's hands. "No wonder," he said, "that misery darkens your doors, and hunger pinches your children's stomachs. Away with you," he cried, "and learn to be honest, thrifty, industrious, and sober, for God alone helps those who help themselves."

There was a twinkle in the old coxswain's eye. He was labouring, like a ship in a gale of wind, under the influence of a joke. A joke is of such a nature that the owner of it cannot keep it in. Like murder it will out. "Master," he said, "your doctrine is a little dangerous. You scold Poverty one moment for what you bid her do the next."

"How so?"

"Why did not her young brat help himself to my bandana and to your superfluous cash?"

The expression on the Buccaneer's face at thus being trifled with, was such that old Jack, to make use of seafaring language, bore away, and mixed amongst the crowd, just as another great hubbub arose from the regions of the disaffected. The grand court was broken up by Demos, who having collected as many as he could of the discontented had raised his standard again and was for enthroning King Mob in the Buccaneer's chair of State. With wild shouts and with flourishes of sticks and other improvised weapons, he came on and demanded a hearing, and many thought there would be just such another to-do as when the old cox'sn so gallantly defended the gorge and regained possession of the Place of Discord.

Demos now in the attitude more of a dictator than a supplicant, demanded of the Buccaneer that capital should be confiscated and divided amongst the people. That luxury should be banished. That all should be made to work for a living and that the hours of labour should be defined, limited, and enforced by law. " By nature," he said, " all are equal, and in the sight of God there is no such thing as class distinction. Every person born is born to an inheritance, and that is a right to live." Demos declared that all property must be common, and all human drones destroyed. He raised the old cry of equality, which history and even nature has proved to be an impossibility.

When the crowd heard the words of Demos there was a great shouting and clapping of hands. This comprehensive scheme somewhat frightened the upper layer of the Buccaneer's society ; some of whom declared that Demos had foreign blood in his veins ; that he was an alien. But Demos cried out, "No alien am I. I am as much your child as those who sit enthroned in high places. They toil not, neither do they spin, but live by the labour of other people. It is against the vampire capital, that I wage my war. That bloodsucker, which feeds upon the industries of your poorer children, who have built up for you your present greatness by the sweat of their brows and by the blood of their bodies."

" And would you, my lad, from sheer envy and hatred," cried the Buccaneer, " pull down in one day what it has taken me so many years of toil to build up ? From what babbling brook have you drunk in your principles ? "

" From no babbling brook," Demos exclaimed, " but from that deep spring which has been handed down to us from ages past. Did not the Great Master, whom yonder old Church Hulk professes to follow, teach us that all men before God are equal, and that all property should be held in common."

Here the High Priest of the Buccaneer rose up and said, " Our Great Master never, by either word or deed taught, or even sanctioned, robbery. On the contrary, He enjoined every man to be contented with that which he had ; not to covet other men's goods. He said, give, but never take. But you are not the first who has tried to distort the Scriptures to serve your own selfish ends."

" Is it not written," said Demos, " him that taketh thy cloak forbid not to take thy coat also ? "

" That neither sanctions nor justifies the confiscation," replied the High Priest. " Is it not also written that the things belonging to Cæsar shall be given to Cæsar ? "

" But who is Cæsar ? " cried Demos. " I am no longer a boy now, to be petted and cajoled, and to be bought over by sweetmeats or a piece of cake. I have a freeman's limbs, give me then a freeman's rights."

It is not to be supposed that on so great an occasion the Buccaneer's old coxswain, Jack Commonsense, was going to remain silent, so he said, as he shoved himself to the front, for he had lost his place in the confusion brought about by the act of robbery on the part of one of Poverty's children. " Master ! " he cried, " I am on in this scene. What rights, my lad," he said addressing Demos, "do you claim that you have not got, except the right of putting your hands into other people's pockets; just because your own happen to be empty or not too full ? This is a robbing of Peter to pay Paul, with a vengeance."

" Who are you," said Demos, " that you should make yourself a judge over us ? "

" Who am I ? " quoth the coxswain. " Who am I, forsooth ! It is a pity, my lad, you should have to ask the question ; but there ; memories the likes o' yours are always short ; who am I, indeed ! why I am Jack Commonsense, very much at your service, my lad, and cox'sn to the honest rover." Suddenly correcting himself, he said, as he lifted his tarpaulin in token of respect, " that is to say, Sea King, that ever ploughed the briny ocean. I have stood by my master, my lad, in fair weather and in foul, and when the stormy winds have blown, and the dark rocks and savage cliffs of danger have been upon our lee, oftentimes I have seized the helm and steered my master clear, and damme, if I will desert him now. Now listen, my lad, and all you whom it may concern, while I spin you a yarn that I picked up on the Spanish Main, ages ago. We picked up many things there, master, did we not ? Dubloons and other treasures. But here's my yarn.

Once upon a time, a man had five sons, and when he was dying he called them round him, and gave to each a fair share of his property, and told them to act to each other as he had acted towards them, and to have all things in common amongst themselves. But one, my lad, so the story goes, d'ye see, was a spendthrift, another was a wine bibber, while another was a glutton; the fourth was a seeker after pleasure, while the fifth was a hard working industrious and sober man. The four first named would do anything but work, and they each gave away their birthright to the fifth; the one for this thing, according to his want, the other for that, until at length the fifth son had possession of the whole patrimony; would you, my lad, were you in his place, divide, and go on dividing amongst your ne'er-do-well brothers to all eternity? Not you, or you are a greater fool than I take you to be. Where then is your community of property? Then as to your equality. That won't wash, my mates. There is no such thing as equality, for one is strong, another weak; one is swift of foot, another slow, while one has more brains than another. Why the hides of asses ain't all of a thickness, and the stick that reaches one, won't touch another; but let that fly stick to the wall, even among thieves and such like vermin, there is no equality, the strongest always getting the lion's share. Take all our master has, and lay it out before you; feast your eyes upon it; gloat over it, and then begin to divide it equally amongst yourselves, and you will be at each other's throats before you know where you are; so much for your brotherly love. Then, my mates, before you commence pulling down, you ought to decide upon what sort of a commonplace hovel you are going to build up. But the first thing you ought to do, is to turn out all the blackguards belonging to our neighbours, for we have enough of our own, and whatever right you think you may have to other people's property, foreign rapscallions can have none, and if you allow them to cry shares, you will be robbing your own honest selves. Trade will languish and die out, for there will be no security for earnings, and no emulation. Ambition, that mighty lever to human actions, will succumb.

Farewell too, to art; and science even will flag for want of nourishment. As luxury is to be banished in our earthly paradise, all carriages will be put down, and all the hands employed in connection with them, will be thrown upon the market. The horses will have to be turned out to grass, and live a life of indolent ease, until they vanish from the land or are turned to a different use, for nature has decreed that nothing useless shall last. The vanities and even the luxuries of the rich furnish thousands of deserving mouths with their daily food ; but all this will have to be stopped, and God alone knows who will benefit. Then I suppose you will occupy the palaces of the rich, as long as they stand, by people of one common level of social standing, and we shall sink into a nation of flats. Let that fly also stick to the wall. Then as no new mansions will be built, for want of wealth, the builders' trade will suffer, and more idle hands will be thrown on the community. Enterprise will die and one trade after another will go, and then farewell to all. The great Sea King upon whose vast empire the sun never sets; the mighty trader, the great pioneer of civilisation ; he whose footprints are to be seen in every part of the universe will sink, unremembered unrespected, and unregretted into the silent tomb of the past and some stronger, and wiser people will take his place.

"Master !" cried the cox'sn turning to the bold Buccaneer, who listened with wonder to old Jack's long-winded harangue. "Master !" he cried, "this Demos is but a boy amongst us yet ; he is a young colt that must be neatly bitted and ridden on the curb, or he will of a surety bolt and fling his rider into the ditch as his forebears have done before him."

Just as things were looking at their worst, the sound of music came over the water from the old Ship of State. It was Pepper, the cheery little cook, the foster father of Demos, playing a tune upon his barrel organ. The strains had a mellowing and soothing influence upon the whole company, and so what at one time bid fair to take a serious turn passed off quietly, and so ends the longest if not the dullest chapter in this eventful history.

CHAPTER XXXVIII.

THE event recorded in the last chapter brought the grand court to a somewhat premature but fortunate conclusion. Though many grievances were made known, it is not recorded that a single one was remedied or redressed, and this perhaps was quite according to precedent.

Dogvane did not see the grand court out; but for reasons of his own, he slipped away and hastened on board of the old Ship of State, where also he found most of his watch; for as the saying is, they seemed to have smelt a rat. He called his merry men on deck. "Mates," he said, "my glass is falling; so likely enough we shall have a strong breeze blowing off shore before long, therefore haul all taught, make all snug, and look out for squalls."

The doughty cook now spoke up, like the bold and clever man that he was. "Captain," he said, "if so be that we are going to have foul weather, why not lighten the ship at once? Chuck over board a couple of dukes, or a brace of earls, or a score or so of common ordinary lords, and the old ship will ride through the storm all the better." It was wonderful, what a dislike Pepper had for the Buccaneer's Upper Chamber, and the people said there must be more in it than appeared on the face of things Nothing the cook would have liked better than to have pickled the whole lot, when the brine would not have been wanting in strength; Billy Cheeks the burly butcher would no doubt have done all the preliminary business with pleasure, for he also had his eye upon the Buccaneer's bloated aristocracy. All this was very strange, for Billy, it was said, had the very best of blood in his veins.

Many thought that beneath the modest bearing of the cook,

there lurked a great ambition, which was no other than to put on old Dogvane's cloak, boots, and collars when nature called that worthy old salt away.

When the cook suggested the lightening of the old ship, Chips the carpenter raised his axe and took up a position beside the hawser that bound the Church Hulk to the Ship of State. The butcher also drew his large knife and felt its edge, for he had quite regained his nerves, and was ready for anything. Old Dogvane smiled approvingly upon their ready zeal; but said, "Steady, my lads, steady. All in good time. No occasion to jettison any of our cargo yet, however useless it may be. You, Billy, who have some smattering of legal knowledge, can explain the meaning of the term. But again, my lads, I ask you, how you came to set that old church drum a beating? The solemn sound as you know will at all times awaken the slumbering feelings of our master. Besides, I myself am considerably affected by it. I should not see that old craft cut adrift without a pang. But see what it has done. It has thoroughly roused our master, and it has raised more devils than we probably shall be able to lay. It's ill to waken sleeping dogs, so says the proverb. The old Squire too is on the tramp, and our master is now for poking his nose into everything. The paint brush, my lads, the paint brush, is at most times better than either the hammer, or the chisel. No offence to your mate, Master Chips." It now came out that Chisel was still ashore, and absent without leave, and many thought he would not come out of it with anything less than a general court martial.

The carpenter now showed a spirit of mutiny that surprised all, and shocked both the cook and the butcher, his, at one time, friends.

"Captain!" he exclaimed, "I've served with you now for many a day, and I've served you well; but the time has come when every honest man should speak his mind. It is all very well for you to put all the blame upon our backs, but let every one bear his own burden. Why did you try the old dodge of throwing dust in our master's eyes? You know he is getting quite accustomed to that sort of thing and can see through it. Why did you tell him all those cock-and-bull stories about contentment, and all that kind of stuff, and induce the old gentleman to hold the Grand Court? Then why did you take him abroad? This it is that has raised all the dust."

"Well, Chips, my lad," cried the old captain, as he dashed a tear from his eye. "This comes hard, very hard from you. For you to turn upon me, cuts me to the very quick. Under the shadow of my wing, you have risen from a low position on board this old craft, to one of great consideration. There was much more in store for you, for I might, in time, have persuaded my master to make either a general or an admiral of you, or you may indeed have risen to be steward of his household. Only that I have a son myself who is the joy of my old age, and the very apple of my eye, and more to me than ever Joseph was to Jacob, it is possible that when I pass away my cloak would have fallen upon your shoulders."

The cook gave the butcher a look and the butcher's breathing became laboured under the weight of suppressed feeling. Old Dogvane continued his address to the carpenter: "Why did I throw dust in the old man's eyes? I am surprised that such a clever lad as you should ask such a simple question. Is it not a time-honoured custom? Have not both the watches done it for ages past? The only error I made was that the dust was not thick enough, and the old man saw through it, and there lies my mistake."

The carpenter was going to answer the captain, for his mutinous spirit was getting the better of him, but the cook seized the carpenter and led him away.

Presently the old Buccaneer was seen slowly walking down to the beach and he was pestered on every side by a swarm of cheap-Jacks of every nation. They hung about him, and as the saying is, they nearly bothered the life out of him. The poor old gentleman seemed to have suffered considerably from recent events, and the sickness of his heart was beginning to pray upon his body. With feeble steps he laboured along and hailed the old Ship of State, but his voice wanted the cheery ring of old.

"Away with you, my lads," cried Dogvane, who heard the Buccaneer's call. "Clear the decks, and each one to his post. Away, and leave the matter in my hands. I will below and look over the chart of public affairs and I will shape a course that will take us out of our difficulties or my name is not William Dogvane. I see the old gentleman has not his busy-body of a coxswain with him, so much the better for my plan. I never could hit it off with that party. Away, my lads, to your posts."

Each one did as he was told, though the carpenter grumbled; but the cook said to him: "Since when, my mate, have you learnt to change your tune?"

"That barrel organ of yours, Master Pepper, may grind away at the same old tune for ever for all I care; but I have my sticking point," said the carpenter. "At any rate I don't shilly-shally about things like old Dogvane does; but I speak out my mind like every honest man should; and look you, my little Pepper, I'm not going to be monkey-led by any man."

"Say you so," replied the cook. "That is a pity; I want a monkey for my organ, and no doubt, you would dance as well as any other."

"Not to your piping, my lad, so stow that. There is a time for all things, Master Pepper. Your jokes and jests are well enough upon a full stomach of contentment, but now they sound flat and feeble. Were I a man easily moved to mirth I might laugh perhaps to-morrow. Look you now! If our little game had come off old William would have been with us heart and soul and then the old fox would have set all sail before a full blast of public opinion, and have taken all credit to himself. But let the wind be doubtful, and he is for ever trimming as if his ship were in a constant sea of doldrums; and what is more, Pepper, he is not above flinging a messmate overboard if it suits his purpose. I'm weary, my lad, of the company I am sailing in."

"Ship of State ahoy!" came from the shore, and interrupted the carpenter's grumblings. A slight breeze came off the land

and shook the shrouds. "Make all taught," cried old Dogvane, "and pipe the pinnace away. I see the cox'sn has put in an appearance after all. I wonder what the devil he wants. I begin to think he is an office-seeker and a place-hunter like the rest of the world." Having said this, Dogvane disappeared below.

Presently the old Buccaneer appeared on board. Not a soul was to be seen. "What!" he cried; "no one on deck. What ho! below there!"

No answer came. He passed by the cook's galley as he went to take a look forward. The cook could be heard reading out the following receipt: "Take one reputation of good social position and pull well to pieces, add one pound of garbage, two ounces of gall and one quart of vinegar, season well with salt and pepper, stew, stir and skim, and serve up when ready."

"A savoury dish that, Master Jack," said the Buccaneer to his coxswain, who replied that at such things the cook of the Starboard Watch had not an equal, and at a dish of scandal he could scarcely be beaten. The Buccaneer, having taken a turn round, came to the after part of the ship, and there he saw old Dogvane with his head just above the after companionway. "Who calls?" he asked in the most innocent manner possible.

"Who calls!" cried the Buccaneer, "and is this the way you look after my affairs? not a soul on deck!"

"Not a soul on deck, sir!" exclaimed Dogvane, in surprise; "then everyone must of a certainty be below." By this time many of the crew had put in an appearance and were busy working away at their respective duties. Chips, having got the better of his fit of ill temper, sang as he worked the following song:

> " My mate is ashore in tow of a lass,
>   Cock-a-doodle,
> A right clever fellow turned into an ass,
>   Cock-a-doodle,
> He's tied by the leg with a petticoat string,
>   Cock-a-doodle,
> And never again will his cheery voice sing
>   Cock-a-doodle."

The look-out man aloft being awakened, no doubt, by the voice of the carpenter, sang out: "All's well." This was official, and Dogvane looked upon it as a good sign. "Your ever watchful man aloft, sir, tells you that all is well; we must perforce believe him, for he is a creditable witness."

"All's well, indeed!" exclaimed the Buccaneer. "What do you mean by telling me that all is well? Are you, Master Dogvane, a knave or a fool; or do you take me to be either the one or the other?"

"God forbid, sir, that I should make so grievous a mistake," replied Dogvane, with humility.

"What did you mean by telling me that my foreign relations were all good, and that my people at home were prosperous and contented?"

"Did I say so much, master? It is on my memory that I did not go so far; I may have said that they ought to be contented. There lies the difference."

"Why, there is not a profession or trade, or even class that is not crying out. My very women are rising in open rebellion. What say you to this?"

"It is passing strange, sir, and only adds one more proof, if it were necessary, of the extreme ingratitude of human nature. There is scarce a thing that we do not take into consideration, and so great is our concern for your welfare that we try to legislate for all your simplest needs, and in time we hope that everything will work with clock-like regularity, and if a man gets drunk even, it shall be by Act of Parliament."

"Pray, sir," asked the Buccaneer, "what business had you below on such an occasion as this?"

"Sir," Dogvane replied, "I was occupied with matters of the gravest importance; something that touches closely upon my master's honour. Master, master," he suddenly cried in an ecstasy of delight, "what think you? I have glorious news; glorious news for you.'

"Glorious news! then out with it, man, for I need something to raise my spirits."

"Sir," cried Dogvane, rubbing his hands with glee. "What think you; I have a concession."

"A concession, man! A concession! that is news indeed. Do you hear, Jack, our honest Dogvane has a concession." The old cox'sn kept his silence; but the Buccaneer was highly pleased for it was now more his custom to grant concessions than to receive them. There was scarcely a neighbour, or foreign relation, no matter however small, who had not got something out of the old man in recent years. At one time he used to thrash his enemy first, and then grant him a concession perhaps, afterwards, and this line of action had its advantages, and in the long-run saved very much time, trouble, bloodshed, and money. The news of the concession brought back the blood to the old Buccaneer's jolly round face, which regularly beamed with enthusiasm.

"Ah! Dogvane," he said, "after all you have served me well, and no matter how you may be reviled you have proved yourself a faithful servant. And so you have a concession!" Then an idea seemed suddenly to strike him, for turning an anxious look upon old Dogvane, he exclaimed, "Stay! Is it a good concession; one worthy of a Sea King? It is not from the Calf of Man is it?" Dogvane shook his head. "Nor from either Jersey, Guernsey, Alderney, or Sark?" Dogvane again shook his head. "Has the Egyptian gipsy sent an apology and withdrawn her curse?"

"My master is wide of the mark," said Dogvane with a smile of satisfaction.

"Well, if the concession comes from neither of these quarters, Master Dogvane, I know not where to look. Stay though. Have the Ojabberaways sent an apology for all their abusive language and unseemly conduct?"

"Not within striking distance yet, sir. Some time since, my master, you were anxious to show our trusty friend here, Jack Commonsense, some mark of your great favour. The matter is not without its difficulties; but still it may be accomplished. Now, if your trusty cox'sn, who is an excellent sailor, no doubt, though deemed for some unknown reason common, has any royal blood in his veins, we can with the stroke of a pen make either an Admiral of him, or a Field-Marshal, or even a Bishop. Then again, if he were only a rich brewer, or a successful trader of any description, or a supporter through thick and thin of our Starboard Watch, we could at once make him a lord of high degree."

"What has this to do, Master Dogvane, with the concession? Why, in the devil's name, do you torment me? Have concessions been of such frequent occurrence in recent years that I can thus afford to dally with them? Speak out, or I will drag that unruly tongue of yours from its roots."

Dogvane, seeing that further trifling would be dangerous, said, "Do you remember, sir, that little dispute we had with the great Bandit of the East upon a small matter of a boundary?"

"Yes, yes, I remember, go on."

"And no doubt you also remember my extreme regret that we had not with us that energetic young wasp, Random Jack, so that we might have either bumped him on the boundary, or whipped him on the breech."

"What has all this to do with it? Your enemies say that you are little better than a wind-bag, and I verily believe they are not far wrong. Has the Eastern Bandit made a concession? Come, yea or nay."

"No other."

"Honest Dogvane, your hand. This is indeed glorious news. So you have brought the mighty Bruin to his senses, and he has knuckled down to the Lion. But go on, Dogvane, the concession."

"If you remember, sir, we placed the matter in the hands of our faithful friend and ally, King Hokeepokeewonkeefum, his august majesty of the Cannibal Islands."

"I remember, man; but that part of the transaction does not give me the satisfaction that perhaps it ought. The concession."

"Still the same old prejudice against colour? but no matter. As—"

"What the devil is in the man! Are we never coming to the

concession? Where is this concession? Out with it, or, by my soul, I will lay my stick across your back."

Dogvane was between two stools; he feared to trifle with his master any longer, and he feared to make known the concession. Though no one could humbug the old Buccaneer like Dogvane, even he could not go too far, and he had now come to the length of his tether.

"Sir," said Dogvane, "we have gained a great diplomatic victory." Directly the Buccaneer heard the nature of the triumph his face fell.

Dogvane came cautiously to the subject again. "With the aid of King Hokee I have settled your dispute without spilling one drop of Christian blood."

"Tell me, man, at once!" cried the Buccaneer, as he raised his stick above his head, "has the Eastern Bandit made honourable amends?"

"He has, sir," replied Dogvane. "He has indeed done all we can in reason expect. The Bandit, though a Christian, is a proud man; and it is not acting generously to humble any man too much."

"Master Dogvane, I too am a Christian, and I have my pride as well as the Eastern Bandit."

"You, sir, are the leader of the Christian world, and as such should set a good example. I did not say, my master, that pride was a Christian virtue, though far too many Christians wear it as their everyday dress. Pride, indeed, is the worst of sins, and through it Satan himself fell. My master is great and noble, and all powerful; he can therefore afford to be magnanimous. Bearing this in mind I made peace when you had been beaten three times in the open. Few other nations, and few other men, would have done this; certainly not the great Bandit of the East. Would your other watch have had the courage to do it?"

Thus did the cunning Dogvane run on, still evading the point of all interest. But his master's patience was now completely exhausted, and he brought his stick across the captain's back.

"Softly, master," cried Dogvane, as he winced under the blow, "my coat needs no dusting. The point is at hand. I have agreed, or arranged, or it may be that I have entered into a sacred covenant with the great Bandit of the East, that for certain considerations, hereafter to be settled and defined, you shall black his boots."

"Black his boots!" cried the Buccaneer in amazement, "and is this your concession, fellow?"

"Stay, stay, sir, not so fast," replied Dogvane. "Make haste is no doubt a very good horse, but hold hard is a better. We have not come to the concession yet. That stick is mighty hard. Stay, sir! I am coming to it. It is this. In consideration for past favours, and to promote a good understanding between you both, the Eastern Bandit graciously condescends to find his own blacking."

"The devil he does," exclaimed the Buccaneer, as his eyes opened wide with astonishment. "What concession is there in that, pray?"

"A very great one, sir, considering the size of the Bandit's boots, it is little less than enormous. You might, sir, had it not been for diplomacy, have been obliged to provide your own blacking. To get the Bandit to concede this cost no end of trouble. One ambassador was quite broken down, and several minor diplomatic officials have been rendered quite useless for the remainder of their lives. Their minds having quite given way, and they are left little better than babbling idiots, and every boot they see they persist in blacking."

The bold Buccaneer that once was, the great Sea King, the mighty trader, was struck for a few moments completely dumb. Indeed Dogvane's concession seemed to have benumbed his brain. His old coxswain, who had kept a respectful silence during this long-winded palaver, now spoke, having first of all cleared his decks, as he called it. "Master Dogvane!" he cried, "the man who stoops to black a boot, will in all probability be kicked by it before the job is finished."

"Who asked you to put your spoke into the wheel?" Dogvane said in an under tone, and then added aloud: "I've been thinking, sir, that we might promote our honest friend here to some sinecure, where he will for the rest of his days have little work and plenty of pay. We have many such posts at our command, but strange to say, they are all full at present. The keeper of the Imperial Hat is a duke; the emolument is barely a thousand a year, but the honour is great and is much coveted. Then there is the custodian of our master's night cap, that is held by one who has royal blood in his veins, and he cannot be sent home, or about his business."

Dogvane's list of high offices was brought to an abrupt conclusion by the sudden awakening of the Buccaneer, who seemed to be possessed with a spark of his old fire. His wrath burst upon Dogvane like an angry gust of wind. "Out of my sight," he cried, as he again raised his stick. Now the keeper of the Buccaneer's stick was another high official, who drew a goodly income for doing so. Dogvane, in his mind, determined that this officer should be at once replaced by one who took better care of his business. He thought, and perhaps rightly, that on such an occasion as the present, the stick should either have been mislaid or sent to be polished, or otherwise repaired. "Out of my sight!" cried the Buccaneer, as he brought his stick down heavily upon old Dogvane's back. "Begone thou veritable wind bag. Do you wish to thrust me down on my knees before all the world? It was not by eating humble pie, fellow, that I have grown to what I am. Get thee hence ere I break every bone in thy body; thou weigher of scruples, thou splitter of straws. Where now is all that money I gave thee over this affair with the Bandit?"

"Master! master!" cried Dogvane as he cowered beneath the anger of the old Sea King, and fell down on his knees before him. "Be not hard upon your servant. Have I not served you faithfully these many long years? When I had charge of your till did you not make more money than ever you have since? Did not your pence grow into shillings, and your shillings into pounds? Have not my eyes grown dim, and my hair sparse and grey, in your service? Then bear with me a little while."

The Buccaneer was slightly mollified. "Ah!" he said, "like

many another old servant, you trade, Master Dogvane, upon the past, and think that your master will bear any amount of carelessness and bungling now for the sake of what has been done before. If in days gone by you made money for me, you have taken very good care to squander it since. But there must be a limit to the endurance even of the best of masters. Have you not dishonoured me in the eyes of my neighbours? Is your memory so short that you have forgotten their reception of me? Have you forgotten the scorn of some? the indifference of others? Have you forgotten the revilings of the Egyptian gipsy? Have you not estranged my friends from me and made me a must elephant of the herd, to wander out into the wilderness? Through you is not the charge laid against me that I have turned my back upon my enemies, and have you not so lowered me in the estimation of my neighbours, that the smallest dog amongst them barks at me?"

"Master—"

"Stay, fellow! I have not finished with you yet. While you prated about economy and peace you have run me deep into debt; while the wake of the old Ship of State, during the time you have been at the helm, has been constantly smeared with blood."

"Good master, the blood rests not upon my head, but upon that of the other watch. All the trouble that I have got into has been owing to the dreadful inheritance they left me."

"That, Master Dogvane, is too stale a cry to be readily believed. It is an old trick, and not altogether a reputable one, for one servant to try and saddle another with the fruits of his own stupidity, or carelessness. But where is that eleven millions I gave you for a certain purpose?"

"Good master, it is true that I have a little outrun the constable; but I have had to recompense Abdur for the damage done, and I have had to buy his friendship. Then the stupendous preparations I made were costly, and though there may not be very much to show for the money, yet no doubt a bloody war was averted, many lives saved, and in the long run, much money."

"A war averted, Master Dogvane, I have been told, is only a

war postponed, and that when once put off it generally comes at a most inconvenient time, and is likely to prove most costly. To strike promptly and hard, experience has proved to be the better plan, and the cheapest both in men and money. Begone from my sight, fellow, for I begin to know thee. I may be s'ow to anger, but when once roused, those who displease me had better beware of me."

Thus it was that old Dogvane, the captain of the Starboard Watch, fell under his master's displeasure. As is always the case directly fortune begins to frown on a man, his enemies crop up by the scores in every direction, and all add a little to the victim's shortcomings, memories for which are long. It is a noble idea that of not kicking a man when he is down; but it seems to be honoured well in the breach. Once let a man trip and he is spared by few. It seems to be a law of nature to attack the wounded. The birds of the air do it and the beasts of the field, and the savage drives his spear into his wounded enemy. Civilisation uses other weapons than the steel-tipped ones; but they are none the less keen and effectual, for a wounded spirit often gets the sharp shaft of scorn sent clean through it. There is no mark of violence on the body, but there is a wound within that never heals.

Things went from bad to worse with old Dogvane until one day he and his watch were kicked, without ceremony, over the ship's side. What brought the final catastrophe about was that Dogvane very unwisely, or some of his hands, tried to tamper with the old Buccaneer's drink. Touch him on his stomach and you made an enemy of him at once. Chips no longer sang, and Billy Cheeks, the burly butcher, was more gloomy than ever. He was not a man of mirth. Even his jokes were heavy, but perhaps his trade affected his disposition; it often does. The cheery little cook never lost heart, and as they rowed ashore he gave them a tune on his barrel organ, and gave them a song in which he ridiculed the prominent men of the other watch, and, as a matter of course, the members of the Buccaneer's Upper Chamber came in for their fair share of good-natured criticism or abuse. As has been said, no one saw a blemish in a neighbour sooner than the cook, and if that neighbour happened to be one of the lords temporal, Pepper prodded him well with jeer, jest, and sneer.

As Dogvane and his mess-mates rowed ashore in disgrace, several heads appeared looking over the bulwarks of the after part of the old ship. These were the occupants of the Upper Chamber, who crawled from their state room like rats from their holes, when the cat is away. The old Church Hulk seemed to awake as from a deep slumber, and presently a hymn of praise and of thanksgiving rose up and was borne upon the breeze all over the Buccaneer's island, and the hearts of all the great Church dignitaries and their many followers rejoiced that the Lord had for the time being saved them from the hands of the Philistines; or in other words from Pepper, and Billy Cheeks. All on board the old Church Hulk, and very many others amongst the Buccaneer's people, fully believed that if once the moorings of the old Hulk were slipped and she was allowed to drift away from the Ship of State, the days of the Buccaneer would be surely numbered. Respectability declared that she could never then go to church, for that she certainly could not listen to a priest, who, no matter however good a Christian he might be, was not a gentleman, for it must be known that all Christians of the various other denominations outside the old Church Hulk, were scarcely deemed to belong to that extremely rare and privileged class.

CHAPTER XXXIX.

As the Starboard went ashore the Port Watch came on board, all with their new brooms. There was the Captain, Bob Mainstay, by name, and his first Lieutenant, Ben Backstay, a good sailor and true. There was also a full compliment of other officers and men. Amongst the rest there was the cheery little midshipman, Random Jack, who was now on the eve of his promotion. It was wonderful how this little fellow had pushed himself to the front.

Wonders, it is known, never cease; but it was a strange sight to see the Port Watch rowed on board by Ojabberaway boatmen. When the weather-beaten old captain of the other watch saw this he smiled in a manner that was peculiar to him and said: "That won't last!" Then, as if speaking to himself, he added, "I wonder now, what was their price. Humph! there is nothing that Bob Mainstay can either promise, or give, that I cannot go beyond. Unless indeed, he and his crew chuck overboard all their principles. Ah! there's the rub. Principles and politics don't always pull together, and politics often, being the stronger of the two, pulls principles round with a bang."

Now there was an animated discussion all along the hard and amongst the Press, as to whether or not the Port Watch had been rowed on board by the Ojabberaways. Many were prepared to swear that it was so; that there could be no mistake about the matter. Others declared it was one of those optical delusions which are for ever happening to surprise and mystify people. Those who see the supernatural in almost everything, declared that this was merely a deception brought about by the devil. The Buccaneer's people were ready to believe almost anything just according to the party they belonged to, or the principles they professed. Indeed their credulity was so great in most things that the cunning rogue frequently reaped a rich harvest out of them. Astrologers were all dead, but the people, some of them, still dabbled in magic and believed in spiritualism.

Before the Port Watch left the shore they promised to do no end of things and their parting with the poor Beggar Woman, Patriotism, was most affecting. They said that so long as they had charge of the old Ship she should want for nothing. In fact everybody was to be made happy and like the ending of all good books, and works of fiction, virtue on all sides was to be rewarded. But the atmosphere of that old Ship clouded the best of memories. Besides, every one knows that promises are quite as cumbersome baggage as a conscience, and all those who wish to get on in the world must unload themselves of the one, as readily as they do of the other.

Many of the crew of the Ship of State kept their consciences on board of the old Hulk alongside, where they were cleaned and repaired and sent for when wanted.

The daily press having had their usual battle, settled down to dictate to the watch in charge what they had to do and what they had not to do. Indirectly it pretty well ruled the roast; told the captain what man he was to put here, and what man there; but Captain Mainstay filled up his different posts according to his own way of thinking, always bearing in view, of course, the Buccaneer's cherished custom. All this took some little time, for you cannot get things to fit on such principles all of a sudden. Accidents will happen, and chance will occasionally put a square man into a square hole and then he has with much difficulty to be pulled out and a round hole found for him.

New brooms invariably sweep clean and the Port Watch set themselves to work to clean up the mess left behind by old Dogvane and his lot. No one kicked up more dust than did the, at one time, little middy, who for his good behaviour was made steward of the household of the Buccaneer's Indian Princess. It was his duty to watch over her; to guard her against her enemies and especially to keep an eye upon the wicked Bandit of the East.

They all agreed for once, and declared that old Dogvane had left things in a terrible state of muddle, and they were unanimous in the belief that they had only stepped on board just in the nick of time to save the old Buccaneer from complete ruin; but this belief was also common to the other watch when they took charge. The cook's galley they said was in a shocking state and full of nothing but cheese parings; while he had scribbled all over the place, "the Upper Chamber must be destroyed." All people have their peculiarities, their whims and their fancies, and the clever little cook was not without his.

When the cook reached the shore, he went about with his barrel organ and sang songs about the iniquities of the other watch; of their indecent haste to get on board the old Ship and grab the emoluments attached to the several offices. The cook being placed in easy circumstances, by the profits he received from his barrel organ, could afford to be virtuously indignant.

Scarcely had the Port Watch settled down to their work than things went wrong with them. They did not in shaping their course make due allowance for the current of Public opinion, which at times set very strong, and the old Ship of State got into difficulties. Over the ship's side they went as quickly as they had climbed on board and the helm was again placed in the hands of that experienced old salt, William Dogvane, who was, however, requested by the Buccaneer to keep his weather eye open, for that if he caught him again napping it would be the worse for him.

"Master," said the captain, "it is no use your putting me on board this old ship unless you give me powers sufficient to keep the wild and mutinous Ojabberaways in order. They are simply playing the very devil."

This to the Buccaneer was a hopeful sign, for Dogvane had always been accused of sympathizing with this people and indeed of playing into their hands. With Dogvane came the conspirators of the cook's caboose. They still held together, though the carpenter was drifting away from his old comrades, into a purer and brighter atmosphere. The cook was like that pattern sailor, Billy Taylor, full of mirth and full of glee.

One fine morning the whole of the Buccaneer's island was awakened by a great hubbub on board of the old Ship. The Church Hulk was slumbering in a peaceful repose after her recent rude shaking. She had again settled down to her usual state.

Notwithstanding what old Dogvane had said to the contrary he soon began intriguing with the Ojabberaways and he made a rapid shift, coming to the conclusion that nothing would make the Ojabberaways eternally happy, but to give them everything they wanted. He said the old Ship thus lightened would ride easily ever afterwards. The cook, however, true to his hobby, said that it would be a great pity to waste the Ojabberaways when there was the whole of the Buccaneer's Upper Chamber weighing the old Ship down by the stern, and generally retarding her progress, and interfering considerably with her steering.

Things looked very bad, and Random Jack who was ashore was most eloquent, and declared for his part he should never be surprised to see a flare up on board the old Ship, when, no doubt, honest sailors would come by their dues. The noise upon the Ship of State roused up the crew of the ship alongside, for if there was to be a mutiny, or any thing of that kind going on, they felt sure they would be boarded, robbed, and cast adrift.

CHAPTER XL.

JUST as people had conjectured; there was a mutiny on board the old ship, and amongst the Starboard Watch, which old Dogvane had allowed to get a little out of hand.

Even the conspirators of the cook's caboose were torn asunder, and the hand of the cook wished to grapple round the throat of the carpenter. The cook abused poor Chips right merrily, and called him every name under the sun, and would allow him no virtue, and very little intelligence. Pepper, with Billy Cheeks the burly butcher, stuck to their captain with an affection that was pleasant to see, and there could not be a doubt that if all went well with the captain, these two would be amply rewarded for their fidelity. But the cabal of the cook's caboose was completely broken up.

The carpenter now behaved in a manner that did him very great credit, and surprised not a few. He turned his back upon the cook and the butcher, and this so displeased them that they never after had a good word to say for him.

It is most fortunate that this mutiny, unlike most other mutinies, was unattended with any bloodshed or loss of life, and of course, this being the case, it lost very much of its interest. Neither was the old Ship of State scuttled and then run on shore, robbed, plundered, and abandoned. Nor did the crew fall upon each other in the division of the plunder, cutting each other's throats and otherwise conducting themselves as is usual on such occasions, though it must be said that the Ojabberaways excited fear in many a breast.

How long the idea of freeing this people had been a quiet occupant of old Dogvane's breast, smouldering there as such things generally do, it is impossible to say. He was sphinxlike and could not be read. Nor was it at all easy to tell which way he would go, or what he would do; for he at all times made what is said to be the true and proper use of language, namely to disguise his thoughts. He also found it a most useful means of either screening an advance into an unknown, and unfriendly country, and also to cover his retreat when beaten. The upshot of the mutiny in the Starboard Watch was, that one fine morning our old Buccaneer woke up to find that Dogvane, his trusted captain, in whom he had placed so much confidence, had gone over bag and baggage to the Ojabberaways, and that he had taken with him Pepper the cook, and Billy Cheeks the burly butcher.

The captain had apparently come to a hurried conclusion, and had risen in the dead of night, and having hastily stowed away his sea chest, and called to his side his beloved son, the small band deserted their old comrades, and turned their backs upon them for ever.

When all these things became noised abroad, very great was the consternation, and it set many tongues wagging, and all kinds of things were said. The carpenter was very much applauded even by those who at one time had plentifully abused him; but in this world of ours nothing lasts long; the sinner of to-day is the saint of to-morrow, and the only thing needful is to wait. Chips, the carpenter, was now thought fit company for the noblest in the land; no doubt, all this was most gratifying, and if it had not been for the constant prods, that the cook kept on giving him with his flesh fork, the prongs of which were dipped in gall; and the occasional sarcasms hurled at him by Billy Cheeks, no doubt Chips would have been a happy man.

As is always the case on such occasions, vague rumours got about, some of which turned out in the end to be true. It was said, upon what was supposed to be very good authority, that Dogvane was to be crowned king of the Ojabberaways, and all, both friends and enemies, wished him joy.

There are those who go about seeking kingdoms; carpet-bag kings in fact, but Dogvane was not one of these kind of pedlars, though if a kingdom was thrust upon him, of course he could not help himself.

It is very much to be regretted that ill-nature did not spare Captain Dogvane; but it did not, and very many most improbable stories now got wind. It was said, amongst other things, that every night before going to bed, when anything had gone wrong with him in the day, that he tore up his night shirt. The story is scarcely worthy of credence, but even if it were true, history affords many examples of a like nature. We are told on the most reliable authority that the Patriarchs of old whenever they were put about invariably rent their garments, and even King David himself, it would appear, was very much given to this practice. A king of course can do no wrong; but amongst people of lower degree the habit should be discountenanced, both on the score of expense, and of decency.

It was also said that Pepper was to be rewarded for his fidelity to his master by being made court jester to Dogvane, king of the Ojabberaways, and that in addition, he was to be chancellor of the exchequer, custodian of the Ojabberaways' morals, and a teacher to them of manners. These offices were brought under one head for the sake of economy, and as Pepper was an enemy to all official extravagance, this combination pleased him. All thought he would have quite enough to do; but then Pepper was an able man, and what to others would have been fraught with very great difficulty, was to him a matter of ease. It is a happy thing to be especially endowed by Providence. Billy Cheeks, the burly butcher, was also promoted from his humble position on board the old Ship of State, so it was said, to be minister of justice to the king of the Ojabberaways, for he had some legal knowledge and gravity enough for a judge, and as things were to be conducted on strictly economical principles, he was also to preside over the Ojabberaways' High Court of Assassination. He was to be also the keeper of the king's conscience. It was thought that he also would have enough to do.

Again did the Port Watch step on board with that jaunty and devil-me-care air, so peculiar to sailors. Random Jack was given a higher post even than that which he had held before; for he was made keeper of the Till and holder of the Buccaneer's Great Purse, offices only held by men of the most approved ability, and integrity. Many believed that he was destined on some future day to command one of the watches, but there seemed to be some difference of opinion as to which. Many indeed there were who pinned their faith to Random Jack, and many there also were who asked themselves how it was that he had thus made his way. Some affirmed that it was by his undoubted ability, but quite as many declared that it was by his unbounded impudence, frequently called self-confidence. Possibly it was by a happy combination of the above two qualities that he had been so successful. Certain it is that no man can expect to rise to a great height unless he has a good share of the last of the above virtues, for it is the only one that the world truly appreciates.

Of all things there is nothing like success. The middy now, instead of being ridiculed, sneered at, and flouted, was taken up, and those who before would have passed him by without bestowing upon him even so much as a supercilious nod now claimed an acquaintance with him, and declared that they had seen all along the superior stuff he was made of.

Those people who know everything, and they are so many that it is little short of a wonder that the world still keeps so uninlightened, said they should never be surprised to find that Random Jack had entered into an alliance with the carpenter, and obtained through him and others the command of the Starboard Watch; but the carpenter was an ambitious man. Upon the old cox'sn being asked his opinion about Random Jack, he gave it, as was his custom, and according to his own fashion. "The lad is good enough, d'ye see. He has parts, and he's got his head pointing in the right direction; if only he has his ballast all aboard. But, my mates, he seems a bit light at times, and does not stand up well to his canvas, but that will come in due course; that will come when he has trimmed his ship a bit. Then he has a knack of steering a bit wide at times; now coming up in the eye of the wind, until he is nearly taken aback; then veering away until he nearly wears round on the other tack, why, his wake, my lads, is about as straight as a cork-screw. Give him more ballast, and a steadier hand at the helm, and the lad will steer a good course through life. Them's my sentiments, mates."

But one fine day when Random Jack was sailing pleasantly along with all plain sail set to a fair wind of public opinion, he suddenly, without rhyme or reason, put his helm down, and everything went by the board, and Random Jack was left a sport to the waves of Fortune, without either sails or rudder, and it was doubtful whether he would ever again make the fair land of Promise.

But before all this a sad thing happened on board the old Ship of State. The first lieutenant of the Port Watch, honest Ben Backstay, had, so many people thought, been treated in a somewhat scurvy manner, not only by the captain of the watch, but by some of his messmates. On one occasion he was tripped up, it was said, by Random Jack and another, and poor old Ben was hurt considerably, though like the brave sailor that he was, he never uttered a word of complaint; but as a slight reward he was kicked upstairs into the Buccaneer's Upper Chamber, thereby falling under the displeasure of the immortal Pepper.

If honest Ben had any feelings he never showed them, and of course, not doing so they were not respected. One morning the whole ship's crew were stricken with sorrow, for Ben, while at his post, heard Him whom all must obey, call his name; so leaving his body below, his soul soared up aloft. The flag of the old Ship of State was half masted, and minute guns were fired. The bells from the church towers tolled out the mournful news, and the Church Hulk sent up to Heaven a requiem on behalf of poor Ben. He was a staunch friend of this old Ship, and she could ill afford, in such perilous times, to lose even one supporter. The Buccaneer mourned the loss of his trusty servant, and he kept a small spot in his heart wherein to plant a few flowers of memory to honest Ben Backstay, and as they towed him to his last moorings, the old Buccaneer said: "Let us all hope that poor Ben Backstay, like poor Tom Bowling, may find pleasant weather, until He who all commands, shall give to call life's crew together the word, to pipe all hands." There was much sorrowing in the land, and many a heart was sad.

Ah! the human heart is but a grave-yard, where lie buried many hopes that never survive even their first childhood; many ambitions cut off in all the freshness of youth, and many friends. As we live, we bear there from time to time, the cherished remains of someone, or of something we love. In our lonely hours we sit by these silent graves, and shed many warm tears of sorrow over them; wishing oftentimes, that we could bring back the dead. Thus we sit, and sit, and mourn, and mourn, day after day, and night after night. At length our sun sets, and our eyes grow dim in the waning light, until at last they close forever. With us we take our little grave-yard, with all its flowers, and bear it away into the great darkness of eternity.

CHAPTER XLI.

THINGS with the Buccaneer had so gone from bad to worse and so preyed upon his mind that his body became affected and he was seized with illness of a lingering kind; but the nature of his illness no one knew.

Now his island was celebrated for men skilled in the treatment of every known disease that man is heir to. Many of these men were specialists, that is to say, they bestowed the whole of their labour and attention upon some one particular disease, or part of the human body. Others again were faddists, that is, they pinned their faith to some particular course of treatment. One of these tried upon the Buccaneer total abstinence, but he got so weak and irritable that this man was shown the door. He went away perfectly well satisfied that the Buccaneer's life was merely a matter of days. Another doctor was called in, who declared he was no advocate for slops and physic. A generous, but plain diet, with plenty of fish to strengthen the brain, the whole washed down by a tablespoonful of whisky diluted well with water, twice a day, was all that was required; but on no account to touch claret, which, he declared, was little better than poison, while sherry was molten lead to the strongest stomach. This advice was not given in the above simple terms, for no little of the physician's skill depends upon a grave deportment, and the use of a language altogether unintelligible to the ordinary mind. Then when by long familiarity the understanding does begin to grasp a name, a new denomination is found for an old complaint, or something fresh is manufactured out of the weakness of the human body. The above treatment was acceptable for a time; but it soon began to pall upon one who had all his life been accustomed to good living, so another doctor had to be tried. When this eminent man heard of the course prescribed by his predecessor, he raised his eyebrows and smiled in a grave and wise manner; there being no approach, however, to coarse and vulgar mirth. "Ah!" he said, as he read over the prescription and order of diet, "brother Grain is a very clever fellow, without doubt, but he has his whims and fancies. Whisky he swears by, because he likes it himself; but I confidently assert that you cannot drink anything very much worse. A little good sound claret, not any of those mixtures, mind you, that are made at home, but a good, pure, wholesome, sound, and not manufactured wine. This, and a diet of game, or fowl, will bring you relief. The nature of your disease is to be explained simply thus: Imperfect mastication and a slight weakness of the salivary glands not bringing about a healthy deglutition there is in consequence a corresponding loss of chymification, followed by imperfect chylification, and thus the food is not properly acted upon before it passes through the pyloric opening into the duodenum. Having had the above explained to you in this simple and unpedantic manner, you will, no doubt, my dear sir, feel very much more at ease." Having thus delivered himself, the doctor took both his fee and his departure.

How sad it is that the poor human body cannot run through its brief span of life, without having to carry about inside it a bottled-up disease of some kind or other, which in time eats through the cork, or stopper, and flows out all over the system, poisoning everything. Taking away all sunshine, all happiness, until at length it dries up the channels of life; not sparing either the great and rich, but attacking the mighty as well as the lowly; not leaving alone so great a man even as our bold Buccaneer. It is sad, but then there is a crowd waiting for us to move on.

After the faddists came the specialists. Each one of these saw in the Buccaneer's illness some one of the symptoms of his own especial disease. Many of these most eminent men met in consultation, and there was a great diversity of opinion. Each of the learned physicians flew at once to his particular part of the Buccaneer's body. One said he was suffering from dropsy and that nothing would save him but immediate tapping. Another said it was stone, while a third was equally sure it was his kidneys that were affected; this happening to be at the time the fashionable disease. The exploring needle was thrust into every part of the patient's body, with the result that some skulking disease was said to be at the end of it, like a base conspirator plotting at the great man's life. They one and all agreed, however, that the patient was suffering from plethora, brought about by a too generous diet, which so often accompanied very great prosperity. So before they left they bled him freely; but still he neither recovered nor did he mend.

Only one set of specialists dare not approach him, and these were the mad doctors; those who treated the human mind. So sensitive was the Buccaneer on this point that it was extremely dangerous to mention the subject of insanity. He allowed all his idiots and maniacs to go about at large, and he never interfered with them until they killed some one, or outraged society by some scandalous act of indecency. They were then locked up to keep them from doing further injury.

The old coxswain stood by his master and prevented him from being either starved, bled, or physiced to death. His neighbours too, all took a kind interest in his welfare. Looked in just to see how he was getting on, and to see how long he was likely to last. Said they hoped he would soon recover; but in their hearts they hoped he never would. On their faces, as is the custom, they wore a deep look of concern; sympathised with all his sufferings, and told him to cheer up, for that they felt confident he would pull through. Inwardly they were considering what of the Buccaneer's property they would lay their hands upon, when the old gentleman became too weak to defend himself. This is not hypocrisy, it springs from that most laudable motive of not wishing to prolong the suffering, or hurt the feelings, even of a rival.

But what caused the poor old gentleman more annoyance than anything was the way some of the members of his family behaved, taking advantage of the old gentleman's state of health to pester him almost to death, and would not take no, for an answer. His daughters even gave him no peace, and their shrill voices were to be heard even above the men's, clamouring for all kind of things.

Some of them put on their nursing caps and bib-aprons and fell to wrangling amongst themselves as to how the sick man was to be treated, while at one end of the room, one Zedekiah Cant, had enthroned himself, and held forth, by way of comforting the sick man's soul, upon the horrors of hell. This reverend gentleman had slipped into the room while two priests belonging to the old Church Hulk fell foul of each other on the door-step over a matter of orthodoxy.

The old coxswain tried his best to keep them all quiet, and he read many of them a lecture; but just as he had succeeded in establishing a little peace in rushed one of the daughters—the one who, at the march-past of the disaffected, had begged that all violent death might be banished from the Buccaneer's kingdom. "Look here, sir," she exclaimed, holding up a pigeon. "It's dead!"

"Who is dead?" cried the old Buccaneer, as he raised himself up in bed, and looked fiercely round like some old terrier who on a sudden smells a rat. "Has anything happened to the Eastern Bandit?" he asked. The ruling passion it is well known is strong even in death.

"Far, far worse, sir," cried his daughter. "In wanton sport your cruel-minded sons have killed this poor, unoffending bird. Its life has been sacrificed to provide a holiday for the idle."

The Buccaneer finding that it was not his old rival who had come to grief, sank down again and appeared quite unconcerned. Miss Progress now requested silence and she at once commenced to lecture the Buccaneer upon the theory of atoms; but even this did not seem to revive the drooping spirits of the sick man. It, however, edified the lecturer to no small degree, therefore it was not altogether barren of results. No sooner had this daughter finished than another came forward, until at length the Buccaneer, who was not ill enough to stand all this worrying, requested his coxswain to pack the whole lot about their business. This he did with extreme pleasure, and he assisted Zedekiah downstairs with the toe of his boot. As he was kicked out of the front door he was attacked and well rated by the two clerical disputants, who dropped their discussion to do battle with him.

The old coxswain took this to be a good sign, "Ah!" he said to himself, "if my old master would only rip out an oath or two, like he used to in our good old fighting days, it would gladden my heart and I would say there's life in the old dog yet."

Now there lived in the Buccaneer's island a celebrated quack, Doctor Politics by name, and there was scarcely anything that this man was not supposed to be capable of doing. He had practised long and with success and he was said to be extremely clever; having a remedy for everything as most quacks have, and as he suited his fees to every pocket he did a very good business, and was becoming more powerful in the Buccaneer's island every day he lived. No doubt this man had worked some very great cures and had brought relief to many suffering bodies; but the great quack, like all great men, had his failings. Having been successful in some things he thought himself skilled in all, and his bearing soon became presumptuous and offensive in the extreme. People, however, believed in him, and that was all that was necessary. Of course he made mistakes at times, and his patients occasionally slipped through his hands, and occasionally the cure was worse than the disease; but accidents will happen even to the cleverest men, and when he made a mistake very little was heard of it.

In an evil hour the Buccaneer put himself entirely in the hands of this physician, who when he entered the sick man's room, began to make great alterations both in medicine and diet. He was a most expensive man and his fees were exorbitant, but to one as wealthy as the Buccaneer, money is no object, and indeed he thought all the better for those things which he paid well for.

"Sir," said the quack, "I have only been called in just in time. You are suffering from a very severe depression, brought about by too good living." In this he seemed to agree with the other physicians. "Your constitution is impaired, and even endangered, and your interior economy is altogether wrong. I will prescribe for you a strict regimen. Every action must be regulated by law, I will lay down for you what you are to eat, and what you are to drink, how much, and at what times. Your hours of labour shall be defined, and also your hours for recreation; the latter I will in time make to equal, or exceed, the hours of toil. Your hours of sleep shall also be regulated, and indeed every action of your life shall be brought under proper control, so that you need never trouble yourself about anything, and any independent thought on your part, or even action, will be quite unnecessary and altogether out of place."

As is well known old servants frequently presume upon their position, and old Jack was no exception to the rule, so he said, "We have enough of your sort of medicine, doctor, on hand already and to spare. What my master wants is a little more freedom."

The doctor looked up from the work he was at and said, "Indeed, may I ask, my good sir, at what college you took your degree? Are you one of those narrow-minded bigots, who not being able to see beyond your own nose, which by the way seems to me to be an unusually long one, declare that all beyond is ignorance and folly? Pray, may I ask if you are homœopath, or allopath?"

The old coxswain took no notice but creeping up to his master he whispered in his ear, "Master, master, have a care. This fellow is weaving a straight waistcoat for you, and God only knows, you are cramped enough as it is."

But the Buccaneer did not understand his old friend and so the quack continued his work, and presently said, addressing the coxswain, "Well, my man, I will have nothing to do with you, and as you are likely to interfere with my treatment with your cut and dried notions, your room will be better than your company. Your master requires no fruit of the medlar kind."

"If your medicine," replied Jack, "is of the same kind as your joke, it won't kill with laughter if it does not cure, and there's comfort in that."

"Begone, thou dotard!" cried the quack, "and mumble your old wives' sayings to old wives' ears." Thus was poor old Jack banished from his master's room. One of the accusations brought against the Buccaneer was that he turned his back upon his friends. About the truth of this it is not necessary to trouble; in such things, and indeed in many others that ill nature floats, there is generally sufficient to give a colouring. One thing is certain, he now allowed a well-tried, and honest old servant, to be put on the wrong side of the door.

Like some faithful old dog, Jack hung about the place and often, and often tried to steal into his master's room, just to see how he was getting on. He swore he would be silent and not utter a word, but poor old Jack's reputation for silence was not great, and the quack doctor kept such an eye upon his patient that he could scarcely dare move, or speak, without his authority. The only consolation that old Jack had was to cry out in the hearing of everybody, "Well, damme! if this is liberty, give me the four iron-windowed stone walls of a prison for choice." But nobody seemed to heed him.

It was a sad sight to see this, at one time, daring old Buccaneer, so fettered and bound. Many a good fight had he fought for the sake of his freedom and after all it had only brought him to this. Evils, it is well known, never come alone, and misfortune after misfortune befell him, for one morning the merry round-faced sun rose with a broader smile than usual upon his jolly red face. It was found that Madam Liberty, of whom people had talked and prated so much, and made such a to-do about, toadying, and flattering her, on even the smallest occasion, had turned out to be no better than she should have been. The precise name by which she was known it is not necessary to mention. Women of her class have at all times played conspicuous parts in the world's history; being even favoured of princes and other noble personages, while one even was made the consort of an emperor and sat upon an Eastern throne. But a greater surprise was still in store for people, for one morning they rose up to find that the modern Phryne had disappeared in a most mysterious manner and many believed that she had been made away with by her son, Demos. This individual had now grown to great consideration in the Buccaneer's island, and under the patronage of the quack he had been made custodian of the household, and keeper of the old Buccaneer's honour; but the latter office under his care soon became a mere sinecure. In turn Demos became the master even of the quack, who had done so much to place him where he was; but is not the story of kicking away the ladder by which you have climbed, a very old one?

The uncrowned queen, Respectability, still held her sway, but her kingdom had become more confined, and she became a most prim, and exclusive sovereign. The great quack doctor treated her with the utmost consideration and politeness, and even Demos, who was for pulling down everything, tried to gain her over, but her majesty became extremely haughty and reserved, and would have little or nothing to do with him.

But now the sorrow of sorrows has to be told. It was a wild and stormy night. The rain swept over the island in blinding sheets. The wind howled amongst the rigging of the old Ship of State, and the wild waves dashed against the rock-bound coast, throwing up clouds of spray, and roaring like hungry monsters, eager to devour their prey. The old signboard over the door of the Constitution public-house laboured to and fro in the blast, and groaned every now and again as if in pain. The light from a feeble lamp shed its uncertain rays upon two forms lying side by side on the cold, damp earth, and the wind as it passed them seemed to sing a funeral dirge to the Buccaneer's two best friends, the Beggar Woman, Patriotism, and the old coxswain, Jack Commonsense.

The two of them had travelled side by side on the road to Misfortune; begging about from door to door, but they claimed neither pity nor sympathy, all people being much too busy with their own affairs to pay them any attention. At length they dragged their starved bodies to die in front of the old house they both loved so well. With the loss of these two the Buccaneer's days, it was believed, were numbered.

CHAPTER XLII.

LITTLE is left to be told now. The sick man occasionally rallied, and he loved to dwell like most old men of every station in life, upon his past. He was also given to occasional fits of boasting, and when he did do anything he took good care to let all the world know it. "Did you see that!" he would cry out in an ecstasy of delight. "Did you see the mighty blow I struck? Never in my palmiest days did I do better. Hide, hide your diminished heads, ye Ramillies, Malplaquet, and Waterloo." These famous battles he loved to talk about.

He also took a strange delight in showering upon all his people all kinds of honours or distinctions, and it was said that men were decorated for doing little or nothing. This was a symptom of decay.

Sometimes as he sat pillowed up in his invalid's chair, with the great quack doctor in attendance upon him, he would mumble to himself, "Aye, aye, I knew thee well. There was Wallop, he swept the seas. There was brave Howard, Hawkins, Frobisher, and the rest, and you, my little man! No, no, I've not forgotten Trafalgar and the Nile. Don't you remember them all, Jack? Jack! Jack! where's my cox'sn, he never used to play the truant," but Jack never answered to his call, and the old man wandered on. "Clack, clack go my windlasses; yo! ho! cry my men. Heave in, my lads. Sheet home and hoist up, and bear away for the main."

The great quack smiled as he glanced his eyes up at the long row of shelves, with their burdens of remedies, all of which had been prescribed to meet some fresh complaint, and many a costly dose had been given, which only aggravated the disease; and of many of the others, all that could be said was, that if they did no good, they at least did no harm; but the straight waistcoat every day received some slight addition, which contracted still more the old Buccaneer's actions, until in time he could scarcely call his soul his own.

Thus did this great man pass his declining years. Ruled over by a tyrannical quack. Worried by his own children, to whom he had given every indulgence, at the recommendation of Madam Liberty, until it could with justice be said that they one and all combined to bring the old Buccaneer's grey hairs with sorrow to the grave.

It is usual in all books, and it is even necessary before you close your pages to kill some of the characters, if not all. Sometimes they die a natural death, at others they are either blown up with gun-powder, or otherwise made away; either with the steel blade, or the leaden bullet of the assassin. The characters who have strutted for a brief space upon the pages of this history must be allowed to die peacefully. The star of Dogvane, the king of the Ojabberaways, after resting for a short while over the green isle of his adoption, set forever in the Western Ocean. His chief jester, the merry Pepper, the man of infinite wisdom and resource, also passed away. Dogvane was never allowed to carry out his grand design of covering the naked population of the Soudan in home-made fabrics. Nor was the cook soothed in his last moments by seeing the object of his life accomplished, namely, the total abolition of the Buccaneer's Upper Chamber; consequently we cannot imagine that his end was peace.

It is a pity that Death is no respecter of persons; had he been, the gifted Pepper, would, no doubt, have been spared to amuse and enlighten the world. Of the other conspirators of the cook's caboose, after having served their allotted time, they also passed away, and it is not recorded that Billy Cheeks, before he died, set fire to the waters of the river that flowed by the Buccaneer's chief city. The carpenter rose high in his master's household, and carried to his grave a goodly load of honour. Of the rest, let history tell what truth or what lies it likes, here no more will be recorded. It will be remembered that our bold Buccaneer was at one time sorely grieved because he only had one general. This seemed to prey so upon his mind in his last days, that he tried to make amends for his past neglect by making generals by the score, whether they were fitted for the position or not; nor did the Buccaneer stop here, for he gave military titles to nearly all his sons, in the hope, no doubt, that amongst the crowd there might be one military genius, or perhaps two.

But stranger things were yet in store for the world, and a graver symptom of decaying power had yet to manifest itself. It has been already said that no man ever did more to degrade noble distinctions and marks of honour than did this, at one time, celebrated Buccaneer, in his declining years. It is true that he had not sunk quite so low as one of his neighbours, who sold such things for a mere money consideration; but he had in his latter years gone some considerable way even in this direction, for he had made money a stepping-stone to preferment. The one who placed drunkenness within easy reach of his people, might reasonably expect to be made a peer. The successful oilman, or grocer, who had made his five talents into ten, need not despair of earning the at one time honourable distinction of knighthood, while any one who served his party well, even if it were to the discredit of his country, was pretty certain to be ennobled. The number of new creations was so great, that his heraldic officers were nearly worn out with finding ancestors and pedigrees for all these great people, and it was wonderful what things their industry, and their ingenuity, brought to light. Frequently they followed the poet's art and gave "to airy nothing a local habitation and a name."

Had he promoted all his cooks to seats in the Council Chamber it would not have been so very extraordinary a thing, considering the part that cooks play in this world of ours. The Buccaneer now put a climax to his folly by one day making all his tinkers lords, and all his tailors knights. Whether this was done in a spirit of irony, or from a deep conviction that, as he had gone so far, he could not in justice draw any hard and fast line, will never be known. He was without doubt the best tinker the world had ever seen, and he had a very large show of tinkered pots, pans, and kettles, always on hand, but many thought he might have stopped here.

These last acts were considered to be of so grave a nature that the priest took the place of the doctor, and when this happens little else remains to be told.

Before closing the pages of this history, another catastrophe must be recorded. In one of those storms which were of frequent occurrence in the Buccaneer's island, the old Church Hulk, which had ridden alongside of the Ship of State for so many years in fair weather and in foul, slipped her moorings one dark night, either by accident, or otherwise, and she drifted on to the rocks of discord, and being broken up was plundered; her own crew being fortunate enough to save some of her cargo of riches for themselves. After all was over they set to work to accuse and abuse each other. Some indeed expressed open satisfaction at what had happened, for the discipline on board the old Church Ship had long been too severe for them, and signs of mutiny and insubordination had long been manifest, as has been already shown. These felt that now they could worship their God how they liked, when they liked, and in what costume they liked; and those who wished it, and there were not a few, could even worship more gods than one.

The loss of the Church Ship was put down to various causes by her crew. Some said it was the work of the devil; others said it was through the wickedness of men; but very few of them thought of applying to themselves the proverb, which the old coxswain and his master had brought from the Spanish Main.

CHAPTER XLIII.

THERE are different opinions as to how the world is to end. ome say it will eventually fall a prey to that rapacious monster, the sun, which seems to be according to these people a veritable gourmand; requiring an enormous quantity of food to keep him going, and thinking no more of a planet than an ordinary individual does of an oyster. Others seem to think that the present inhabitants are to be frozen out, while others again think that the balance of things is to be upset, and that some day we shall, world and all, be flung into unlimitable space, waking up eventually perhaps the peace and quiet of some far off system. Whatever the method, the result will be the same, so far as the inhabitants are concerned. All people are selfish enough to hope that things will last their time, for no matter how the world is abused, and called all sorts of bad names, but few leave it willingly, and if they could look out upon the many beauties with which they are surrounded; if they could be cured of their blindness, they would see something fresh every day to give them pleasure.

It was equally a matter of doubt as to how this brave old Buccaneer was to make his final exit. Frequently the last stroke of death is not given by that ailment that has been threatening through life. But as to the Buccaneer? Would his neighbours step in, and taking advantage of his weakness, knock the old gentleman on the head, and then divide his riches amongst themselves, and thus save all further trouble to administrators and executors? Would Demos, taking advantage of the position his wanton mother Liberty had placed him in, club the old gentleman, and so give him the finishing stroke? Such a thing has happened before now, in the world's history, and it may happen again. Children petted and spoiled, have ere now risen against their parents, and have cruelly treated them. Was the old Buccaneer, the prosperous trader, to have the last drop of blood sucked out of him, by the foreign parasites and cheap-Jacks, or was he doomed to have the last spark of life trampled out of him by the Ojabberaways? Again, what if this old Buccaneer, who had sailed for so many years under the death's head and crossbones, were destined to end his days under Petticoat Government? There would be a strange irony in this, and such a thing would go far, no doubt, to rectify the many injustices that the fair sex from the beginning has been subjected to. Revenge is sweet, and no doubt if this were to happen, the last moments of the Buccaneer would not be passed in peace. But of his end who can tell? It would be but waste of time further to surmise, for we must say farewell to our brave old friend. We will leave him in the hands of the great quack doctor and his numerous attendants. What matters it, whether after lingering for a while below, he was taken up to heaven on a snow white cloud, the fringe of which was illumined by the glowing embers of a world he loved so well, and in which he had played a by no means insignificant part? What if he passed away before the final consummation of all things, leaving his spirits behind to walk the earth, and to encourage some weary traveller who, commencing life as a Buccaneer, lives in after years under the protection of the great uncrowned queen Respectability, and takes for his fancy dress the cowl and frock of a monk?

The last moments of the great and powerful are sad to contemplate, and are not lightly to be intruded upon. We see the mighty intellect impaired, and the babbling tongue let loose. We see the strong arm that was once the terror of all those who came within its reach lying listless on the counterpane, with emaciated fingers whose strength is not sufficient to crush a fly. Character, virtue, intellect, all that goes to make a man great, have to retire into the shade of the sick chamber, and wait patiently there, silently watching the ravages that are being made. Then with the last breath of the dying man, Reputation spreads her wings, soiled perhaps, and torn by slander, and pierced by the sharp pointed shafts of ill-nature, and takes refuge in the marble palaces of History, where things are cleansed and purified, or condemned to everlasting obloquy.

We drop the curtain, and wish this celebrated Buccaneer a long good night.

THE END.

S. Cowan & Co., General Printers, Perth

1

www.ingramcontent.com/pod-product-compliance
Lightning Source LLC
Chambersburg PA
CBHW031928230426
43672CB00010B/1852